2/20/14

To: Joyce

with admiration

for all your devoted

efforts for city

schoolchildren,

Buzzy

"There's too much dogma in American education, both within the 'establishment' and among 'reformers.' In this book, Kalman R. Hettleman crashes both parties with a clear and contrarian call for far-reaching changes. His prescriptions will make all sides uncomfortable, which is one indication that they warrant close attention." —**Michael J. Petrilli**, vice president for national programs and policy, Thomas B. Fordham Institute

"Prepare to be enlightened and provoked by one of America's most original thinkers on education reform. In *It's the Classroom, Stupid*, Hettleman draws on his deep experience in urban education to take on sacred cows and naked emperors wholesale. I fervently hope that his call to focus reform on research-based classroom teaching finds a receptive audience." —**Robert E. Slavin**, director, Center for Research and Reform in Education, Johns Hopkins University

"*It's the Classroom, Stupid* is perfect reading for anyone who wants a primer on the last half century's worth of urban education reform. Hettleman challenges us to rethink the fault lines of education's battles and refocus our efforts on improving the core technology of teacher and learning. It's a radically unsexy idea that is our only hope for radically improving our children's lives. —**Justin C. Cohen**, senior advisor to District of Columbia Schools Chancellor Michelle Rhee

i

New Frontiers in Education
A Rowman & Littlefield Education Series
Edited by Dr. Frederick M. Hess

This Rowman & Littlefield Education series provides educational leaders, entrepreneurs, and researchers the opportunity to offer insights that stretch the boundaries of thinking on education.

Educational entrepreneurs and leaders have too rarely shared their experiences and insights. Research has too often been characterized by impenetrable jargon. This series aims to foster volumes that can inform, educate, and inspire aspiring reformers and allow them to learn from the trials of some of today's most dynamic doers; provide researchers with a platform for explaining their work in language that allows policymakers and practitioners to take full advantage of its insights; and establish a launch pad for fresh ideas and hard-won experience.

Whether an author is a prominent leader in education, a researcher, or an entrepreneur, the key criterion for inclusion in *New Frontiers in Education* is a willingness to challenge conventional wisdom and pat answers.

The series editor, Frederick M. Hess, is the director of education policy studies at the American Enterprise Institute and can be reached at rhess@aei.org or (202) 828-6030.

Other titles in the series:

Social Entrepreneurship in Education: Private Ventures for the Public Good
 by Michael R. Sandler

Choosing Excellence in Public Schools: Where There's the Will, There's a Way
 by David W. Hornbeck with Katherine Conner

It's the Classroom, Stupid

A Plan to Save America's Schoolchildren

Kalman R. Hettleman

ROWMAN & LITTLEFIELD EDUCATION

A division of

ROWMAN & LITTLEFIELD PUBLISHERS, INC.
Lanham • Boulder • New York • Toronto • Plymouth, UK

Published by Lexington Books
A division of Rowman & Littlefield Publishers, Inc.
A wholly owned subsidary of The Rowman & Littlefield Publishing Group, Inc.
4501 Forbes Boulevard, Suite 200, Lanham, Maryland 20706
http://www.lexingtonbooks.com

Estover Road
Plymouth PL6 7PY
United Kingdom

British Library Cataloguing in Publication Information Available

Library of Congress Cataloging-in-Publication Data

Hettleman, Kalman R., 1935–
  It's the classroom, stupid : a plan to save America's schoolchildren / Kalman R. Hettleman.
    p. cm.
  ISBN 978-1-60709-548-4 (cloth : alk. paper) — ISBN 978-1-60709-549-1 (pbk. : alk. paper) — ISBN 978-1-60709-550-7 (electronic)
  1. School improvement programs—United States.   2. Public schools—United States.   I. Title.
  LB2822.82.H5 2010
  371.2'070973—dc22   2009031853

Printed in the United States of America

Dedication

Most of all to my wife Myra, for more than written words can say. And to our four sons, daughters-in-law, and grandchildren: Jeffrey, Neil, Daniel, Robert, Shelly, Kerry, Ayelet, Susan, Jonathan, Rachel, Grant, Jesse, Gabriel, Eliana, Anna, and Julia. And to the memory of my parents.

Contents

Acknowledgments

To get a book published these days is no easy matter, particularly if you're a first-time author and a wonky one at that. So I have many people to thank.

Rick Hess believed in the book, and his writings on education policy are the gold standard in the field. I am indebted, too, to his assistant Juliet Squires. At Rowman and Littlefield Education, Tom Koerner and Maera Stratton had faith in the book, greatly improved it, and have been a pleasure to work with.

Several colleagues and friends read the entire manuscript and were enormously helpful. They included Ulrich Boser, Justin Cohen, David Schimmel, Kenneth Greif, and Neil Didrickson. My wife Myra and our sons read through draft after draft, as I tested their patience and endearment. Bob Embry deserves special mention: he not only critiqued the manuscript, but for a long time he has been my closest colleague and sparring partner in education battles, and a dear friend.

Many others—educators, persons in the writing business and friends—helped in various large or small ways, from reading part of the manuscript to offering advice to answering my questions. I received a mixture of encouragement and, not infrequently, critical comments. Given the often contrarian content of the book, it is an understatement to say that not all agree with all I wrote. My honor roll includes Andres Alonso, Cecelia Cancellaro, John Q. Easton, Eve Heyn, David Hornbeck, Karen Houppert, Ray Jenkins, Rick Kahlenberg, Susan Lattimore, Mary Levy, Gene Maeroff, Lewis Noonberg, Mike Olesker, Linda Perlstein, Mike Petrilli, Andy Rotherham, Bob Slavin, Sam Stringfield, Sue Torr, and Russ Whitehurst.

I also want to single out two friends who performed above and beyond the call of duty or friendship. Sarajane Greenfeld proofread with an extraordinary eagle eye every word of the manuscript *twice*. Renee Zuckerbrot, a literary agent, was unstinting in support.

And finally, there is not enough space to properly thank the hundreds and hundreds of teachers and other educators with whom I have had close contact over the years. They, like those acknowledged above, have taught and inspired me, and the faults in this book are my own doing.

Preface

In 2003 I applied to the Maryland State Board of Education to become a member of the Baltimore City school board. Under state law, the state board selects among applicants and sends a list of names to the governor and to the mayor of the city who must jointly fill vacancies from the list. After the state board forwarded my name to the mayor and governor, a strange thing happened. I am a lifetime, activist Democrat, yet the conservative Republican governor was ready to appoint me but the liberal Democratic mayor wasn't.

I had no prior adverse dealings with the mayor, and my qualifications weren't in dispute. I had served on the city school board in the 1970s, had been the top aide for education and social services to two earlier mayors of Baltimore, and had been active in education policy analysis and advocacy for decades. However, insiders told me that my reputation for being independent and outspoken scared the mayor and officials of the school system, and one top administrator threatened to resign if I were appointed. On the other hand, the state superintendent of education and governor had their own motives for hoping that I would shake up the distressed system.

The mayor passed over me and did the same for similar reasons a year later. Months after that, however, an unexpected vacancy arose, and the mayor approved my appointment. Apparently by then the mayor was also fed up with how the city school system was doing, and he was willing to take a chance on someone who might rock the boat.

That's what this book is intended to do. It turns upside down the conventional wisdom about K–12 public education in America, particularly for poor urban schoolchildren, and proposes a contrarian plan for reform. Nothing less is needed if all children are to fulfill their potential and partake in the American dream.

A NATIONAL TRAGEDY

The plight of American public schools seems incomprehensible. Why has the richest, most powerful nation in the history of mankind failed to educate all its children, particularly low-income children of color? Why do we allow this shameful and self-destructive injustice? Who's to blame? What can be done? And, as I have been asked countless times, is there any hope?

There is hope. The problem is not that Americans, because of racism or indifference to the poor, lack the will. Public school reform has become something of a national obsession. Virtually everyone—from educators to policymakers to parents to your next-door neighbor—wants to see schools improved. Most have a strong opinion about why things have gotten into such a mess and what needs to be done to clean it up.

The rub is that we disagree, frequently disagreeably, over causes and cures. But if truth be told, no one, no matter how expert, knows how to assure that all children will succeed academically. There's no proven blueprint. In particular, no urban school system has come close to enabling most of its students to meet high standards or to substantially reducing the achievement gap between disadvantaged students and others.

Still, there is hope of great progress if we come to a fresh understanding about what works in school reform and what doesn't work, and if we uproot entrenched mindsets and management practices that stand in the way. We must probe beneath the false certainties and ideological extremes that dominate public discussion. "The real difficulty in changing the course of any enterprise is not in developing new ideas," wrote John Maynard Keynes, "but in escaping old ones."

Towards those ends, this book is intended for educators, policymakers, parents, and the general public. Mountains of words have been said and written about the plight of public schools, but I hope the book lights a few sparks that ignite a more informed national debate.

Some parts of the analyses and recommendations will seem more familiar than others. But taken as a whole, the book presents what might be called an unconventional, unified theory of school reform. The book is less a top-10 wish-list of program remedies and more an analysis of bedrock barriers to reform and cornerstone strategies for overcoming them.

To make it more readable, I have borrowed from philosopher Blaise Pascal who famously wrote to a friend that he had made the letter longer than usual because he lacked the time to make it short. I have had plenty of time to write this book. It has germinated in my mind for years, and there is no excuse for it not to be succinct.

MY BACKGROUND AND PERSPECTIVE

For most of my professional life, I have been actively involved at the intersection of urban policy, program administration and politics. My background includes positions as a lawyer in the federal "war on poverty" legal services program, as director of the Baltimore welfare and social services department, and as Maryland cabinet secretary responsible for welfare, social services and employment programs. In addition, I have managed or been closely engaged in numerous political campaigns at the state and local levels.

My immersion in public school reform has been interspersed through the years and consuming for the last ten years. In the early 1970s, the Baltimore mayor, for whom I was liaison to the school system, appointed me to the school board to try to heal bitter racial divisions. In the 1980s, I served as an advisor to the then-superintendent of the Baltimore schools, during which time I helped to initiate the Success for All program that became one of the nation's best-known and most successful school reforms. Thereafter in addition to being an education policy consultant, I became a pro-bono attorney for students with disabilities and wrote a series of nationally disseminated reports on special education. Then came my appointment to the school board in 2005. Last but not least, I have wrestled with issues of public schooling as the father of four and the grandfather of eight children.

In writing this book, I have relied on policy research and analysis but also on personal experience and judgment. And I have bent over backwards to make clear which is which. My political worldview is generally to the left of the mainstream Democratic Party. However, any tendency to tilt too far ideologically is offset by the fact that on education policy, far more than any other issue, I am sometimes on the side of conservatives. In fact, when it comes to the political and ideological education wars, I often find myself a man without a country.

One other prefatory note about writing the book: It was painful to reach the conclusion that, while there is more than enough blame to go around for the failure of public schools, educators are their own worst enemies. The reference is only to educators who are policy-makers in the top tiers of the education establishment in federal, state and local departments of education, teacher colleges, and national associations including teachers' unions. Frontline teachers are my heroes. From my mother, a public school teacher, to my own teachers as a student in the Baltimore public school system, to the incalculable number of teachers and administrators I have interacted with over the years—my admiration for them knows no bounds. My goal is to honor these heroes by revealing how the "system" betrays their ideals and how it can be reformed so they can enable many more children to succeed.

Part I

Introduction

Chapter 1

A New Lesson Plan

This book proposes to turn on its head conventional wisdom about how to reform the education of America's poorest students. A lot that we know about our public schools is true. Their condition is dire. Over half a century after the best-selling book "Why Johnny Can't Read"[1] shocked the nation, poor Johnny still can't read, or compute. Neither can poor Tyesha or Juan or millions of other predominantly low-income children of color.

We also know that this national tragedy is not because of lack of will or effort. For the past twenty-five years, the condition of K–12 education has been regarded as a national crisis. Public opinion polls reveal strong belief that public schools are failing to maintain their historical mission to drive economic growth and foster social cohesion. Political candidates promise solutions and vie to become the next "education president" or governor or mayor. The public cries out for reform and is willing to pay steeper taxes if that's what it takes.

In the name of reform, countless strategies have proliferated, most famously, or infamously, the federal No Child Left Behind Act of 2001 (NCLB) with its mandate for rigorous student testing. It is impossible to find a classroom anywhere in the country that has not been affected by NCLB or a single public school system that has not been flooded over the years by an overflowing stream of reform initiatives. But nothing has succeeded in large measure.

The big unknown is why. Why—despite our wealth, miraculous technology, and imperfect but abundant democracy—this failure? Why, in a cliché that has haunted us for at least four decades, have we been able to put a man on the moon but not every child on a ladder to success?

This book debunks conventional explanations and excuses peddled by educators and ideological combatants, left and right, in the "education wars."

3

Their reform theories rely on obsolete ideas and false certainties that are most evident in a trinity of dogmatic misbeliefs. First, that education leaders know best how to improve our schools. Second, that we need to retreat from NCLB and restore more local control. And third, that political officials must be kept out of public education.

Wrong, wrong, wrong. This book specifies why they are wrong and how to get school reform right. The analyses and recommendations apply nationwide. American public schools as a whole come up short. At the same time, the main focus is on the problems of poor schoolchildren in urban school systems. As the saying goes, when the nation catches cold, the poor get pneumonia. The large majority of students from low-income families, especially those concentrated in large cities, are truly left behind and left out of the American dream. They don't come close to meeting high standards, and there is a vast achievement gap between African-American and Hispanic children and White children. This educational underclass is growing: poor children are projected over the next ten years to be a majority of all public school enrollments.

MAJOR RECOMMENDATIONS

First, the stranglehold of the education establishment over school reform must be weakened. To make this happen, the federal government must exercise more control over public schools and become the national guarantor of equal opportunity and strict accountability for student achievement.

The education establishment—defined as the top tier of officials in local, state and federal departments of education, teacher-education colleges, teachers' unions, and national educational associations—resists reform. Most conspicuously, it has sought to undermine the provisions of NCLB that require state standards, tests, and sanctions on failing schools. But rather than go too far as the public furor indicates, NCLB doesn't go far enough. States and local districts are still able to lower standards, dumb down tests, and go soft on sanctions, and most have.

Of equal concern, NCLB does nothing to address the "savage inequalities"[2] in funding that deny students equal opportunity and allow the education establishment to divert attention from its own failures.

To address these problems, the nation needs a more muscular, coherent K–12 education framework. I define it as a New Education Federalism in which the role of the federal government is to:

- Mandate a single national set of high-level academic standards and tests;
- Guarantee adequate funding for high-quality classroom instruction; and

- Ensure that teachers and students receive the benefits of first-class research and development into the most effective instructional programs and methods.

These federal intrusions on state and local control are less radical than they appear. They leave room for a comfortable intergovernmental balance. The federal government sets national standards for *what* every child is entitled to: an equal opportunity to be prepared for the work force and civic participation. States and local governments and departments of education still have great leeway in *how* federal standards are met: how students are taught, teachers are trained, and federal aid is spent.

Second, local school boards should be eliminated, and mayors put in charge of local school policy.

As another building block of the New Education Federalism, local school governance must be overhauled. This should begin with the abolition of local school boards. It's true that local boards, whether elected or appointed, are good in theory. They are close to their communities and are intended to insulate schools from partisan politics. But in practice, no matter how dedicated, volunteer board members lack the time and knowledge to make smart policy decisions and frequently, particularly when elected, engage in raw politics themselves. Worst of all, they prevent clear executive accountability: a single person who can be held responsible for local performance.

Mayors are best suited to assume this authority and be held accountable. Historically City Halls have been happy to avoid the headaches that come with running the public schools. But modern mayors recognize that schools are indispensable to urban renaissance, and most are ready to accept hands-on responsibility. With their political necks on the line, mayors will be more prone to challenge school-system bureaucracies and to bring in fresh leadership. Some mayors have already stepped up and taken charge with encouraging results.

Third, outside leadership, featuring non-educators, must be brought in to retool and manage instructional support systems for classroom teachers.

Professional educators lack management know-how. This hardly comes as a surprise. The public is aware of rampant bureaucratic deficiencies pertaining to budgets, data systems, facilities, and other operational matters.

But the management deficiencies are far worse than that. Below the public radar and most lethal to school reform is mismanagement of instruction itself. School administrators fail to provide classroom teachers with solid curricula, training, lesson plans, supervision, and program evaluations. These tasks are crucial, particularly in urban schools where veteran teachers are in short supply.

Yet, the education establishment is oblivious to these management failures. Educators are able, often heroic frontline teachers and principals. But, as a profession, they lack the training, culture and temperament to be strong managers. As they leave the classroom and rise through the ranks to establishment positions, their professional DNA rejects management skills and systems that are the norms in business, science, and other fields.

As a result, management leadership for local school systems must be imported from the outside. This includes hiring non-educators as superintendents and high-level managers, bringing in management consultants, and nurturing a new breed of education entrepreneurs. Their skills and boldness must be used to revolutionize management where it is insidiously inept: in the design and delivery of classroom teaching and learning.

CONTRARIAN GUIDING PRINCIPLES

The major recommendations are driven by a set of principles that contradict the conventional wisdom of educators and politicians. To introduce these principles, I contrast the "Conventional Wisdom" with my "Contrarian Views." Of course, educators and politicians often fiercely disagree on theories of reform. But the Conventional Wisdom expresses the prevailing point of view among the education establishment. At the other pole, the Contrarian Views add up to an unconventional and unified set of principles for how to reform K–12 public education.

The Uncertainty Principle

Chapter 2 documents what I call (with apologies to Werner Heisenberg, founder of the uncertainty principle in physics) the Uncertainty Principle. The Conventional Wisdom is that we—educators, political officials, and parents—know how to fix public schools: we just lack the wisdom or the wallet to get it done. Most people preach certainty about the road to salvation for public schools. Many liberals declare the answer to be more money and less testing. Many conservatives think redemption can occur only if public school systems are privatized.

The Contrarian View is that no one knows for sure how to fix schools on a large scale. But how can I be so sure of this uncertainty since most school systems, including those in large cities, have made some progress in recent years? Because the progress is relatively slight. In particular, in no large city have most students achieved academic proficiency measured by national tests. Further, while any casual observer can find hundreds of innovative ideas that have been planted in schools across America, the research pickings are scant. There is only a small body of scientific knowledge that identifies the exact formula of reforms that *might* work if well implemented.

To borrow from John Kenneth Galbraith's swipe at economists, school reform is too often a debate between those who do not know and those who do not know that they do not know. Do I claim to be the only one who knows for sure what will transform public schools, especially for poor children? No. But the book's unorthodox and often politically incorrect theory of reform is a break with the past. The analyses and recommendations can jump-start a fresh national debate that steers clear of the false certainties and flaws in current reform agendas.

It's the Classroom, Stupid

As exposed in chapter 3, one fundamental and unappreciated reason why urban school reform has not succeeded is because most ambitious reforms do not focus squarely on the only place where they can ultimately succeed: in classroom instruction. Conventional Wisdom holds that current reform movements will significantly raise achievement. The most prominent across the ideological spectrum include school choice (charters, vouchers, and privatization), accountability (stiffer standards, testing, and sanctions on failing schools), more money (especially for smaller class sizes, teacher pay, and instructional interventions for struggling students), suppression of teachers' unions, and decentralization of decision-making from central bureaucracies to individual schools.

Some of these strategies make more sense than others. But all have inherent limits that are evident, not just in their lack of significant success so far, but in their structure. They do not focus *directly* on how to improve teaching and learning in the classroom. For example, student testing is necessary to identify which schools are failing. But it doesn't tell policy-makers how to improve them. Another example is charter schools. While worthwhile endeavors, they are small in number, have a mixed record, and haven't lived up to their promise to become incubators for instructional practices that can be widely transplanted into public school systems.

Many high-visibility reform strategies are popular with policy-makers because they are relatively inexpensive (with the exception of "more money") and can be sold as quick fixes. On the other hand, transforming teaching and learning in the classroom trenches is arduous, incremental, and difficult to manage. David Tyack and Larry Cuban, in their classic history of American public schooling *Tinkering Toward Utopia—A Century of School Reform,* write: "Change where it counts the most—in the daily interactions of teachers and students—is the hardest to achieve and the most important."[3]

The Contrarian View uncovers and confronts this mismanagement of classroom instruction. The most dedicated teachers need much more management support than they get. They aren't given well-designed, teacher-friendly curricula and lesson plans. Instead they are buried under layer after layer of incoherent directives and held to unrealistic and demoralizing expectations. There is little supervision, monitoring and evaluation to determine if teachers are implementing the curricula as intended and if the curricula are working as they are supposed to. The magnitude of this mismanagement and what to do about it is a pivotal and, despite the vast literature on school reform, original theme of this book.

Educators are Their Own Worst Enemies

Conventional Wisdom holds that educators aren't mainly to blame for poor student achievement. Liberals say the true causes are poverty and unequal opportunity. Conservatives point the finger at parents for not pushing their children to study harder and for not being more supportive of teachers.

The Contrarian View concedes that the schools can't do the job by themselves, as spelled out in Chapter 6, "A Nation at Risk, and at Fault." But educators are hardly guiltless. Chapter 7 pinpoints how student learning could soar if the education establishment weren't so hidebound in its thinking and weak in leadership and management. This establishment does not include frontline teachers and administrators who, like students, are largely the *victims* of the establishment "system." It's the top ranks of departments of education, teacher colleges, and other professional associations that protect bureaucratic incompetence and create a policy vacuum made to order for faddish ideologues.

A related guiding principle is that teachers' unions, while pillars of the education establishment, are often scapegoated. According to Conventional Wisdom, the unions are politically powerful, self-seeking organizations that defend incompetent teachers and obstruct reform. Political conservatives see the crusade for charters, vouchers and privatization as a way to break the unions' power. Even some liberal Democrats, including Barack Obama, have grown critical of the unions' influence.

The Contrarian View points out, however, that while critics are not wholly wrong, the evidence doesn't support the harshest allegation against the unions: that their contracts make it near-impossible to fire unsatisfactory teachers. School administrators have ample disciplinary authority that they don't exercise because of their professional collegiality and management inertia.

The Folly of Local Control and the Imperative of a New Education Federalism

One underlying reason education reform isn't cooking is because no one is in charge of the kitchen. Who *is* in charge of K–12 public schooling anyway? The local school board or mayor? The fifty governors and state departments of education? The president, the Congress, and the U.S. Department of Education? It's all of the above, which means no one. The buck is passed among educators and elected officials at all levels, and the public doesn't know who, if anyone, to hold accountable. How, as laid out in chapters 8 through 10, do we sort this out and fix it up?

At its roots is the most historically sacrosanct Conventional Wisdom: the fervent belief in local control of public schools. It is so indoctrinated that most liberals and conservatives sing in this rare instance from the same education hymnal. The refrain is that since students, teachers, and communities are diverse, those closest to the schools know best how to run them.

My Contrarian View is that conventional dogmatists have got things backward. For school reform to succeed nationally, local control should be severely limited, and more, not less, federal authority should be imposed. How does it make sense for 14,000 or so local school districts in the U.S. or even the 100 largest urban or suburban ones to go their own way in deciding what to teach and how to teach it? Compared to how other countries govern schools, the U.S. is an educationally underdeveloped nation.

The New Education Federalism recognizes this reality. It calls for national standards and tests to end the duplication of effort and carte blanche that states now have to "race to the bottom"—meaning to lower academic standards and inflate test results to avoid sanctions under NCLB, as many have shamelessly done. It also makes the federal government, for the first time, the guarantor of adequate funding. The nation must end the deep inequalities that exist between funding in poorer and wealthier school districts. At the same time, the federal government must provide vastly improved research and development (R&D) that guides where the money can be best spent.

Local school systems still have key parts to play in the New Education Federalism. But figuring out how to measure up to federal standards will require a different kind of local executive authority and accountability, and it should be vested in mayors. Conventional Wisdom says that schools must be kept out of the political reach of mayors and policy-making entrusted to elected or appointed local boards. But the Contrarian View puts City Halls in charge and abolishes school boards. This transition is beginning to happen in many large cities headed by strong mayors, with Michael R. Bloomberg in New York City and Adrian M. Fenty in Washington, D.C., blazing the trail.

Thus, the architecture of the New Education Federalism places the White House and Congress at the top and City Hall at the base of the school governance chain of command. State governments have not been accidentally overlooked. Governors can exert leadership. Some have. But as a whole, states have defaulted in their obligation to remedy unequal educational opportunity. State departments of education are bastions of the education establishment and can't be counted on to challenge the status quo. The "race to the bottom" under NCLB is just the latest proof.

One Size Fits Most

Conventional Wisdom is that no matter who governs school policy, individual schools and teachers must be given maximum autonomy to do their own instructional thing in the classroom. "One size doesn't fit all" is the mantra heard more than any other among educators. School districts aren't all alike. Nor are schools, teachers and students.

But think about it. In other fields like medicine, it's called malpractice if professionals do not follow established, science-based practices. Therefore the Contrarian View is that the ABC's of teaching should be largely determined by R&D that prescribes the core of how most students should be taught most of the time. There is a balance to be struck that autonomy zealots are reluctant to acknowledge. One-size-fits-most leaves plenty of room for principals and teachers to tailor (in educational language, "differentiate") instruction to fit individual student needs.

One rub, however, is that educators are not trained to appreciate and utilize research. Rather, they abide by what I call an *ethic of individualism.* Most experienced teachers want to close their classroom doors and go their own instructional ways. Scholar Richard F. Elmore observes: "[Educators] subscribe to an extremely peculiar view of professionalism:

that professionalism equals autonomy in practice. So when I come to your classroom and say, 'Why are you teaching in this way?' it is viewed as a violation of your autonomy and professionalism."[4] This ethic may be changing. Younger teachers are more open to instructional mandates and guidance than veteran teachers.

Equity Trumps Excellence as a National Priority

The nation faces a wrenching predicament. Conventional Wisdom is that the nation can close the achievement gap ("equity") and bring all students up to world-class standards ("excellence") at the same time. That's what we want to believe because the national interest requires both. But as revealed in chapter 4, it isn't easy do both. Fickle public attention and scarce funding lead to conflicts between economic class interests. Better-off parents want their children to be included in costly programs like pre-kindergarten, all-day kindergarten, and summer school, despite research showing that these programs primarily benefit low-income students. Also, student testing under NCLB benefits low-income, low-achieving students more than other students.

NCLB attempted to break this pattern. Its signature provision is the requirement that 100 percent of American children achieve at high levels. But it turned out that the president and Congress tried to bite off more than the nation's educational system could chew. Its effort to lump all students together for accountability purposes complicated the law's design and provoked the storm of controversy that now rages.

It is unrealistic to believe that this political standoff between economic classes can be reconciled soon. Consequently, the Contrarian View insists that equity be given the higher priority. The nation's history teaches us that while theoretically a rising tide of excellence lifts all boats, poor people and minorities of color, largely clustered in big cities, will continue to miss the boat unless their plight is in the forefront of the national debate.

FUTURE POSSIBILITIES

Chapter 14 assesses the feasibility of the recommendations in the book. Will our nation rise to the challenge of school reform? It's natural to be skeptical and immobilized when there is so far to go, there are no certain directions for how to get there, and there have been so many false starts. Leadership, however, can overcome the obstacles. But as the book explains, the education establishment is not the place to find it. That does not rule out the possibility that more openness and dynamism can be infused into its top officials. Those who populate its institutions are drawn to education because they care deeply about children. But the spark of educational leadership is not there and must be lit from the outside.

Bright spots on the horizon, illuminated in chapter 13, are the groundbreaking reform initiatives in cities like New York, the District of Columbia, and Baltimore, where outside leadership is shaking up the inside bureaucracies. Nonetheless, political leadership at the national level will remain an urgent prerequisite for nationwide reform. One would suppose that liberal Democrats would be the first to enlist for the campaign. Democrats led the passage of Social Security, Medicare and Medicaid, the Great Society, and civil rights laws addressing racial and economic injustice. Yet conservative Republican George W. Bush pushed through NCLB, the most radical attempt to use the federal government as the guarantor of the rights of low-income students. And Democrats have been mainly on the sideline engaging in educational fratricide.

Although the terms "liberal" and "progressive" are often used interchangeably in political contexts to describe worldviews that are politically to the left, political liberals and education progressives are often not one and the same. They unite to support more funding and oppose vouchers. They usually align with teachers' unions. But they splinter over charters, testing, and other provisions of NCLB. And they habitually are on opposite sides on pedagogy, particularly in the reading wars.

To the extent that labels can capture belief systems, I am among the political liberals who tend to agree more with educational conservatives than educational progressives. As a political activist, I have felt strange and uncomfortable lining up behind conservatives like president George W. Bush on NCLB. But I am not alone. President Obama and true-blue liberal leaders like Senator Edward Kennedy and Representative George Miller are among those who have departed from educational progressives in their backing for NCLB. And in other audacious ways, president Obama has shown signs of aspiring to be educator-in-chief. The $100 billion for education in the American Recovery and Reinvestment fiscal stimulus bill enacted in early 2009 is remarkable in its size and its intent to condition much of the money on innovative reform in states and local districts. It could be a big step in the direction of the New Education Federalism.

But it won't work if the education establishment's defensiveness and management incompetence continue to stand in the way of reform. The chapters that follow lay out a road map to keep that from happening. It is unconscionable to wait any longer to get started. The nation has already created a legacy of inequality in public education that future generations will see as inexplicable and shameful.

NOTES

1. Rudolf Flesch, *Why Johnny Can't Read* (New York: Harper & Brothers, 1955). In this introductory chapter, sources are omitted and not noted except for direct references or quotes. The sources are cited in later chapters where the issues are more fully discussed.

2. Jonathan Kozol, *Savage Inequalities: Children in America's Schools* (New York: Crown Press, 1991).

3. David Tyack and Larry Cuban, *Tinkering Toward Utopia: A Century of Public School Reform* (Cambridge, MA: Harvard University Press, 1995), 10.

4. Richard F. Elmore, "The Limits of 'Change'," *Harvard Education Letter,* January/February (2002), http://www.edletter.org/past/issues/2002-jf/limitsofchange .shtml, 2.

Chapter 2

The Uncertainty Principle

Is it accurate to say, as I did in the prior chapter, that education reform is largely a debate between those who do not know and those who do not know they do not know? How can I be so certain about uncertainty? And so what? Why make such a big deal of uncertainty since almost everyone agrees that we have a long way to go to raise student achievement to acceptable heights?

To answer the so-what question at the outset, school reform has no chance unless we expose the false certainties that obscure the hard road ahead and lull us down the wrong paths. Generations of school reformers, no matter how well-intentioned, keep repeating the same mistakes. There is a big difference between school "reform" and student "progress." It's easy to reform, reshape, redo how schools operate. We do it all the time. But constant change has usually meant a passing parade of fads, innovations that blossom and wither, and broken promises.

This chapter documents the Uncertainty Principle in two parts. First, through student test data that are dismally low nationwide, especially in large urban districts. A study in 2006 by the Harvard-based Public Education Leadership Project summed up the failure of *all* urban districts to enable the great majority of students to meet high-level standards: "While [various reforms] have had a dramatic impact on individual schools, they have failed to produce a single high-performing urban school system."[1]

Second, the chapter looks at uncertainty in the light of the most prominent current reform movements, among them accountability under NCLB and school choice, including charter schools. Unfortunately, neither of these offers substantial hope of near- or longer-term leaps in student achievement that would disprove the Uncertainty Principle.

STUDENT TEST DATA

NCLB mandates testing but does not require states to give the same or comparable tests. Each state devises its own standards and tests, and they vary widely. Comparisons are also elusive because of differences in student demographics, school funding and other variables. However, there is one well-established independent barometer: the National Assessment of Educational Progress (NAEP) tests.[2] Under the regular NAEP protocols, large samples of students nationwide are tested in a variety of subjects, primarily reading and math at grades four and eight. Students are graded as Basic, Proficient (in effect passing), or Advanced. Because regular NAEP test results are reported for the nation as a whole and individual states, not for individual school districts, in 2002 the NAEP Governing Board initiated the Trial Urban District Assessments. Valid samples of students in selected cities were chosen for testing, and in the 2007 assessments, 11 large cities were included.[3]

The results overall are appalling. In 2007 nationwide, only 33 percent of fourth-graders met the Proficient standard for reading, 39 percent for math; for eighth-graders, 31 percent met Proficient in reading, 32 percent in math. In large cities, only about 20 percent of fourth-grade and eighth-grade students were Proficient in reading, about 25 percent in math. The figures are even more dreadful for low-income, Black, and Hispanic students, reflecting huge White-Black and White-Hispanic achievement gaps.[4]

The data on high school completion rates (an inexact but close mirror of dropout rates) is another touchstone of failure. Methods of calculating the rates vary widely, but they range as low as 50 percent for African Americans and 52 percent for Latino students.[5] By any measure, the rates are a national catastrophe.

The Testy Controversies

Despite the NAEP test score data, many liberals believe that the plight of American public schools—and by implication the Uncertainty Principle—is exaggerated. They point to much higher student test scores on *state* tests, and say that national NAEP standards are unrealistically high. They also claim that doomsayers, mainly conservatives, discount the promising arc of progress over the years. Each of these arguments has provoked bitter debate.

The average disparity between students who score Proficient on NAEP tests and students who score the equivalent of Proficient on state tests is, for the nation as a whole, an astonishing forty-plus percentage points in reading and about thirty-five points in math.[6] And the disparities are usually larger for urban students, particularly low-income minorities.[7]

In Texas, proclaimed by its former governor George W. Bush as a "miracle" of progress, as of 2005, the difference between NAEP and state scores since 1994 was 56 percent in reading and 52 percent in math.[8]

What explains the phenomenon of such vast disparities? Are state tests too easy or NAEP tests too hard? Some education experts across the ideological aisle validate NAEP. To the Education Trust, a liberal-leaning think tank, the disparities show that state test scores give students and parents "a false sense of promise."[9] A 2007 study published by the Thomas B. Fordham Institute, a leading conservative think tank, is titled *The Proficiency Illusion*. "Those who care about strengthening the United States' K–12 education should be furious [at the easy state tests]," the authors of a Foreword to the study charge.[10]

On the other hand, well-reputed defenders of the state tests argue that the NAEP "gold standard" is more than a bit tarnished. They—including centrist think tanks like the Center on Education Policy and Education Sector—say that NAEP sets the bar too high.[11] In addition, researchers employed by the Council of Chief State School Officers, an association of state departments of education, argue that state tests aim to set realistic goals for improvement, whereas NAEP tests specify "lofty long-term goals."[12]

The data is also the subject of ideological fireworks over the rate of past and present progress—the stronger the pace of progress, the weaker the Uncertainty Principle. Since the 1970s, low-income students have made notable gains under state and NAEP tests, and the achievement gap between whites and children of color has narrowed. For example, a University of California study, using NAEP long-term trend data for the nation as a whole, showed that Blacks made "remarkable gains" in reading in fourth grade between 1971 and 2004, and the White-Black achievement gap closed significantly.[13]

But the news is not so good if the lens is focused on the results since NCLB went into effect in 2002. According to the Center on Education Policy, the number of states with gains in reading and math on *state* tests "far outstripped" the states showing declines.[14] But the picture using NAEP data is much darker. The University of California study found that nationwide, "the chasm between state and [NAEP] estimates of proficiency has grown wider since NCLB,"[15] and "No progress has occurred since 2002 in closing Black-White or Latino-White gaps."[16]

The conflicting data leaves room for ideologues to put their own spin on the trajectory of progress. And they do, with vehemence. Most conservatives think schools haven't gotten that much better and can't get much worse, whereas many liberals take their cue from professors David C. Berliner and Bruce J. Biddle, authors of the 1995 book, *The Manufactured Crisis: Myths,*

Fraud and the Attack on America's Public Schools. Doomsday attacks on the schools, they wrote, were "nasty lies" by conservatives who are "ignoring, suppressing, and distorting evidence" of progress.[17] Why would anyone do such a dastardly thing? According to Berliner and Biddle, to pursue a political agenda "promoted by specific groups of ideologues who were hostile to public schools and who wanted to divert attention from America's growing social problems."[18]

In rebuttal, Diane Ravitch, who is an education conservative (though political liberal), asserted that it was *The Manufactured Crisis* "which blithely disregards ample evidence" contrary to its arguments.[19] Lawrence C. Stedman, a researcher and self-styled political progressive, found Berliner and Biddle's "achievement analysis deeply flawed and misleading . . . As progressives, we should admit that achievement is low. But that does not mean we have to embrace a conservative agenda."[20]

The tenor of the debate has not changed much over the years. Chester E. Finn, Jr., the majordomo of education conservatives, argued in 2007 that K–12 education "has been in a long-term recession from which it seems unable to emerge."[21] On the opposite side, well-known liberal researcher Gerald W. Bracey wrote in 2006 that many Americans have "The Neurotic Need to Believe the Worst" about public schools, in large measure because they want to advance their goal of privatization of public schooling.[22]

Yet for all the bombast, neither side can prove its point. As the University of California researchers put it: "Many governors and state school chiefs cannot honestly tell parents whether their schools are getting better and which student subgroups are making progress over time."[23] My view, through the statistical haze, is that conservatives have the better of the argument. They are more in tune with the unacceptably low test score data before and since NCLB, especially the NAEP results. That said, I also believe that their tendency to believe in privatization as the cure-all for what ails public schools is unjustified.

In the next section of this chapter, we examine the track record of privatization and other major reform movements. Despite all the disheartening data, is it foreseeable that any of them, if given a chance, could grow in the future and provide reasonable certainty about how to make school reform work?

THE PASSING PARADE OF SCHOOL REFORMS

The predominant reform movements now are accountability (testing and other measures under NCLB and state laws) and school choice, especially charter schools. They have monopolized the national reform agenda for nearly twenty years and pervade almost every chapter in this book. But neither offers an antidote to the Uncertainty Principle.

Accountability under NCLB has so far not lived up to expectations, as the test data since its passage shows. It's not just that student achievement has lagged. It's also that educators have had virtually no success in turning around failing schools. For example, the Maryland Department of Education, a national leader in trying to impose accountability, tried a series of restructuring routes with the Baltimore City public schools, but they all led to blind alleys.[24]

In the minds of conservatives, public school systems are incapable of reforming themselves. Only market-based competition—school choice, mainly through charter schools and vouchers—can. As famously expressed by John E. Chubb and Terry M. Moe, "Reformers would do well to entertain the notion that choice *is* a panacea (italics in the original)."[25] But they and other conservative crusaders for choice have been guilty of, to borrow a market term, "irrational exuberance." The results so far have not lived up to expectations. Still, charters, vouchers and other forms of privatization are in relatively early stages of development, and their potential merits close attention.

Charter Schools

Charter schools enjoy considerable bipartisan backing, including president Obama (although some liberals, especially teachers' unions, are resistant).[26] And they have mushroomed, enrolling more than one million students in about 4,000 schools in over forty states.[27] But their record on student achievement is modest at best. Two scholars recently concluded after a survey of the research that charters have performed only slightly better, if at all, than regular public schools.[28] The Public Education Leadership Project at Harvard University reported, "Student-achievement levels have varied greatly across all charter schools; as a result, their average performance is only slightly better than that of all traditional U.S. schools."[29] The National Charter School Research Project, an arm of the University of Washington Center on Reinventing Public Education, finds that any verdict "is far from settled, and is likely to remain so for some time."[30]

The Charter Project also acknowledges the movement's growing pains. Political and bureaucratic resistance and insufficient funding are parts of the problem but so are internal management challenges, like finding suitable principals and teachers and providing services to students with disabilities. Many charter school proponents don't hide their disappointment. Paul T. Hill, one of the leaders of the movement, wrote in 2007 that, "it is time to acknowledge that getting dramatic results from school choice will be harder than expected—and that the actions that must be taken will be more difficult than some supporters had hoped."[31] Chester E. Finn, Jr. has conceded, "Early zealots of the charter-school movement, myself included, were naive . . . we paid too little attention to whether those vying to launch charter schools were up to the challenge, whether those authorizing them were performing due diligence and oversight, whether curricular and instructional plans were sound and accountability instruments adequate."[32]

Many attempts to increase quantity and quality are underway.[33] And that's good, I believe, for public education. Charters have parental appeal and offer fresh leadership, ideas and ideals. Still, they are not the millennium for school reform. They show little capacity to grow in scale into a nationwide system, idealized by conservatives, that could put regular public schools as we know them out of business.

Vouchers

Vouchers would be the most potent choice weapons of all, say choice partisans. By enabling parents to choose public or non-public schools, vouchers will bust the public monopoly controlled by teachers' unions and mismanaged by bureaucrats. The "invisible hand" of competition will work its wonders, and students—whom choice advocates identify as "consumers"—will profit academically.[34]

Could it happen? It's extremely improbable. Most voucher initiatives have been smothered by liberal opposition led by teachers' unions, including the resounding defeat of statewide referenda in California, Michigan and conservative Utah. Moreover, the research on the handful of programs that have gotten off the ground is unpromising. As two researchers concluded in 2007, the evidence is "decidedly mixed, leaving policy makers with few reasons to push for voucher reform or expend time and effort rallying support."[35] A recent study of the groundbreaking initiative begun in Milwaukee in 1995 found "relative parity" between voucher students and comparable public school students.[36] And evidence on the large, federally-funded District of Columbia voucher program is contested and in a state of flux.[37]

Still, education conservatives think vouchers "are alive and well."[38] Public opinion is about evenly divided for and against them,[39] and the door may be open, as contemplated in chapter 14, for political compacts in which liberals get more money and conservatives get more choice, including vouchers for low-income families. But from the experience to date, there is no credible basis to cast vouchers as a primetime player in nationwide school reform.

Other Privatization Initiatives

School choice allied with privatization is blossoming beyond charter schools and vouchers. Most notably, bold urban superintendents—notably in Chicago, New York, Baltimore, D. C., and New Orleans—have been bringing in outside companies to operate schools under contracts. Contract schools overlap more or less with charter schools, and operators are a mixed bag of for-profit and non-profit organizations. Some operators are local enterprises. Others are regional or national networks. What they have in common is substantial autonomy from school system regulation and competition with each other and regular schools.

Contract schools are even newer on the scene than charter schools, and so their effectiveness and growth potential are unknown. The same uncertainty applies to instances where privatization of classroom instruction *within* regular schools is gaining a foothold. For example, private management consultants are working with school systems to design curriculum, data-driven assessments and intervention strategies. And private companies are directly providing tutoring and teacher training. These outside-in reforms are in their infancy and deserve support, but, like charters, their capacity to dramatically alter the K–12 landscape seems limited.[40]

The Rest of the Passing Parade

There are numerous other current, widespread reforms. For example: alternative certification and merit pay for teachers, smaller class sizes, smaller high schools and middle schools, schools with grades K–8 replacing separate elementary and middle schools, all-day kindergarten programs, instructional technology, restrictions on "social promotion" of students who don't meet passing standards, and after-school and summer school academic programs. The list grows exponentially if lesser but other budding initiatives are included—like school uniforms, single-gender schools, better food programs, and incentives to students for good grades or attendance.

Unfortunately, this long reform parade is likely to pass by failing schools and students without leaving behind much impact. It isn't that the majority of these big and little proposals aren't worth trying. It's that, first of all, there are simply too many of them. According to one estimate, there were 3,000 reform measures of one kind or another enacted in the 1980s alone.[41] That is too many for even able administrators to manage and to evaluate. What's more, too many stray from a sharp focus on classroom instruction, as explored in chapter 3. In addition, the so-called priorities keep changing. Teachers and administrators are driven to distraction by the constant changes forced upon them.

Moreover, excavation of the research on past and present reforms yields only fragments of know-how and hope. That, as we have seen, is the case with accountability and school choice. It is also true of the instructional "best practices" that are backed by a fair amount of relatively reliable research. These "best practices" include smaller class sizes, pre-school programs, certain early reading programs, summer school, tutoring for low-performing students, and classroom-based coaches for teachers. But even there, the weight of the evidence of effectiveness is often disputed.

For instance, smaller class sizes. If any education policy would seem to be a commonsense win-win, smaller class size would be it. Teachers as a rule would opt for smaller classes over higher pay. Parents and the general public are enthusiastically supportive. And the thrust of the research, summarized by the Brookings Institution in 2006, is that reducing class size substantially in early elementary grades pays off academically, especially for Black students.[42]

Nonetheless, the Brookings articles also cite a lot of expert skepticism. California embarked on the nation's largest class size reduction program, but encountered problems recruiting enough teachers and providing classroom space; the research on the initiative is inconclusive. The research is also confined for the most part to class size reductions in elementary schools, leaving unknown the possible benefits in middle and high schools.[43]

An even more surprising debate is over pre-school programs such as Head Start and pre-kindergarten classes. These, like smaller class size, would seem candidates for landslide acclaim based on common sense and well-publicized research. Yet, controversy is rampant. All sides agree on the importance of pre-school readiness. But which readiness traits are most important for three- and four-year olds and how to impart them are controversial, with strong ideological undertones. Social-emotional readiness is favored by liberals; academic readiness, especially early language and literacy development, is favored by conservatives.[44]

Keep in mind that smaller class sizes and pre-school programs are examples of the lingering uncertainties and disputes over "best practices" with a fair amount of science behind them. It only gets worse from there. The horizon is cloudier for many other high-flying initiatives where the research is either mainly negative or inconclusive. To mention a few: initiatives to improve middle schools,[45] to break up high schools into smaller schools,[46] and to devise merit pay incentives for teachers.[47]

Wishful Thinkers

The absence of proof of what might change the course of K–12 public education does not deter many people from self-assured certainties. Out front are ideologues who believe that their respective agendas—for liberals, more money spent on schools and social programs and on progressive teaching methods; for conservatives, more school choice, emasculated teachers' unions and traditional teaching methods—will lead us to the educational promised land.

But they aren't the only ones. Another school of thought—populated by pragmatists—believes that we know what to do, but just don't do it. Bill Clinton, a consummate centrist, proclaimed as president that "Nearly every [education] problem has been solved by somebody somewhere and yet we can't seem to replicate it anywhere else."[48] However the president, rarely at a loss for policy prescriptions, was uncharacteristically vague about what exact school policies and programs were to be replicated. John L. Anderson, head of the then highly touted New American Schools Development Corporation (NASDC), bemoaned: "After a lot of years of trying to improve schools, we don't have one district of any size or diversity of population where good schools are the norm not the exception. And that runs contrary to the fact that we know how to create good schools."[49] But he, like Clinton, didn't spell out how it could be done, and the NASDC, which had a congressional mandate to create good schools on a national scale, was a failure.[50]

More than a decade later, many in educational and political high places still haven't learned the NASDC lesson. In 2005, education entrepreneur Chris Whittle wrote in *The Wall Street Journal:* "After 15 years of up-close involvement with public education, I have heard the same refrain: 'We know what to do to improve schools. Our problems are just a failure of execution.'" But Whittle's own take was "I don't buy that."[51] Neither do I. But the notion persists. Bill Gates opined in 2007 that the basic problem is "the lack of political and public will."[52] However, the will has been amply demonstrated by reams of public opinion polls, earlier noted, that show overwhelming support for reform and the electorate's willingness to pay higher taxes to bring it about. It's further demonstrated by the endless reforms that have been tried and by the national, state and local politicians from both sides of the aisle who run for office on education platforms.

Another slim reed for wishful thinkers is the heartwarming stories of heroic individual teachers. Each of us has personally encountered some, we hear about them in the media, and we see movies based on their lives like *Up the Down Staircase, Stand and Deliver, Conrack and Mr. Holland's Opus.* If they can do it, why can't all teachers? The obvious answer is because super-nova teachers who burst on the scene and light up the despairing lives of poor students are rare. Their stories are inspirational but we don't know how to clone Jaime Escalante or the cherished teachers that each of us remembers. To become stars, most teachers require a galaxy of support that doesn't exist.

The public seems ahead of ideologues and other certaintists in recognizing the reality of uncertainty. A national poll in 2007 revealed that sizable portions of the public remain un-persuaded by liberal or conservative reform platforms.[53] Still, uncertainty doesn't mean we can't substantially improve public schools. We just haven't figured out well enough how to do it. Which is where this book fits in. Many hopeful steps can be taken, and they are delineated in later chapters. But on the way to specific recommendations, we must be on the lookout for basic factors—I call them "bedrock barriers"—that stand in the way. These stumbling blocks are brought to light next.

NOTES

1. Stacey Childress, Richard Elmore and Allen Grossman, "How to Manage Urban School Districts," *Harvard Business Review,* November 2006: 55–68, 55.

2. The National Center for Education Statistics, "About the Nation's Report Card," http://www.nationsreportcard.gov/about_nrc.asp.

3. The cities are Atlanta, Austin, Boston, Charlotte, Chicago, Cleveland, District of Columbia, Houston, Los Angeles, New York City, and San Diego. Cities to be added in 2009 are Baltimore, Detroit, Fresno, Louisville, and Milwaukee.

4. National Center for Education Statistics, *Reading 2007: Trial Urban District Assessment Results At Grades 4 and 8,* http://nces.gov/nationsreportcard/ pubs/dst2007/2008455; National Center for Education Statistics, *Mathematics 2007: Trial Urban District Assessment Results At Grades 4 and 8,* http://nces. gov/nationsreportcard/pubs/dst2007/2008452. Comparisons of students in the U.S. against our international competitors are inexact and controversial, but in general we are "failing to ensure that our children are academically prepared to compete with their international peers." The Commission on No Child Left Behind, *Beyond NCLB: Fulfilling the Promise to Our Nation's Children* (Washington, DC: The Aspen Institute, 2007), 11. This includes low-income U.S. students who perform worse than low-income peers in other countries. See, for example, David C. Miller and others, *Comparitive Indicators of Education in the United States and Other G-8 Countries: 2006* (Washington, DC: U. S. Department of Education, 2007). Compare Gerald W. Bracey, "Believing the Worst," *Stanford Magazine,*

July/August 2006, http:www.stanfordalumni.org/news/magazine/2006/julaug/features/nclb.html.

5. Nancy Kober, *A Public Education Primer* (Washington, DC: Center on Education Policy, 2006), 28.

6. Derived from data in Center on Education Policy, *Has Student Achievement Increased Since 2002?* (Washington, DC: Center on Education Policy, 2008).

7. Disparities of fifty or more percentage points are found, especially in reading, in Atlanta, Charlotte, Chicago and Cleveland. U.S. Department of Education, *Reading 2007;* U.S. Department of Education, *Mathematics 2007;* Jason Snipes and others, *Beating the Odds VIII: An Analysis of Student Performance and Achievement Gaps on State Assessments* (Washington, DC: Council of Great Cities Schools, 2008).

8. Bruce Fuller and others, "Gauging Growth: How to Judge No Child Left Behind?" *Educational Researcher,* vol. 36, no. 5 (June/July 2007): 268–278.

9. Sean Cavenagh, "State Tests, NAEP Often a Mismatch," *Education Week,* June 13, 2007: 1, 23.

10. John Cronin and others, *The Proficiency Illusion* (Washington, DC: Thomas B. Fordham Institute, 2007), Foreword by Chester E. Finn, Jr. and Michael J. Petrilli, 3.

11. Center on Education Policy, *Has Student Achievement Increased Since 2002?*; Margery Yeager, *Understanding NAEP: Inside the Nation's Education Report Card* (Washington, DC: Education Sector, 2007).

12. Cavenagh, "State Tests, NAEP Often a Mismatch." Other extenuating circumstances for the disparities between the NAEP and state results are offered. NAEP is not aligned to state curricula and classroom teaching as state tests are. Student and teacher motivation differ because state tests have high stake consequences (under NCLB, for example) whereas NAEP tests don't. And there is much more test-prep for state tests. Center on Education Policy, *Has Student Achievement Increased Since 2002?,* 62; Cronin and others, *The Proficiency Illusion,* 35. Despite a growing cry to find middle ground, the debate drags on. When Diane Ravitch and Deborah Meier, luminaries of the education right and left respectively, were convened for a dialogue, they found many areas in which they could bridge differences. But neither gave ground on NAEP. Meier condemned "its cuts scores and norms as . . . politically determined and, at present, absurdly high;" Ravitch countered that NAEP's "assessment standards are entirely nonpolitical and benchmarked to international standards." Deborah Meier and Diane Ravitch, "Bridging Differences: A Dialogue Between Deborah Meier and Diane Ravitch," Commentary, *Education Week,* May 24, 2006: 36–37, 44.

13. Fuller and others, "Gauging Growth," 270.

14. Center on Education Policy, *Has Student Achievement Increased Since 2002?* 25.

15. Fuller and others, "Gauging Growth," 273.

16. Fuller and others, "Gauging Growth," 270. See also Sam Dillon, "'No Child' Law Is Not Closing a Racial Gap," *The New York Times,* April 28, 2009: A1.

17. *The Manufactured Crisis: Myths, Fraud, and the Attack on America's Public Schools* (Reading, MA: Addison-Wesley, 1995), xi–xii, 144.

18. Berliner and Biddle, *The Manufactured Crisis,* xii, 343. See also Richard Rothstein, "The Myth of Public School Failure," *The American Prospect,* no. 13 (Spring 1993): 20–34, 33.

19. Diane Ravitch, "Are American Schools Better Than We Think?" Education Review, *The Washington Post,* November 5, 1995, 16.

20. Lawrence C. Stedman, "Putting the System to the Test," Education Review, *The Washington Post,* November 5, 1995, 16, 17.

21. "Risky business," *The Education Gadfly,* vol. 7, no. 34 (September 9, 2007): 2.

22. Bracey, "Believing the Worst."

23. Fuller and others, "Gauging Growth," 277.

24. For further discussion of the shortcomings of NCLB and state accountability laws, see chapter 9.

25. *Politics, Markets and America's Schools* (Washington, DC: The Brookings Institution, 1990), 217.

26. In a national poll in 2007, 65 percent of the public favored and 35 percent opposed charter schools, and the support is increasing each year. Lowell C. Rose and Alec M. Gallup, "The 39th Annual Phi Delta Kappa/Gallup Poll of the Public's Attitude Toward The Public Schools," *Phi Delta Kappan,* vol. 89, no. 1 (September 2007): 34–45, 38.

27. For general background on their growth: Robert Bifulco and Katrina Bulkley, "Charter Schools," in Helen F. Ladd and Edward B. Fiske, eds. *Handbook of Research in Education Finance and Policy* (New York: Routledge, 2008); Robin J. Lake, ed., *Hopes, Fears, & Reality: A Balanced Look at American Charter Schools in 2007* (Seattle, WA: University of Washington Center on Reinventing Public Education, 2007).

28. Bifulco and Bulkley, "Charter Schools," 436, 440.

29. Childress, Elmore and Grossman, "How to Manage Urban School Districts," 58.

30. Erik W. Robelen, "Project Aims to Cut Through Fog of Studies on Charters," *Education Week,* August 29, 2007: 12.

31. "Waiting for the 'Tipping Point'," Commentary, *Education Week* (September 5, 2007): 26.

32. Chester E. Finn, Jr., *Troublemaker* (Princeton, NJ: Princeton University Press, 2008), 266.

33. In the forefront are the think tank Educator Sector and the National Charter Schools Research Project.

34. An excellent balanced overview is Roy Zimmer and Eric P. Bettinger, "Beyond the Rhetoric: Surveying the Evidence on Vouchers and Tax Credits," in Ladd and Fiske, *Handbook of Research in Education Finance and Policy.*

35. Chad d'Entremont and Luis A. Huerta, "Irreconcilable Differences? Education Vouchers and the Suburban Response," *Educational Policy,* vol. 21, no. 1 (2007): 40–72, 49. See also Zimmer and Bettinger, "Beyond the Rhetoric," 458.

36. Alan J. Borsuk, "Voucher study finds parity," *The Milwaukee Journal Sentinel JS Online,* February 25, 2008, http://www.jsonline.com/story/index .aspx?id=721737.

37. Maria Glod, "Study Supports School Vouchers," *The Washington Post,* April 4, 2009, B1; Maria Glod and Bill Turque, "Report Finds Little Gain From Vouchers," *The Washington Post,* June 17, 2008, B6.

38. Lisa Snell, "Vouchers: Alive, Well and Working," Opinion, *The Los Angeles Times,* February 13, 2008. For a recent all-out defense of vouchers (and choice strategies in general), see Jay P. Greene and others, "Is School Choice Enough?" *City Journal,* vol. 18, no. 3 (Summer 2008), http://www.city-journal.org/2008/forum0124.html.

39. The wording of the question affects the responses. Compare Rose and Gallup, "The 39th Annual Phi Delta Kappa/Gallup Poll," 37; and William G. Howell, Martin R. West and Paul E. Peterson, "What Americans Think About Their Schools," *Education Next,* vol. 7, no. 4 (Fall 2007): 13–26, 17.

40. For a further account of the capacity of privatized school operators, including charter and contract schools, see chapter 12.

41. Fredrick M. Hess, *Spinning Wheels: The Politics of Urban School Reform* (Washington, DC: Brookings Institution Press, 1999), 9.

42. Tom Loveless and Frederick M. Hess, eds., *Brookings Papers on Education Policy, 2006/2007* (Washington, DC: The Brookings Institution, 2007).

43. Class size illustrates how school policy issues are too often presented as false dichotomies. The class size issue is usually posed: Would you prefer more students with an excellent teacher or less students with a poor teacher? But, even putting to one side the difficulty in calibrating the continuum between "excellent" and "poor" teachers, it is obvious that urban school systems in particular do not have enough excellent or anywhere near-excellent teachers with current large classes. So the real-world choice is between more or less students with mainly average teachers.

44. For a sampling of the voluminous literature on early childhood education: National Research Council, Robert T. Bowman, M. Suzanne Donovan and M. Susan Burns, eds., *Eager to Learn: Educating Our Preschoolers* (Washington, DC: National Academy Press, 2001); and an exchange "Young Einsteins," by David Elkind, "Much Too Early," and Grover J. Whitehurst, "Much Too Late," *Education Next,* vol. 1, no. 2 (Summer 2001): 9–21.

45. Debra Viadero, "No School Improvement Models Get Top Rating From AIR," *Education Week* (October 11, 2006): 9; Kathleen Kennedy Manzo, "Motivating Students in the Middle Years," *Education Week* (March 19, 2008): 22–25.

46. Loveless and Hess, *Brookings Papers on Education Policy;* Erik W. Robelen, "Schools-Within-Schools Model Seen Yielding Trade-Offs," *Education Week* (September 19, 2007): 10.

47. Vaishali Honawar, "Performance-Pay Studies Show Few Achievement Gains," *Education Week* (March 12, 2008): 7; Lynn Olson, "Teacher-Pay Experiments Mounting Amid Debate," Education Week (October 8, 2007): 1.

48. Lynn Olson, "Growing Pains," *Education Week* (November 2, 1994): 29.

49. Olson, "Growing Pains."

50. Mark Behrends, *Assessing the Progress of New American Schools: A Status Report* (Santa Monica, CA: RAND, 1999); Debra Viadero, "Research Group, New American Schools Merge," *Education Week* (May 5, 2004): 12.

51. "S.O.S. (Save Our Schools)," Opinion, *The Wall Street Journal,* November 4, 2005.

52. David M. Herszenhorn, "Billionaires Start $60 Million Schools Effort," *The New York Times,* April 25, 2007, http://www.nytimes.com/2007/04/25/education/25schools.html.

53. William G. Howell, Martin R. West, and Paul E. Peterson, "What Americans Think About Their Schools," *Education Next,* vol. 7, no. 4 (Fall 2007): 12–26, 17.

Part II

Bedrock Barriers to Reform

American public schools fail for myriad reasons. In the next three chapters, I uncover several whose harmful impact is most concealed. These bedrock barriers might be likened to dominant genes in the DNA of public education that are insufficiently mapped and understood. The first of these barriers is the failure of school reform to focus directly on teaching and learning in the classroom. The second is the conflict over competing priorities for reform: should it be "equity," to bring low-achieving, predominantly minority students up to acceptable standards, or "excellence," to raise all students to world-class benchmarks? The third is the never-ending warfare between political and educational ideologues that wrecks most reform efforts.

Chapter 3

It's the Classroom, Stupid

You would think that school reform would be all about improving teaching and learning in the classroom. But it isn't. There is a vast difference between reforms that focus *directly* on the classroom, and those that don't. Just ask the prestigious Koret Task Force on K–12 Education, made up mainly of conservative education bigwigs. It convened a debate in 2007 that cast a rare, illuminating light on a bedrock obstacle to school reform that runs through the history of U.S. public education: the failure of most reforms to focus first and foremost on classroom instruction and the daily interactions between teachers and students.

The Koret debate topic was "Resolved: True School Reform Demands More Attention to Curriculum and Instruction than to Markets and Choice."[1] It signified unrest among education conservatives that the market-based choice movement was not living up to expectations, and several of its long-time leaders thought the reason was its neglect of teaching and learning in the classroom. They were right. And liberals have been no less guilty than conservatives of this neglect.

The Public Education Leadership Project has studied urban school districts across the country. Its conclusion: there is an overriding need for system-wide reform to concentrate on "the instructional core."[2] The Project's lead scholars write that "most external forces pull public school districts away from their focus on student achievement. Thus, a district must . . . begin at the nucleus of its organization: teaching and learning."[3] Education historian Jeffrey Mishel observes that a procession of school reforms devoted to organization, governance, and funding have related more "to the context of education than to what goes on in classrooms."[4]

31

The lack of success of the most influential school reform strategies illustrates the point. Again accountability is a prime example. High academic standards and tough tests that measure what students have learned are indispensable. Otherwise, it is impossible to hold educators accountable for dismal student outcomes. In chapter 9, I go a big step farther than most accountability supporters in urging the adoption of national standards and tests. Still, standards and tests only set *what* is to be learned; they don't address *how* teachers are to teach so students learn what they should.

They don't address what instructional programs should be used, how much classroom time is needed, how students should be grouped, the pace of instruction, and many other aspects of teacher interactions with students. They don't address what resources are needed—for example, teacher training, manageable teacher-student ratios, academic and behavioral interventions for struggling students, and sufficient supervision, monitoring, and evaluation of instruction.

Despite these limitations, many accountability champions hold out the promise that standards and testing are enough by themselves to significantly improve student achievement. NCLB's strict expectations and sanctions are supposed to put schools and teachers on the hot seat; teachers are pressured to teach to the tests; and presto, so the theory goes, test results will soar. But this kind of levitational magic hasn't occurred, as witnessed by the massive failure of schools and students since the accountability movement began. As the saying goes, you can't fatten a calf by weighing it.

Charter schools suffer from the same disconnect with the core of teaching and learning in the classroom. Beyond the evidence showing that they have produced only modest gains in student achievement (as summarized in the prior chapter), they do not seem to be on the road to fulfill another paramount objective: that they will be incubators for breakthrough instructional practices that can be transplanted into public schools.[5] Successful charter schools demonstrate exceptional leadership, school climate and high expectations, but not distinctive "innovations of educational delivery," in the words of charter advocate and policy analyst Frederick M. Hess.[6] Therefore, the best charter schools are not easily replicated, and their overall ripple effect on public schools has been slight.

Accountability and choice are the biggest and most visible reform strategies that are structurally insufficient because they have little direct impact on the classroom. But there are many others. For instance, replacing large high schools that enroll 1000–2000 students with smaller ones with 200–500 students. The theory is impeccable: smaller schools enable teachers, students and parents to create closer learning communities, and the advantages outweigh the higher per-pupil costs that result when economies of scale are lost. Yet the Gates Foundation, after spending more than $1 billion promoting small schools and realizing little success, was compelled to concede that fewer classrooms in a more compact environment don't change the quality of teaching that goes on in the classrooms.[7]

The same holds true for the spreading popularity of combining K–5 elementary schools and 6–8 middle schools into K–8 schools. The hypothesis makes sense. It keeps vulnerable young adolescents longer in neighborhood, nurturing elementary school settings. Middle schools have long been even more difficult to reform than high schools. So the Baltimore public school system, with my active support as a school board member, has been a national leader in making the transition. But the execution in Baltimore and elsewhere has been faulty, largely because the organizational structure has been modified but classroom instruction hasn't. Evidence of the effectiveness of K–8 schools, as in the case of smaller schools, is unproven.[8]

This is not to say that these organizational changes should be scrapped. They can help to improve teacher collaboration, student behavior and other facets of school climate, all of which bear on teaching and learning. But the benefits are bound to be marginal unless simultaneously there are changes in classroom instruction.

Another telltale illustration of a heralded reform that fails to reach into the classroom and thus falls short of its goals is the popular quest to end "social promotions"—that is, the practice in virtually every school system (though the numbers are much larger in urban districts) of promoting students from one grade to the next even though they don't meet passing standards. Few reforms seem to make so much sense. Yet, good intent collides with reality, and policies that seek to curtail social promotions have not succeeded.

The main explanation for this policy failure is that while social promotion doesn't usually work, neither does retention. Flunking students and retaining them in the same grade is no guarantee that they will catch up with their peers, particularly if they get the same instruction in the same way a second (or third) time around. The only sure ways to prevent social promotions *or* retentions are timely instructional interventions that keep students from falling behind in the first place.[9]

Baltimore is a case study. In the late 1990s, Chicago and New York undertook well-publicized initiatives, and Baltimore sought to follow suit. As a consultant, I drafted its policy that turned out to be the most far-reaching in the country. Baltimore put "promotional gates"—meaning students had to meet stringent standards to be promoted to the next grade—in grades one through eight, whereas Chicago and New York had instituted them in only a few grades. The intent was for retained students to be brought back up to their age-appropriate grade level through intensive instructional interventions. But the resources—the knowledge about research-based instructional practices, the better-trained teachers, and the money—weren't there to deliver.

As a consequence, as many as 50 percent of all flunked students were subject to being retained more than once in the same or different grades. Falling farther behind academically and becoming more overage, discouraged, and disruptive in the classroom, students who are retained twice are almost certain to become dropouts. In the face of these facts and the inability to deliver the necessary instructional interventions, Baltimore and other urban school systems have gradually watered down their policies, and social promotions are still widespread.

What about governance reforms? In chapter 10, I put a lot of stock in proposals to give mayors control of local school systems and to eliminate school boards. Mayors are of course remote from the classroom. But this cornerstone strategy is an exception to the rule because it is probably a pre-condition for instructional reform. It is likely to lead to clearer lines of executive authority and accountability, the infusion of stronger managers and management systems, and a political buffer zone. These will enable educators to focus more effectively on what they should know and do best: classroom instruction.

WHY IS THE INSTRUCTIONAL CORE NEGLECTED?

It is no mystery why most school reformers, despite good ideas and intentions, slight teaching and learning. For one thing, teachers want to be left alone to do their own thing. They avow it's their professional right to reject any restrictions on their autonomy. So inside the classroom is where reformers least dare to tread.[10] Another basic reason is that reform movements that don't directly affect classroom learning are relatively easy to understand and communicate. Proposals like school choice, accountability, and reorganizations make good sound bites for politicians and an education establishment desperate to appear to be "doing something" to bring about change. On the other hand, changing the instructional core requires professional knowledge, arduous work in the classroom trenches, and a lot more money. All are in short supply, and mismanagement of instruction, as detailed in chapter 11, is the least recognized but most fatal damage done by bungling school bureaucracies.

As a result, there are many missing links between most policy reforms and classroom practice. Susan H. Fuhrman, dean of the University of Pennsylvania Graduate School of Education, thinks instruction is so complex and dependent on the dynamics between individual teachers and students that it "is very difficult to implement through policy."[11] Education historians David Tyack and Larry Cuban have captured it best: "Change where it counts the most—in the daily interactions of teachers and students—is the hardest to achieve and the most important."[12]

How will such change be achieved? First, by learning the lesson in this chapter that for school reform to succeed, "it's the classroom, stupid." Second, the other bedrock barriers, next described, must be exposed. And third, the cornerstone recommendations in later parts of the book, including proposals to overhaul the management of the design and delivery of classroom instruction, must be implemented.

NOTES

1. The debate was not transcribed. For a link to the audio, see http://www.hoover.org/research/taskforces/education. The debate is recounted in Sol Stern, "School Choice Isn't Enough," *City Journal,* vol. 18, no. 1 (Winter 2008), http://www.city-journal.org/2008/18_1_instructional_reform.html.

2. Stacey Childress, Richard Elmore, Allen Grossman and Caroline King, *Note on the PELP Coherence Framework,* undated, http://agi.harvard.edu/conference/09_PELP2%20Coherence%20Framework%20Note% 2007, 2.

3. Stacey Childress, Richard Elmore and Allen Grossman, "How to Manage Urban School Districts," *Harvard Business Review* (November 2006): 55–68, 60.

4. Jeffrey Mirel, "Urban Public Schools in the Twentieth Century: The View from Detroit," in Diane Ravitch, ed., *Brookings Papers on Education Policy 1999* (Washington, DC: The Brookings Institution, 1999), 52.

5. Paul T. Hill, "Waiting for the 'Tipping Point'," Commentary, *Education Week,* September 5, 2007, 26–27.

6. Frederick M. Hess, "The Supply Side of School Reform," in Hess, ed. *The Future of Educational Entrepreneurship: Possibilities for School Reform* (Cambridge, MA: Harvard Education Press, 2008).

7. Childress, Elmore and Grossman, "How to Manage Urban School Districts;" Linda Shear and others, "Contrasting Paths to Small-School Reform: Results of a 5-year Evaluation of the Bill & Melinda Gates Foundation's National High Schools Initiative," *Teachers College Record,* vol. 110, no. 9 (2008), http://www.tcrecord.org/Content.asp?ContentID=15180.

8. Debra Viadero, "Evidence for Moving to K–8 Model Not Airtight," *Education Week* (January 16, 2008): 1, 12.

9. Kalman R. Hettleman, "Study of Promotion/Retention Policies in Urban School Districts," unpublished study submitted to the Baltimore City Public School System, November 1998; Robert M. Hauser, Carl B. Frederick and Megan Andrew, "Grade Retention in the Age of Standards-Based Reform," in Adam Gamoran, ed.,

Standards-Based Reform and the Poverty Gap (Washington, DC: The Brookings Institution, 2007).

10. For fuller analysis of the insularity of teachers and their hostility to encroachments on their classroom turf, see chapter 11.

11. Susan H. Fuhrman, "Less than Meets the Eye: Standards, Testing, and Fear of Federal Control," in Noel Epstein, ed., *Who's in Charge Here: The Tangled Web of School Governance and Policy* (Washington, DC: Brookings Institution Press, 2004), 142.

12. David Tyack and Larry Cuban, *Tinkering Toward Utopia: A Century of Public School Reform* (Cambridge, MA.: Harvard University Press, 1995), 10.

Chapter 4

Which Children Get Left Behind?

Yogi Berra supposedly said, when you come to a fork in the road, take it. If only education reform were that easy. Any explanation of our country's failure to focus on the classroom and to close the achievement gap between races and economic classes must take into account the bedrock conflict over the most urgent goal for American school reform. Is the highest priority to close the achievement gap—that is, to bring low-achieving, predominantly poor and minority students up to basic competencies? That goal is commonly referred to as "equity." Or is the goal to bring all students up to world-class standards, the goal known as "excellence"?

We shouldn't have to choose. Public opinion says we can and should do both.[1] If all students were brought up to world-class benchmarks, disadvantaged students would benefit. A rising tide of excellence would lift all students to where they can meet high standards and compete successfully for good jobs in a global economy.

Of course that hasn't happened. Many education policy analysts think we are doing well enough on the whole: it's the low-income students concentrated in big cities who are the big problem and cause all public schools to be unfairly condemned. Education professor Larry Cuban finds fault with "the flawed logic of those who tar all public schools with the urban brush."[2] However, others believe the entire system is broken and needs an overhaul. The psychologist and popular writer Howard Gardner writes a dreary "Tale of Three Systems," all of which need revival: inner cities, rural areas and working-class suburbs, and under-performing elites.[3]

The origins of the dilemma lie in the multiple missions that public schools have been called on to undertake. These missions extend beyond the acquisition of core academic knowledge. As far back as the "common school"

37

pioneered by Horace Mann in the early 1800s and through much of the twentieth century, public schools were asked to shoulder the assimilation of immigrants, preparing them for citizenship and promoting social cohesion and economic growth. In the process, as policy scholar David Gamson chronicles, educators tried to adapt the curricula to the differing "aptitudes, abilities, and ambitions of students."[4] It was a delicate balancing act between high-level coursework for some, "life adjustment" or vocational education for others. Controversy over IQ burst on the national scene, and "tracking" of students according to their ability became a dirty word.

The goal of excellence got a big boost when, following Russian launch of the space vehicle Sputnik, the National Defense Education Act of 1958 cast math and science education as vital to our national security. But the goal of equity rebounded through the 1960s and 1970s, as the civil rights era concentrated the nation's attention on assuring equal educational opportunity for poor children, especially Blacks. The landmark 1965 Elementary and Secondary Education Act, that initiated large-scale federal aid for schools serving low-income students, was enacted as part of the Great Society programs under President Lyndon B. Johnson.

Then in 1983 another shift occurred, signaled by the famous warning in the *A Nation at Risk* report that "a rising tide of mediocrity . . . threatens our very future as a Nation and a people."[5] The threat was primarily international economic competition, and equity took a back seat.[6]

Equity stayed in the rear until passage of NCLB in 2001. As analyzed in detail in later chapters, NCLB was an ambitious attempt to wrap equity and excellence within one legislative package. Every child is supposed to meet demanding standards by 2014 in literacy, math and science. But that lofty aspiration complicated the legislative design and caused much of the ongoing furor over the law's rigorous mandates.

CLASS WARFARE

In the real world of K–12 school policy-making, the best interests of low-income students often clash with the best interests of higher income students. Examples of this economic class competition begin with a closer look at how it has affected the course of NCLB.

Leave My Child Alone

Middle- and upper-class parents spearhead the criticism of NCLB. They object to its preoccupation, as they see it, with testing that emphasizes academics at the expense of broader, life-enriching educational experiences. And many are fleeing public schools. Abundant evidence confirms that since NCLB, the curriculum has been narrowed and subjects like art, gym and music crowded out.[7] Two commentators allege that NCLB "forces a fundamental educational approach so inappropriate for high-ability students that it destroys their interest in learning, as school becomes an endless chain of basic lessons aimed at low-performing students."[8] A report published by the Thomas B. Fordham Institute finds, on the basis of data analysis and a national teacher survey, that NCLB and state accountability laws have helped low-performing students while the performance of top students has been "languid."[9]

It's not that Americans of all economic stripes don't support special efforts to help poor students. They do. But non-poor parents want to be left alone and left out of NCLB testing and other mandates. A recent study confirmed that lower-income parents are more in favor of what NCLB is trying to accomplish than other parents.[10] And for good reason. School accountability doesn't matter as much to middle- and upper-income children who, through their families, learn a lot more outside of school than do low-income children.

A stunning demonstration of this is "summer learning loss." The hallmark research on point is by Johns Hopkins University sociologists who found that Baltimore's poor children tend to keep up with middle class peers during the regular school year but fall behind over the summer when their peers benefit from out-of-school enrichment.[11] Simply put, NCLB and other attempts to raise academic standards and impose rigorous student testing are more crucial to the success of at-risk, lower-income children than other children. The net result is swelling middle- and upper-class sentiment to repeal or substantially weaken NCLB. Some equity advocates, on the defensive, think that NCLB should abandon the target of universal proficiency and zero in more narrowly on closing the achievement gap.[12]

Some of the same tensions bedevil states' efforts, not covered by NCLB, to raise the bar for high school graduation exams from minimum competency to world-class standards. Many states are backpedaling or finding loopholes to prevent large numbers of students, predominantly low-income children of color, from failing to graduate.[13]

Dueling for Dollars

The simultaneous embrace of equity and excellence is also thwarted by the competition for scarce funds. Equity partisans zero in on the inequitable funding for poor urban districts.[14] Yet, wealthier suburbs complain that their schools too are under-funded. This friction plays out in many ways. Should expenditures for preschool, all-day kindergarten, summer school and smaller class sizes be provided for all students, or just those at risk—even when research shows that the benefits accrue mainly to minority and disadvantaged students?[15]

For example, Maryland, a wealthy state, mandates and provides substantial funding for all-day kindergarten statewide, despite lacking any evidence of gains for children who are not at risk of school failure. The funds, by any cost-benefit calculus, would be more productively spent on instructional interventions for at-risk students. But upper-income parents don't see it that way. They want their kids to get every possible edge, particularly now that college admissions are more competitive than ever. Yet, resources earmarked to achieve equity are already so limited that triage rears its ugly head even among low-performing students. Those closest to passing state exams— "bubble kids"—receive more assistance than those at the bottom who are written off as having no chance of passing.[16]

Advocates of programs for "gifted and talented" students add their voices to the chorus of complaints that low-performing students receive a dispro-portionate share of funds. I was confronted as a school board member in Baltimore with an excruciating vote when the CEO (superintendent) recom-mended, as part of a per-student funding formula for individual schools, that "advanced" students were entitled to the same per-student amount as "fail-ing" students. The advanced students, many of them low-income children of color, deserve the chance to fulfill their full potential. Moreover, since many other advanced students are from middle-class families, serving their needs helps to stem the exodus of such families from city schools. These rationales carried the day, and the CEO's recommendation was passed. But I dissented on the grounds that the weight for failing students should be several times greater than for advanced students. In my view, there is simply not enough money to go around, and the academic poorest of the poor needed assistance most desperately.

School systems nationwide are struggling with the same dilemma. In many local districts, especially in the face of complaints that NCLB is causing programs for "gifted" students to be crowded out, parents are pressing states to widen eligibility and boost funding for such programs.[17] Inevitably, the expansion of gifted programs will be largely at the expense of extra help for low-performing students.

Other Class Conflicts

It's hard to find a major school reform issue where the equity versus excellence equation doesn't factor in. For instance, a battleground in the "reading wars" is the claim that "phonics" methods better meets the needs of struggling, disproportionately low-income learners than "whole language" methods.[18] Economic class struggle also lurks beneath disputes over vouchers and charter schools. Persons suspicious of choice programs argue that no matter how great the effort to assure that all students have equal chance to participate, some "creaming" will occur: that is, the poorest families with the lowest-performing students have the least savvy and will take the least advantage of choice opportunities.[19]

The economic class divide even affects the cutoff age of entry into pre-kindergarten and kindergarten. Low-income students, because of less enriching home environments, benefit more than other students from enrollment at the earliest possible age. At the other extreme, many middle- and upper-income families are holding back their four- and five-year-olds a year in the hopes the delay will pay off years later in the competition for gifted programs and even college admissions.[20]

EQUITY MUST COME FIRST

The nation will remain stuck with winners and losers in the competition between equity and excellence as long as we persist in not finding the way to achieve both at the same time. History will continue to show "that the ascendance of one tends to distract attention paid to the other,"[21] with equity usually winding up on the short end. The enduring plight of poor and minority Americans shows that they are almost invariably the losers when economic class interests, typically interwoven with racial issues, clash.

Given this political reality, this book's recommendations dwell on policies to achieve equity. The percentage of low-income students in public schools across the country is growing rapidly,[22] and the achievement gap is the most important civil rights issue of our times. Inequitable educational opportunity is the shame of our nation and the root cause of most of our social and economic shortcomings.

NOTES

1. Lowell C. Rose and Alec M. Gallup, "The 38th Annual Phi Delta Kappa/ Gallup Poll of the Public's Attitudes Toward the Public Schools," *Phi Delta Kappan,* vol. 88, no. 1 (September 2006): 46–47. Many low-income students do well academically and also lose out if excellence for all is not attained. Joshua S. Wyner, John M. Bridgeland and John J. Dilulio, Jr., *Achievement Trap: How America Is Failing*

Millions of High-Achieving Students from Lower-income Families (Lansdowne, VA: Jack Kent Cooke Foundation, 2007).

2. Larry Cuban, "How Systemic Reform Harms Urban Schools," Commentary, *Education Week* (May 30, 2001): 48, 34.

3. Howard Gardner, "E Pluribus...A Tale of Three Systems," Commentary, *Education Week* (April 23, 2008): 40, 30–31.

4. David Gamson, "From Progressivism to Federalism: The Pursuit of Equal Educational Opportunity, 1915–1965," in Carl F. Kaestle and Alyssa E. Lodewick, *To Educate A Nation: Federal and National Strategies of School Reform* (Lawrence, KS: University of Kansas Press, 2007), 182, 183.

5. The National Commission on Excellence in Education, *A Nation At Risk: The Imperative for Educational Reform* (Washington, DC: U.S. Government Printing Office, 1983), 5.

6. The authors of *A Nation At Risk* did not intend that equity should be slighted: "We do not believe that a public commitment to excellence and educational reform must be made at the expense of a strong public commitment to the equitable treatment of our diverse population." The National Commission on Excellence, *A Nation At Risk*, 13. Yet that's what happened.

7. Center on Education Policy, *Instructional Time in Elementary Schools: A Closer Look at Changes for Specific Subjects* (Washington, DC: Center on Education Policy, 2008).

8. Susan Goodkin and David G. Gold, "The Gifted Children Left Behind," Opinion, *The Washington Post,* August 27, 2007, A13.

9. Ann Duffett, Steve Farkas, and Tom Loveless, *High Achieving Students in the Era of No Child Left Behind* (Washington, DC: Thomas B. Fordham Institute, 2008).

10. Goodkin and Gold, "The Gifted Children Left Behind." Parents in high-poverty schools value a teacher's ability to improve student achievement significantly more than parents in low-poverty schools; the latter are more interested in "student satisfaction." Brian Jacob and Lars Lefgren, "In Low-Income Schools, Parents Want Teachers Who Teach," *Education Next,* vol. 7, no. 5 (Summer 2007): 59–65.

11. Doris R. Entwisle, Karl L. Alexander, and Linda Steffel Olson, "Summer Learning and Home Environment," in Richard D. Kahlenberg, ed., *A Notion at Risk: Preserving Public Education as an Engine for Social Mobility* (New York: The Century Foundation Press, 2000).

12. David J. Hoff, "Researchers Ask Whether NCLB's Goals for Proficiency Are Realistic," *Education Week,* Nov. 29, 2006, 8.

13. Michele McNeil, "Exit Scramble," *Education Week* (August 23, 2008), 21–23.

14. For more on inequitable funding, see chapter 9.

15. Goodwin Lui, "Interstate Inequality in Educational Opportunity," *New York University Law Review,* vol. 81, no. 6 (2006): 2044–2128, 2079–2082. See also David Grissmer and others, *Improving Student Achievement* (Santa Monica, CA: RAND, 2000), xxviii.

16. I have seen this occur often in Baltimore. And see Richard Rothstein, "Leaving 'No Child Left Behind' Behind," *The American Prospect,* vol. 19, no. 1 (January/ February 2008): 50–54, 51. Compare Debra Viadero, "Study Finds No 'Educational Triage' Driven by NCLB," *Education Week* (October 31, 2007): 11.

17. See, for example, Liz Bowie, "The others left behind," *The Baltimore Sun,* November 18, 2007.

18. See further discussion in chapter 5.

19. Roy Zimmer and Eric P. Bettinger, "Beyond the Rhetoric: Surveying the Evidence on Vouchers and Tax Credits," in Helen F, Ladd and Edward B. Fiske, *Handbook of Research in Education Finance and Policy* (New York: Routledge, 2008); Robert Bifulco and Katrina Bulkley, "Charter Schools," in Ladd and Fiske, *Handbook of Research in Education Finance and Policy.*

20. Elissa Gootman, "Those Preschoolers Are Looking Older," *The New York Times,* October 19, 2006.

21. Frederick M. Hess and Andrew J. Rotherham, "NCLB and the Competitiveness Agenda: Happy Collaboration or a Collision Course?," *Phi Delta Kappan.* vol. 88, no. 5 (January 2007): 345–352, 346.

22. Debra Viadero, "Low-Income Students are Public School Majority in South, Study Finds," *Education Week Online,* October 30, 2007, http://www.edweek.org/ew/articles/2007/10/30/10poor_web.h27.html.

Chapter 5

Child Victims of Ideological Warfare

The familiar reference to "education wars" is not rhetorical overkill. In 2008 Charles M. Payne, a distinguished professor at the University of Chicago School of Social Work and a long-time activist in reform movements in the Chicago public schools, published a brilliant, unsparing indictment, *So Much Reform, So Little Change: The Persistence of Failure in Urban Schools.* In a chapter titled "A Curse on Both Their Houses: Liberal and Conservative Theories of Reform," Payne harshly criticizes the "disability of ideology and the way it distorts much of the discussion" on school reform.[1] To historian David Tyack, the education wars have long "resembled the battles of the old Chinese warlords, who assembled their armies, hurled insults at each other, and then departed, leaving the landscape as it was."[2]

That landscape is littered with the broken dreams and ruined lives of generations of innocent schoolchildren. These ideological warriors must be stopped. To borrow from the movie *Network,* Americans must cry out, "We're mad as hell, and we're not going to take it anymore."

THE WARRING SIDES

On the right are political conservatives and education traditionalists who usually are one and the same. They espouse market solutions, particularly school choice. They think public schools squander money and are captives of greedy teachers' unions. On pedagogy, they line up behind what are called "traditional" ways of teaching. Where they diverge somewhat is over the powerful federal role under NCLB: political conservatives oppose its sweep, while education traditionalists tend to be ambivalent.

45

The situation on the left is less lockstep. Although the terms "liberal" and "progressive" are often used interchangeably to describe those on the political left, political liberals and education progressives sometimes disagree. They unite to fight for more funding. They oppose vouchers and school privatization. They usually but not invariably support teachers' unions. But they splinter over charters, testing and NCLB, and "progressive" versus traditional pedagogy.[3]

I am among the small band of political progressives who side more often with educational traditionalists than with educational progressives.[4] I take my cue from arguably the twentieth century's greatest educational leader, Albert Shanker. Shanker, the legendary and leftist head of the American Federation of Teachers union who died in 1997, often broke liberal ranks and fought alongside education traditionalists to gain high ground on behalf of poor and minority students.[5]

Historical Perspective

How ironic that education, which is supposed to stand for reasoned inquiry, is held hostage to ideological irrationality. That's nothing new, however. In 1902 John Dewey wrote about "two 'sects' fighting over the curriculum."[6] In the past, however, the nation remained more united than divided over education's broadest goals, which were to improve society and to grow the economy. These unifying goals kept the cyclical conflicts over school policy confined within narrow, non-ideological boundaries. It used to be said that in the United States, unlike Western Europe, political parties have "not differed very much in their views of education even if they had quite different policies in other domains."[7]

This started to change dramatically in the 1960s and 1970s as the nation's social and cultural turmoil spilled over into public schools. Desegregation, prayer in school, teachers' strikes and youth counterculture—these and other upheavals evoked partisan political responses. Liberals put the blame on society's failure to address poverty and provide schools with enough money. Conservatives blamed families for not doing more to rein in and motivate their children and school bureaucracies for wasting money and kowtowing to teachers' unions. By the 1980s, as education historian Diane Ravitch concluded, "School politics became more like American politics in general . . . the consensus that had undergirded American education for most of its history seemed to be dissipating."[8]

It imploded altogether during the mid-1980s. The accountability and school choice movements, largely driven by conservatives, transformed the national debate. Even before the passage of NCLB in 2001, political writer

E. J. Dionne, Jr. cited education policy as an example of how the nation's cultural wars cause the false polarization of major political issues: "As a country, we don't care about education nearly as much as we enjoy using the education issue as an opportunity to grind our favorite ideological axes, whether against inequality or against teachers' unions or against the lousy values said to permeate our society."[9] Education scholar E. D. Hirsch, Jr. observes that "educational policy is confused with political ideology. In the United States today, the hostile political split between liberals and conservatives has infected the public debate over education—to such an extent that straight thinking is made difficult."[10]

Though now hard to imagine, there was a lull in the fighting when NCLB was enacted with strong bipartisan backing. While that bipartisanship has frayed, the ideological dynamics of NCLB pale in comparison to the polarized debates over school choice and classroom instruction.

THE CHOICE CRUSADERS

The school choice movement has been used in this book to illustrate both the Uncertainty Principle and the failure of school reform to sufficiently focus on classroom instruction. It's also a notorious example of ideological warfare. Andrew Rotherham, co-director of the Education Sector think tank that tries to build bridges between ideologues of the right and left, calls school choice the most divisive issue in American education: "The politics of the issue are not empirical but rather ideological," he writes.[11]

The premise of school choice, which underlies proposals for vouchers, charter schools, and tuition tax credits, derives more from economic theory than education policy analysis. Its founding father is Milton Friedman, the icon of conservative economics.[12] What public schools lack, conservatives assert, is market competition and discipline. They envision an educational "field of dreams": build competition for public schools and parents, students, and teachers will come. Public funds should follow the child to non-public schools. The successful schools will thrive, and the bad ones will lose their customers and fold. Choice is also deeply embedded in the sanctions on failing schools under NCLB. Such schools are to be dismantled, and conservatives push charter and other privately operated schools as the most potent alternatives.

In fairness, some forms of choice have some liberal support. Notably, charter schools are supported by president Obama and many liberals. On the other hand, most liberals are almost as fervently against vouchers, tuition tax credits, and privatization as conservatives are for them. Many on the political left see choice as an attempt by anti-government conservatives to eliminate public schools altogether, making public education just another marketplace commodity. Education writer Peter Schrag imagines some future conservative politician saying, "What, you want socialized education?"[13]

Other observers point out that choice has been used as a political weapon by Republicans since President Richard M. Nixon, beginning with its lure to segregationist whites in the South and North.[14] Its constituencies now include religious communities, most of them politically conservative, seeking grants or vouchers for their schools. And for decades, conservatives have not disguised their hope that choice would topple the power of teachers' unions.

Yet, as summarized in chapter 2, neither charters nor vouchers has amassed compelling evidence of student achievement or growth potential on a national scale. Still, liberals should not become too optimistic. Most choice crusaders can be expected to hold firm to their convictions. Vouchers and tax credits, in particular, are the kind of ideological "big idea" that enthralls the conservative rank and file and philanthropies.

CONFRONTATION INSIDE THE CLASSROOM

The 100 Years War seems a skirmish compared to the endless conflicts between education traditionalists and education progressives over what students should learn and how they should learn it. If there is a saving grace, it's that they are fighting over classroom terrain that matters the most. Still, that's small consolation given the damage inflicted on teachers and students who are caught in the middle.[15]

What Courses Should Be Taught?

Education traditionalists and progressives have probably been fighting the longest over the goals of public education. Progressives believe that classroom subjects must attend to the "whole child": that is, the social, emotional and moral domains of learning as well as academics. Their guiding spirit John Dewey proclaimed in 1897 that public schools were the primary means of social reform and the teacher was "the prophet of the true God and the usherer in of the true kingdom of God."[16] The contrasting philosophy is voiced by traditionalist Diane Ravitch. Dewey's "messianic belief" in the power of schools, she writes, encourages "ideologues of every stripe to try to impose their social, religious, cultural, and political agendas on the schools," thereby preventing "a clear definition of what schools can realistically and appropriately accomplish for children and for society."[17] Traditionalists cite criticism in the *A Nation at Risk* report of the "cafeteria-style curriculum [in high schools] in which the appetizers and desserts can easily be mistaken for the main course."[18]

But these conflicts over curriculum content arise as early as pre-kindergarten and kindergarten. In the wake of the blast-off of the Russian space vehicle Sputnik, famed U.S. Navy admiral and nuclear engineer Hyman Rickover commented, "Sure the Russians beat us—they're studying to be engineers, and our kids are finger painting."[19] Most illustratively, the Head Start program from its conception has been the center of a custody battle between progressives and traditionalists. Progressives sought to focus it on the child's health and family well-being while traditionalists wanted to place more emphasis on academic readiness. That battle is still raging. In public schools, instructional content has been pushed down from the early elementary grades into kindergarten and pre-kindergarten. This trend has left progressive early childhood educators fuming and fighting a rearguard action.

Clashes over *what* should be taught are intermingled with clashes over *how* teachers should teach, except that the warfare over the latter—classroom pedagogy—causes even more academic casualties.

Methods in Their Madness

At least since the 1940s, education progressives and traditionalists have bitterly competed for dominance over teaching methods in the classroom. The tide has ebbed and flowed, but the terms of engagement haven't changed very much. Each side claims to have science in its corner. Each side engages in false dichotomies. And each side contends that the other is responsible for the instructional mess in American public schools.

Progressives think children must be allowed to follow their own interests and learn at their own pace. They say traditionalist pedagogy is just the opposite: too much rote memory, drill-and-kill, and testing that stifle curiosity, creativity, and the love of learning. The main focal point for their ire now is NCLB. As advanced by education professors Marilyn Cochran-Smith and Susan L. Lytle, NCLB's approach to teaching is "remarkably narrow . . . out of date and as insufficient as a telephone made from two tin cans and a piece of string."[20]

Traditionalists are no less scornful of progressives. E. D. Hirsch, Jr. portrays progressives as living in a "Thoughtworld" of romantic, utopian intentions that ignore the realities of how children learn.[21] Learning, say traditionalists, must be teacher-centered rather than child-centered and build upon layers of age-appropriate factual knowledge. Traditionalists argue that Dewey-eyed progressives foster a learning environment in which if it feels good to students and teachers, anything goes.

Another reason why progressivism falters, they assert, is that, when it rejects standardized curricula, it places too much of a burden on teachers to grow their own. Traditionalists claim the burden is heaviest on the disproportionate number of inexperienced teachers in urban school districts. Progressives insist that the "one-size-fits-all," prescriptive curricula and lesson plans favored by traditionalists go too far in the opposite direction, tying too tightly the hands of teachers and devaluing their professional autonomy.

Math, science, and other subjects have not been neutral territories in the clashes over teaching methods.[22] But the "reading wars" between progressive "whole language" and traditionalist "phonics" approaches have been in a class by themselves in perpetual partisanship. Ravitch mentions a historical account of sixteenth century European educators disputing the best way to teach reading, and dates the earliest debates in the United States to the 1820s.[23] These days a prominent progressive accuses the phonics camp of a "flat-earth view of the world, since it rejects modern science about reading and writing and how they develop."[24] A prominent traditionalist accuses whole-language adherents of relying on "superstition, tradition, and untested assumptions about how kids learn to read."[25]

The most recent escalation in the conflict came when, with traditionalists in the administration of president George W. Bush calling the shots, the Reading First program was enacted as part of NCLB. Reading First provided grants for reading instruction to states that followed research favoring the "phonics" approach. But, predictably, it became an ideological lightning rod, and after its administrators were alleged to have improperly steered contracts to particular vendors and overlooked conflicts of interest, Congress in 2008 cut off further funding.

And so it goes, back and forth, with both sides missing chances to find common ground. A tale of two authors illustrates this foolishness. Hirsch, a well-known traditionalist, and Theodore Sizer, an equally well-known progressive, published new books at about the same time in the late 1990s.[26] A number of book reviews and other articles highlighted conflicts in their beliefs, while failing to note that Hirsch was focusing almost exclusively on elementary schools, Sizer on high schools.

A dispassionate reading of the books shows that Hirsch and Sizer leave lots of classroom space for agreement on the need for an age-appropriate instructional continuum. Usually that means a gradual shift in emphasis from traditional to progressive methods as students go from learning the basics in elementary schools to more self-directed, experiential learning in high school. Nonetheless, to borrow a line from Middle East diplomacy, progressives and traditionalists never miss an opportunity to miss an opportunity.

WILL THERE EVER BE A TRUCE?

Lisa Delpit, an African-American educator who won a MacArthur award in 1990, expresses the frustration of those fed up with the polarization. Low-income Black children are capable of higher-order thinking, she writes, but "schools must provide these children the content that other families from a different cultural orientation provide at home."[27] In other words, poor children of color need the best of both pedagogies. Delpit concludes: "[T]he debate is fallacious; the dichotomy is false . . . those who are most skillful at educating Black and poor children do not allow themselves to be placed in 'skills' [traditionalist] or 'process' [progressive] boxes. They understand the need for both approaches."[28] Education writer Harold Henderson, author of a history of the Open Court reading program, observes that American public education "maintains a status quo that is mediocre by either standard."[29]

So a truce is imperative. But on whose terms? As noted earlier, I am one of the rare birds who is politically liberal on almost every issue except education policy where I often flock with education conservatives. But both the right and left flocks must remove their ideological blinders so they can home in on sensible middle ground. It shouldn't be that hard. A symbolic start in breaking the stalemate was a public dialogue between traditionalist Ravitch and progressive Deborah Meier. While not masking their "deep and important differences," they agreed that "What unites us above all is our conviction that low-income children who live in urban centers are getting the worst of both of our approaches."[30]

How do we get the best of both? Hybrid content and methods are one way of driving towards a balanced approach (while saving lots of useless ideological energy). For example, more and more early childhood programs combine academics and social and emotional development. And going up the grade staircase, many programs in reading and math are being written in ways to blend traditional and progressive pedagogy. The "hybridization" of instructional methods by classroom teachers has long been a theme in school reform. Teachers adapt and stabilize the old with the new as curricular innovations come and go.[31] Charter schools too may be a bellwether. One journalist found the best charter schools to be "a counterintuitive combination of touchy-feely idealism and intense discipline."[32]

An irony that should give impetus to a peace process is the tendency of progressives and traditionalists alike to think that the other is on the verge of final victory. The progressive author of a recent book suggests that in the wake of NCLB, traditionalists "are very much in control" and progressives "seem to be an endangered species."[33] On the other hand, a traditionalist luminary believes that "status quo reformers" who are mainly progressives "run the school systems, fill the schools of education, lead the professional associations, and dominate the education bureaucracies."[34] These mutual apprehensions underscore the wisdom of the advice offered by Ravitch: "Both sides should declare victory and go home."[35]

NOTES

1. Charles M. Payne, *So Little Change, The Persistence of Failure in Urban Schools* (Cambridge, MA: Harvard Education Press, 2008), 192.

2. David Tyack, "School Reform is Dead (Long Live School Reform)," *The American Prospect Online,* November 30, 2002, http://www.prospect.org/web/printfriendly-view.ww?id=5454.

3. Educational ideologies and conventional political ideologies are not a perfect match, but they are usually aligned. Tom Loveless, "Introduction," in Loveless, ed., *The Great Curriculum Debate* (Washington, DC: Brookings Institution Press, 2001), 11.

4. As expressed throughout the book, I depart particularly from the conservative tendency to disparage the need for more school funding and to view school choice as the be-all, end-all solution to the problems of public education.

5. Shanker is further discussed in chapter 7.

6. Loveless, "Introduction," 1.

7. David Tyack and Larry Cuban, *Tinkering Toward Utopia: A Century of Public School Reform* (Cambridge, MA: Harvard University Press, 1995), 45.

8. Diane Ravitch, *The Troubled Crusade, American Education 1945–80* (New York: Basic Books, 1983), 323, 316.

9. E. J. Dionne, Jr., "The First Lesson: Parents Matter Most," Opinion, *The Washington Post,* April 2, 1996.

10. E. D. Hirsch, Jr., *The Schools We Need and Why We Don't Have Them* (New York: Doubleday, 1996), 5.

11. Andrew J. Rotherham, "Empiricized Ideology: Research and School Choice," paper prepared for the American Enterprise Institute Conference, "The Politics of Knowledge: Why Research Does (or Does Not) Influence Education Policy," May 21, 2007, 4.

12. For a brief history of its lineage, Rotherham, "Empiricized Ideology," 6–8.

13. Peter Schrag, "The Great School Sell-Off," *The American Prospect,* no. 12 (Winter 1993): 34–43, 41.

14. See, for example, Michael Lind, *Up From Conservatism: Why the Right is Wrong for America* (New York: The Free Press, 1996), 165.

15. For general background on the "curriculum wars:" Loveless, *The Great Curriculum Debate,* particularly the chapter by William Lowe Boyd and Douglas E. Mitchell, "The Politics of the Reading Wars;" Diane Ravitch, *Left Behind: A Century of Failed School Reforms* (New York: Simon & Schuster, 2000).

16. Dewey is quoted in Ravitch, *Left Behind,* 459.

17. Ravitch, *Left Behind,* 459.

18. The National Commission on Excellence in Education, *A Nation At Risk: The Imperative for Educational Reform* (Washington, DC: U.S. Government Printing Office, 1983), 18.

19. Rickover is quoted in Deborah Perkins-Gough, "Giving Intervention a Head Start: A Conversation with Edward Zigler, *Educational Leadership,* vol. 65, no. 2 (October 2007): 8–14, 9.

20. "Troubling Images of Teaching in No Child Left Behind," *Harvard Educational Review,* vol. 76, no. 4 (Winter 2006): 668–697, 674.

21. Hirsch, *The Schools We Need and Why We Don't Have Them,* 69–126.

22. Tom Loveless, "A Tale of Two Math Reforms: The Politics of the New Math and the NCTM Standards," in Loveless, *The Great Curriculum Debate:* The National Mathematics Advisory Panel, *Foundations for Success, Final Report* (Washington, DC: U.S. Department of Education, 2008); Paul R. Gross, *Politicizing Science Education* (Washington, DC: The Thomas B. Fordham Foundation, 2000).

23. Diane Ravitch, "It Is Time to Stop the War," in Loveless, *The Great Curriculum Debate,* 210.

24. Professor Kenneth Goodman is quoted in Ravitch, "It is Time to Stop the War," 221.

25. G. Reid Lyon, "How to improve Reading First," *The Gadfly,* vol. 7, no. 15 (April 19, 2007): 2.

26. Hirsch, *The Schools We Need and Why We Don't Have Them;* Theodore R. Sizer, *Horace's Hope: What Works for the American High School* (Boston: Houghton Mifflin Company, 1996).

27. Lisa Delpit, *Other People's Children: Cultural Conflict in the Classroom* (New York: The New Press, 1995), 30

28. Lisa D. Delpit, "The Silenced Dialogue: Power and Pedagogy in Educating Other People's Children," in Lauren I. Katzman and others, *Special Education for a New Century* (Cambridge, MA: Harvard Educational Review, 2005), 138.

29. Harold Henderson, *Let's Kill Dick & Jane: How Open Court Publishing Company Fought the Culture of American Education* (South Bend, IN: St. Augustine's Press, 2006), 2.

30. "Bridging Differences: A Dialogue Between Deborah Meier and Diane Ravitch, *Commentary, Education Week* (May 24, 2006): 36–37, 37.

31. Tyack and Cuban, *Tinkering Toward Utopia,* 9, 109, 138. Also Cuban, "'Hugging the Middle': Why Good Teaching Ignores Ideology," *Commentary, Education Week* (April 29, 2009): 30–31.

32. Paul Tough, "Still Left Behind: What It Will Really Take to Close The Education Gap," *The New York Times Magazine,* November 26, 2006, 9.

33. William Hayes, *The Progressive Education Movement: Is It Still a Factor in Today's Schools?* (Lanham, MD: Rowman & Littlefield, 2006) xv.

34. Frederick M. Hess, *Common Sense School Reform* (New York: Palgrave Macmillan, 2004), 8.

35. Ravitch, "It Is Time to Stop the War," 226.

Part III

Who's to Blame?

There is no shortage of suspects for who's responsible for what's gone wrong with K–12 public education. Politicians, school bureaucrats, and parents all come under fire. And deservedly so. But their degree of culpability differs and, in my analysis, has two principal dimensions.

The first involves the fundamental question: Can public school systems *by themselves* solve the problems of low academic achievement, especially among poor and minority children? Stated another way, to what extent are schools limited by external factors that impede student readiness and ability to learn? These questions, explored in the next chapter, "A Nation at Risk, and at Fault," raise vexing questions about poverty, race and the responsibility of society as a whole.

The second dimension is examined in the chapter after that, "Educators Are Their Own Worst Enemies." It covers the most precarious contrarian terrain. An unmistakable distinction must be drawn between those educators I hold blameworthy and those I don't. It is educators in the *education establishment*—persons in high places in departments of education, teachers' colleges, national associations and unions—who are very culpable. And it is frontline teachers and principals who are overwhelmingly blameless. *Teachers are my heroes, and they, along with schoolchildren, are victims of the education establishment's weak leadership and management failings.* In this analysis, I strive to do justice to their hard, often thankless work and valiant commitment to their students.

Chapter 6

A Nation at Risk, and at Fault

The most famous words about public education in the twentieth century are found in the 1983 report of the National Commission on Excellence in Education, *A Nation At Risk: The Imperative for Educational Reform.* The report declared: "[T]he educational foundations of our society are presently being eroded by a rising tide of mediocrity that threatens our very future as a Nation and a people . . . As it stands, we have allowed this to happen to ourselves . . . We have, in effect, been committing an act of unthinking, unilateral educational disarmament."[1]

As a nation we are still disarmed. And as a nation we—all of us together in the fifty states and over 14,000 local school districts—are still collectively at fault. Our collective culpability lies in the enormous impact of social and economic factors outside the schools on teaching and learning inside the schoolhouse. This reality came to contemporary light in 1966 when James S. Coleman, then a sociologist at Johns Hopkins University, produced research showing that school resources meant less in determining student achievement than the family's economic and educational background.[2] The Coleman report remains, regrettably, an un-impeached fact of education life. And its lessons are deeply embedded in our public consciousness. In opinion polls over the past thirty years, over 70 percent of the American people consistently agree that the problems of public schools result much more from societal problems than from the quality of schooling.[3]

Today the evidence of a causal relationship between poverty and student academic achievement is indisputable and stark. As detailed in chapter 2, there are huge gaps between the performance levels of low-income students and other students. To make matters worse, low-income students of color are rapidly growing as a percentage of total public school enrollments, and the gaps in achievement are not shrinking.

Still, the existence of a causal relationship between poverty and student achievement doesn't answer the knottiest and most contentious root issues of all: Who and what account for family poverty? How much is attributable to lack of *individual* effort, compared to *society's* failure to provide poor families and children with the opportunity to overcome economic and social disadvantages? And what can be done that will alleviate these disadvantages and reduce the achievement gaps?

The poverty puzzle was a staple of social policy debates in the 1960s and 1970s, often framed in terms of whether there was a "culture of poverty." The same issues persist today in attempts to solve the causes and consequences of welfare dependency, teenage pregnancy, drugs, violence, and other urban pathologies, as well as school failure.

The exact answers are uncertain and debatable. But beyond doubt is that, in recent decades, the nation has faltered in efforts to remedy impoverished family and neighborhood environments. Nor is the political outlook promising. Conservatives and liberals agree that schools are burdened by economic and social circumstances beyond the control of educators, but they disagree on which are most important and what to do about them.

CULTURAL FACTORS

Conservatives emphasize that family culture counts more than teachers or other education resources. Better parents, in their view, make for better schools. And the political right isn't alone in this feeling. Just ask many African-Americans and other liberals who don't think Bill Cosby is so funny any more.

In 2004 in a speech at a 50th anniversary commemoration of the *Brown v. Board of Education* decision, Dr. Cosby (he holds a regular, not honorary, doctor of education degree from the University of Massachusetts[4]) electrified the debate over responsibility for the problems of African-American families. He pinned most of the blame for undereducated African-American children on African-Americans. In his words, "Brown versus the Board of Education is no longer the white person's problem . . . [People] marched and were hit in the face with rocks and punched in the face to get an education and we got these knuckleheads walking around who don't want to learn English. I know you all know it. I just want to get you as angry [as] you ought to be."[5]

Other African-Americans had uttered similar sentiments, but they were mainly doctrinaire conservatives. Cosby reached a much larger audience and gained surprising support. For example, liberal Henry Louis Gates, Jr., a heavyweight scholar and public intellectual at Harvard University who is African-American, wrote in the wake of Cosby's comments, "[V]alues matters . . . We can't talk about choices people have without talking about the choices people make."[6]

And Barack Obama, in his keynote address to the Democratic National Convention in 2004 when he first came to fame nationally, declared: "Go into any inner-city neighborhood, and folks will tell you that government alone can't teach kids to learn; they know that parents have to teach, that children can't achieve unless we raise their expectations and turn off the television sets and eradicate the slander that says a black youth with a book is acting white."[7] Nor has Obama backed off. He stated in a presidential campaign speech in 2008 that "too many [Black] fathers are AWOL, missing from too many lives and too many homes."[8]

Across the country, Cosby ignited simmering differences of opinion among African-Americans, most of whom are liberals, and other Americans over whether individuals or society as a whole are more responsible for the educational failures and other problems of minorities and the poor. Michael E. Dyson, a professor at the University of Pennsylvania and an African-American, set the tone for Cosby's critics. Cosby's "bitter gospel," Dyson writes, is that poverty is "the fault of the poor themselves . . . By convincing poor blacks that their lot in life is purely of their own making, Cosby draws on harsh conservative ideas that overlook the big social factors that continue to reinforce poverty."[9]

A flash point in the controversy is the alleged phenomenon of young African-Americans (and Hispanics) who slack off in school because of fear of being ridiculed by their peers for "acting white." There are different theories for why and how widely it occurs. The most common explanation is that some minority youth put down striving peers because of their own feelings of insecurity and resentment. However, some researchers cast doubt on the prevalence of the syndrome. Ronald F. Ferguson, an education scholar and director of the Achievement Gap Institute at Harvard University and an African-American, underscores that youth lifestyle in general is more of a contributing factor to lack of learning effort than racial differences. The nation needs to support youth of all races with alternative self-images, Ferguson advises, and a lot of this character rebuilding must be done outside of the schools.[10]

There is no disputing, however, many other ways in which class culture hinders student achievement. The most well-known study of child-rearing differences among families prior to school entry is by developmental psychologists Betty Hart and Todd Risley. They discovered that before children were four years of age, parents who held professional jobs had spoken 45 million words to them, compared to middle- and working-class parents who had spoken 20 million words and lower-class parents who had spoken 10 million words. The quality as well as quantity of the words was astonishingly different. The ratio of encouragement to discouragement in words between parents and children was 6 to 1 in families of professional parents, 2 to 1 in working class families and 1 to 2 (that is two discouraging comments for one encouraging comment) in families on welfare.[11] These divergences in language exposure correlate strongly with later academic outcomes.

Class differences also clearly show in the "summer learning loss" that poor children experience. The leading evidence in this area, earlier noted in chapter 4, is a large, multi-year study of children in the Baltimore City public schools by researchers at the Johns Hopkins University. They found that low-income students learn as much or nearly as much as upper-income children during the school year, but fall behind over the summer when they don't receive equivalent educational enrichment.[12]

Overall, as summarized by sociologist George Farkas, "Research supports the idea that black-white differences in social class, family structures, and child-rearing behaviors explain much of the test score gap."[13] The Educational Research Service in a report *Culture and Learning* attempted to walk the tightrope between identifying distinctive cultural characteristics that affect academic performance and not reducing the poor to stereotypes. "Culture does *not* determine a child's ability or intelligence. But it can produce many different ways of knowing and learning (emphasis in the original)," the report concluded.[14]

Still, the differences of opinion over the impact of culture seem irreconcilable, in part because of the chicken-or-egg nature of the debate. That is, if individual family behavior and culture are to blame, aren't they caused or exacerbated by societal factors? Ferguson observes, "[N]o matter what we think about youth cultures, they are products of our own society, and societal responses are required when they go awry."[15]

Orlando Patterson, another renowned scholar and an African-American, laments the "'cool-pose culture'" of young Black men, while pointing out "The important thing to note about the subculture that ensnares them is that it is not disconnected from the mainstream culture."[16] Patterson mentions hip-hop, professional basketball, and homeboy fashions. He could have added violence and sexuality in movies, television, video games, and other heavily advertised commercial products. Poor youth and adults are less economically and educationally inoculated than other Americans against the pop-culture viruses that are rampant across America.

But national culture is only partly to blame for school failure. Worse is the inequality of opportunity for adults and children that has stained our nation for generations.

INEQUALITY OF OPPORTUNITY

Dyson's rebuttal to Cosby expresses the conventional liberal position that the problems of poor people are not of their own making. They arise, in the liberal viewpoint, from financial and social deprivation, including the vestiges of slavery, segregation, and inferior schooling. Many liberals oppose NCLB on the grounds that it creates the delusion that academic standards, tests and sanctions by themselves are powerful enough to erase the achievement gap. Not true, liberals say. Poor children of color won't pass the tests and succeed in school until family and community poverty and inequality of educational opportunity are remedied. And that, they assert, the nation has been unwilling to do.

They cite too the unfulfilled promise of school integration. Public schools are still de facto segregated by race, perpetuating the sense of isolation and inferiority that the *Brown vs. Board of Education* decision and the Coleman report recognized as depressing academic achievement. What's more, efforts over the past decade to integrate schools based on economic class (family income) rather than race have not gained much ground either.

Education analyst Richard D. Kahlenberg compellingly recounts the "forty American school districts, with some 2.5 million students" where economic status is a factor in student assignments to particular schools and where the results are positive.[17] The unfortunate reality, however, is that socioeconomic integration, although sound in theory and practice, is unlikely to spread much farther because of fierce political opposition to "busing" or attendance zone gerrymandering of any kind, socioeconomic as well as racial.

There are other profound impacts of economic and social class on educational attainment. In his landmark book, *Class and School: Using Social, Economic, and Educational Reform to Close the Black-White Achievement Gap*, Richard Rothstein brilliantly illuminates the many ways in which academic growth is stunted by impoverished family and neighborhood environments.[18] Inferior health care worsens vision and hearing problems that directly affect learning, while asthma and other illnesses cause chronic school absenteeism. Lead-paint poisoning decreases cognitive ability.

In addition, when low-income families flee to escape dilapidated conditions or are evicted for non-payment of rent, their children are forced to change schools and lose the benefits of continuity of instruction. About half of inner-city students change schools at least once during a year and about one-quarter transfer at least three times during a year.[19] In the Baltimore public schools, about 10 percent of the students are homeless or under the care of the Department of Social Services.[20]

All told, as summarized by the Mass Insight Education and Research Institute, "[A] wide body of research shows that persistent and extreme poverty, and related social, environmental, and psychological factors . . . affect both the cognitive development and school achievement of individual children."[21] Education professor Iris C. Rotberg finds that socioeconomic status "accounts for about three-quarters of the variation in student performance among schools in the United States."[22]

LETTING SCHOOL SYSTEMS OFF THE HOOK?

Does all this evidence of our nation's collective fault exonerate public schools from being held responsible for poor student achievement? Rothstein concludes, "The influence of social class characteristics is probably so powerful that schools cannot overcome it, no matter how well-trained are their teachers and no matter how well-designed are their instructional programs and climates."[23] He has been the most powerful voice for the pessimistic prognosis that schools can do relatively little by themselves.

Education Week threw fuel on the fire by issuing in 2008 for the first time a comparison of the fifty states on what it called a student's "Chance-for-Success Index." The Index gave great weight to the economic and educational circumstances of parents,[24] provoking a conservative analyst to complain that it was "defeatist" and "gives comfort to an education establishment desperate to blame 'poverty' for its failings."[25] The education writer Peter Schrag, who is usually found in the same liberal corner as Rothstein, replied that "It saddens me to see my friend . . . sinking so far into social determinism that he's ready to leave millions of poor children, many of them black or Latino, in dead-end schools with unqualified teachers, insufficient textbooks, and sometimes none at all, and facilities that hell wouldn't have."[26]

Rothstein's defense, echoed by other liberals, is that the emphasis on external factors should not be misinterpreted "as implying that better schools . . . will not make a contribution to narrowing the achievement gap."[27] He advocates school improvements like early childhood, after-school and summer school programs. However, while he would "never say public school can't do better . . . [he would] say they can't do much better" unless social and economic ills are cured.[28]

The Rothstein perspective puts all liberals in a political hot seat. The predicament is how to address the external circumstances that restrict school success without appearing to absolve the schools of their share of responsibility. Any emphasis on the economic and social causes of student failure is used by sizable numbers of educators and the public to excuse the failures of school systems. Too many people, including educators, already have too-low expectations for poor and minority students that become self-fulfilling prophecies in the classroom.

The liberal split personality flared up during the 2008 elections when two national coalitions issued conflicting manifestos for school reform. One group, called the Education Equality Project, included political officials and educators across the ideological spectrum (for example, Republican governor of California Arnold Schwarzenegger and Democrat civil rights activist Reverend Al Sharpton). Its agenda centered on school policies like raising teacher quality and pay, accountability, and maximizing parents' options.[29] The other group, a task force that included equally well-known educators and academics, mostly liberals, published a "Broader, Bolder Approach to Education" statement. Its thrust was that the keys to student success were reforms beyond the schoolhouse and conventional schooling: large-scale economic and social programs were paramount.[30]

Neither group denied that the other made some valid points. Arne Duncan, then superintendent of Chicago schools and soon to be appointed U.S. secretary of education by president Obama, signed both manifestos. But their platforms—one which placed the onus on the schools, the other which didn't—were clearly at odds, with Democrats sharply divided.

OUTSIDE AND INSIDE THE SCHOOLHOUSE

What is to be learned from these controversies over how much culture, race, and social and economic class affect school reform? For one thing, it's politically incorrect to talk about them, as Cosby, Rothstein and others have found out. When I was a member of the Baltimore school board and drafted an article on this subject, several colleagues advised me to back off; they thought that I would be seen as making excuses for the board and the entire school system.

The second and more important lesson is that no one knows for sure, or even with plausible probability, how to quantify the proportional impact of outside and inside factors. The "culture of poverty" matters. Individual and family responsibility matter. Inequality of opportunity matters. But if a lot more money to eliminate the achievement gap suddenly appeared, there are no sophisticated cost-benefit comparisons to guide whether it would be better spent on social welfare and community development programs, or directly on schools.

Still, in the final analysis, it is indisputable that poor students will do much better in school if the nation does a better job of addressing the causes and consequences of poverty outside as well as inside schoolhouses. More health care, jobs, drug treatment, housing and other family and neighborhood programs are desperately needed. I am a liberal activist in favor of greatly expanded governmental actions to alleviate economic inequality and injustice.

Nonetheless, this book does not attempt such a mammoth policy sweep. Its focus is on inside school reforms and what schools can do for themselves. In particular, the education establishment must own up to its own culpability and reverse its historical pattern of self-inflicted harm, as revealed in the next chapter.

NOTES

1. The National Commission on Excellence in Education, *A Nation At Risk: The Imperative for Educational Reform* (Washington, DC: U.S. Government Printing Office, 1983), 5.

2. James S. Coleman and others, *Equality of Educational Opportunity* (Washington, DC: Government Printing Office, 1966).

3. Lowell C. Rose and Alec M. Gallup, "The 38th Annual Phi Delta Kappa/Gallup Poll of the Public's Attitudes Toward the Public Schools," *Phi Delta Kappan,* vol. 88, no. 1 (September 2006): 41–47, 43.

4. His doctoral thesis was titled "The Integration of Visual Media Via Fat Albert and the Cosby Kids Into the Elementary Schools Culminating as a Teacher Aid to Achieve Increased Learning." http://aalbc.com/authors/bill.htm.

5. Transcript published by Cosby's public relations representatives, http://www.eightcitiesmap.com/transcript_bc.htm.

6. Henry Louis Gates, Jr., "Breaking the Silence," Guest Columnist, *The New York Times,* August 1, 2004.

7. Barack Obama, 2004 Democratic National Convention Keynote Address, http://www.americanrhetoric.com/speeches/convention2004/barackobama2004dnc.htm, 5.

8. Julie Bosman, "Obama Calls for More Responsibility From Black Fathers," *The New York Times,* July 16, 2008.

9. Michael E. Dyson, "The Injustice Bill Cosby Won't See," Opinion, *The Washington Post,* July 21, 2006, A17.

10. Ronald F. Ferguson, *Toward Excellence with Equity: An Emerging Vision for Closing the Achievement Gap* (Cambridge, MA: Harvard Education Press, 2007), 296.

11. Betty Hart and Todd R. Risley, *Meaningful Differences in the Everyday Experience of Young American Children* (Baltimore, MD: Paul H. Brookes Publishing, 1995).

12. Doris R. Entwisle, Karl L. Alexander, and Linda Steffel Olson, "Summer Learning and Home Environment," in Richard D. Kahlenberg, ed., *A Nation at Risk: Preserving Public Education as an Engine for Social Mobility* (New York: The Century Foundation Press, 2000).

13. George Farkas, "The Black-White Test Score Gap," *Contexts,* vol. 3, no. 2 (Spring 2004): 12–19, 17.

14. *What We Know About: Culture and Learning* (Arlington, VA: Educational Research Service, 2003), 5.

15. Ferguson, *Toward Excellence with Equity,* 296.

16. Orlando Patterson, "A Poverty of the Mind," Op-ed, *The New York Times,* March 26, 2006.

17. Richard E. Kahlenberg, "The Century Foundation Issue Brief," November, 2006, http://www.tcf.org/list.asp?type=PB&pubid=592, 2.

18. Richard Rothstein, *Class and Schools: Using Social, Economic, and Educational Reform to Close the Black-White Achievement Gap* (Washington, DC: Economic Policy Institute, 2003).

19. Kieran M. Killeen and Kai A. Schafft, "The Organization and Fiscal Implications of Transient Student Populations," in Helen F. Ladd and Edward B. Fiske, eds., *Handbook of Research in Education Finance and Policy* (New York: Routledge, 2008), 632, 633, 638.

20. Unpublished Baltimore City school system data presented to the Baltimore City Board of School Commissioners, May 6, 2008.

21. Andrew Calkins and others, *The Turnaround Challenge: Supplement to the Main Report* (Boston, MA: Mass Insight Education and Research Institute, 2007), 76.

22. Iris C. Rotberg, "Myths That Continue to Confound Us," Commentary, *Education Week* (June 11, 2008): 32.

23. Rothstein, *Class and Schools,* 5.

24. "Quality Counts 2008," *Education Week* (January 10, 2008): 6, 40.

25. Liam Julian, "Quality doubts," *The Gadfly,* vol. 7, no. 2 (January 11, 2007).

26. Peter Schrag, Stephan Thernstrom, Reply by Richard Rothstein, "'Must Schools Fail?': An Exchange," *The New York Review of Books,* vol. 52, no. 3 (February 24, 2005).

27. Rothstein, *Class and Schools,* 9.

28. Diane Jean Schemo, "It Takes More than Schools to Close Achievement Gap," *The New York Times,* August 9, 2006, A15.

29. http://educationequalityproject.org.

30. http://www.boldapproach.org/statement/html.

Chapter 7

Educators Are Their Own
Worst Enemies

Pogo could have had the education establishment in mind when he famously said, "I have seen the enemy and they is us." This realization requires careful explanation. The last thing I want to do is unfairly tar all educators with a broad brush of culpability. Nonetheless, the risk must be run.

School reform is sure to continue to fail unless the self-destructive ways of the leaders of the education profession are exposed and rectified. E. D. Hirsch, Jr. has grasped this truth. Teachers, he writes, are "some of the most dedicated and sympathetic members of our society. No, the enemy is the controlling system of ideas that currently prevents needed changes from being contemplated or understood. It is the enemy within that needs to be defeated."[1]

The enemy within is the education establishment. The term "education establishment" sounds familiar, but is rarely defined. I define it as educators in the top echelons of organizations that are most influential in the development of public school policy. In an establishment class by themselves in importance are local, state and federal departments of education. Other influential organizations are teacher-education programs in universities and colleges, teachers' unions, national associations of educators, and education think tanks.

Though the education establishment is amorphous in structure, its leaders (except in think tanks) tend to act alike. They fail to exert dynamic leadership. They cherish the status quo, blaming the shortcomings of public schools on everyone but themselves. The sum and substance is a policymaking vacuum that ideologues, political officials, and other non-educators, including lay school boards, try to fill. Politicians may be chicken when it comes to bold action to pull school reform out of its rut, but the education establishment laid the egg first.

Consider two major areas in which the education establishment has been conspicuously negligent and inept. One is school accountability. Legislators enacted NCLB and state laws mandating strict accountability because education leaders had refused to be accountable on their own. It's all well and good to criticize NCLB, as almost everyone does, but why weren't educators in high places out in front and regulating themselves before the laws were passed? Why didn't the education establishment blow the whistle when generations of earlier federal reforms, notably the Elementary and Secondary Education Act to provide compensatory aid to low-income students and the Individuals with Disabilities Act for students with learning handicaps, were grossly mismanaged?

Why, even now, hasn't the education establishment proactively put forth workable proposals for dealing with thorny issues under NCLB like testing? Instead, many states have hunkered down and engaged in the shameful "race to the bottom" in which academic standards have been lowered and test results inflated to avoid being cast in an unfavorable light.[2]

A second glaring example of the default of the education establishment is its neglectful mismanagement of classroom instruction, which, as exposed later, is the least recognized but most direct cause of poor academic achievement. The public is aware of botched budgets, student records, school maintenance and many other school operations. But below the public radar is how school system officials mismanage the design and delivery of instruction in the classroom itself, depriving teachers, especially less experienced ones, of the support they need. Why have education chiefs allowed classroom instruction to be so loosely designed and so laxly implemented? Why have they been so insular and resistant to research findings on how to improve instruction? Why have so many been holy warriors in the ideological "education wars"?

These breakdowns are rarely scrutinized or even perceived. On the contrary, a comment by John Merrow, a leading education journalist, is typical: he sharply criticized what he considers the onerous testing provisions of NCLB but said, "'[D]on't put the blame on educators."[3] A blue-ribbon commission advocating a radical overhaul of public schools alleged, "The problem is not with our educators. It is with the system in which they work."[4] But aren't educators themselves the "system" and doesn't the education establishment bear responsibility for it?

Very few observers come right to the point like Leon Botstein, a university president engaged in K–12 education policy. In discussing the 50 percent or so dropout rate among minority students, he observed: "The system is broken. No one would keep a fleet flying if half of the planes crashed. So the country is derelict, [President George W. Bush] is derelict, and his predecessor Mr. Clinton was derelict, the Congress is derelict, state legislators are derelict, *and the education establishment is routinely committing a kind of crime* (emphasis added)."[5]

Another maverick on the subject is Jane C. Owen, a university professor in education leadership, who has written that educators have been "disempowered, disenfranchised, and deprived of our professional status and our voice because *we have allowed this to happen* . . . Where is our voice? It is time for the sleeping giant to stir, awaken with a roar, and take back our profession (italics in the original)."[6]

Agreed, but who exactly should be the voice of the sleeping giant? What is a finer-grained dissection of the spineless anatomy of the education establishment? Which parts are more blameworthy than others?

GIVING TEACHERS AND PRINCIPALS A PASS

I draw a clear line between the leaders of the education establishment and frontline teachers and principals. But should teachers and principals be excused from blame altogether? Teachers interact directly with students and are universally regarded as the single most important school factor in student success or failure. Further, as professionals, they have an obligation to speak out not just on pay and tenure but on instructional policies and practices that affect their ability to teach.

Yet, they are not well-suited by personal nature or professional nurture to stir the pot. As amplified in chapter 11, those who go into teaching tend temperamentally to shy away from organizational regimen and conflict. On top of that, bureaucratic norms, to put it mildly, place the highest premium on not making waves. Teachers learn that to get along on teaching assignments and promotions, they had better go along with the system's leadership.

Similar constraints apply to principals. True, they are leaders in their schools. But they have been culturally conditioned as teachers, their job involves little policy-setting (even when they have considerable control over operations within their individual schools), and they are subject to the same pressures to conform as teachers. If anything they are on a shorter leash, because, as administrators, they are supposed to be part of the system's leadership team. The relative insignificance of principals and teachers in policy-making becomes more evident as the colossal failings of superior officers in departments of education are uncovered.

DEPARTMENTS OF EDUCATION—ONE FOR ALL

Together, local, state and federal departments of education are the nucleus of the education establishment. Their leaders—local superintendents, state superintendents, the secretary of the U. S. Department of Education (DOE) and hand-picked deputies and other top executives—exert the greatest influence at any moment in time. Still, they come and go (as do school reforms). And so the permanent bureaucracies—the near-top administrators and middle managers, many protected by civil service personnel laws or administrators' unions—also contribute heavily to the institutional resistance to change.

Since the passage in 2001 of NCLB, if not before, DOE seems to be in the driver's seat, with its authority to promulgate rules, enforce laws, and occupy the bully pulpit. The Editorial Projects in Education Research Center, an arm of the publishers of *Education Week,* conducted a study in 2006, *Influence: A Study of the Factors Shaping Education Policy.*[7] Education authorities were asked to compile a top-ten list of the most influential organizations in education policymaking. The study, wrote its authors, "offers a first attempt at untangling the complex web of influence that has helped to shape education policy over the years."[8] In second place on the list, topped only by the U.S. Congress, was DOE.

That ranking would seem to confirm DOE's dominance over local and state departments of education (LEAs and SEAs). But the system doesn't work in such a hierarchical way. Instead the relationships are interwoven and interdependent. LEAs are the farm system for the bigger-league SEAs and DOE. Educators work their way up and sometimes back through the spiraling staircases and revolving doors among LEAs, SEAs and DOE. They carry with them habits of mind and practice shaped on the local frontlines (as well as by teacher colleges).

Moreover, LEAs and SEAs are the ones who create the mess that federal legislators and DOE bureaucrats try to clean up. Chester E. Finn, Jr., arguably the nation's most influential education policy intellectual, put it aptly: "Keep in mind that today's highest priority reforms—closing the learning gap, converting low-performing schools into good ones . . . —wouldn't be necessary if the SEAs and LEAs had done their jobs right in the first place."[9]

Local Departments

There are few sure things in public education, but the incompetence of local school bureaucracies is one of them. Not just the daily snafus, but worse, an underlying "system" in which administrators avoid clear lines of authority and accountability and try to conceal their ineptitude in a dense forest of jargon and red tape. All that notwithstanding, local bureaucracies for the most part only mismanage education policies; they don't set most of the policies they mismanage. Chapter 8 particularizes how in recent decades federal and state laws, regulations, and regulators have steadily closed the window of "local control." But this seismic shift in power occurred because local boards, superintendents, and bureaucracies did such a poor job when they controlled their own destinies.

For example, local ineptitude undermined the two most powerful pre-NCLB attempts by the federal government to improve the academic fortunes of disadvantaged students: the Elementary and Secondary Education Act enacted in 1965, and the Education for All Handicapped Children Act enacted in 1975 (now the Individual with Disabilities Act). LEAs failed abjectly to carry out these laws as Congress intended.[10]

State departments of education were complicit in these failures because under the federal laws, they were supposed to approve LEA plans and oversee their implementation. However, their inaction was no surprise.

State Departments

An odd couple, the liberal think tank Center for American Progress and the conservative U.S. Chamber of Commerce, teamed up for a 2007 state-by-state report card on how states are educating their children. Its "unambiguous" conclusion: that "the states need to do a far better job of monitoring and delivering quality schooling." The report cited the tendency of many states to "systematically paint a much rosier picture of how their schools are doing than is actually the case."[11] Even a study by the Education Commission of the States, an organization of state officials, conceded that SEAs are regarded as "too hierarchical, bureaucratic and compliance-oriented."[12] All in all, SEAs, while less visible to the public than local or federal bureaucracies, have generally been as weak-kneed and ineffective.[13]

Early in the twentieth century, SEAs acted minimally but hardly anybody noticed or cared: SEAs were supposed to play second fiddle to LEAs and the tune of local control. This low profile changed gradually over the years, beginning with the powers delegated to them under federal laws. Many states also legislated their own aid programs targeted at low-income and other at-risk students. At the same time starting in the 1970s, states were forced by court orders or the threat of lawsuits to dramatically increase state aid to low-wealth, primarily urban, school districts.[14] With more money came more strings, and SEAs, whether they wanted to or not, became enmeshed in regulating LEA expenditures.

Next came the movement to raise academic standards and impose greater accountability on LEAs.[15] Some states took modest steps on their own, and federal laws, even before NCLB, pressured SEAs to get increasingly involved in local teaching and learning. In 2004 education historian Michael W. Kirst summarized the metamorphosis of SEAs: "[P]erhaps the most striking change in U.S. education governance in the last forty years has been the growth of centralized state control and the ascendance of governors over school policy in most states."[16]

But while SEAs were given more power, most tried to avoid using it. This was educationally inbred: state bureaucrats didn't know much more than their local counterparts about how to turn around failing schools, and even if they did, they were disinclined to rock the collegial boat. Also governors and legislators pushed them to go easy because of the politics of local control.

Some progress occurred in some states. But not nearly enough to stem the tide of nationwide disillusionment with SEAs and LEAs that led to the passage of NCLB and its revolutionary federal dictates. Under NCLB, SEAs had to create sophisticated testing systems and networks of curriculum and instruction experts who were supposed to write world-class academic standards and provide local districts with technical assistance on how to improve teaching. And they had to administer sanctions that were supposed to apply when schools failed to improve.[17]

In assigning this tough homework to SEAs, the framers of NCLB were aware that SEAs had never shown the will or management capacity to complete the assignment. But states' rights and local control were political dogma, so, to gain enough votes for passage, administration and enforcement were left with the states. On their end, states were fearful of the NCLB mandates and the responsibilities thrust upon them. They could opt out, but it would cost them lots of federal aid. Therefore they huffed and puffed and resisted, but were not ready to blow their own fiscal houses down. They took the money and then sought to figure out how to cope.

That frantic effort quickly deteriorated into the "race to the bottom" to lower standards and exaggerate student progress. The clearest proof, as summarized in chapter 2, is that while test scores soared on state tests, students progressed little if at all on the more reliable National Assessment of Educational Progress (NAEP) tests given to students across the states. After NCLB, the huge disparity between state and NAEP scores actually widened.

Anecdotally, Paul Vallas, who was superintendent of the Chicago public schools before taking on the same job in Philadelphia, quipped that to really improve test scores in Philadelphia, he could undertake various school reforms or "give everyone the [less demanding] Illinois test."[18] The head of the Council of Chief State School Officers (state superintendents) conceded that states were evading the rigorous mandates of NCLB; the states, he said, are "trying to survive."[19]

There is little reason to believe that SEAs will ever rise to the challenge of school reform.[20] The twenty-first century award for wishful thinking by knowledgeable people who should know better goes so far to the blue-ribbon Commission on the Skills of the American Workforce. Its 2007 highly-publicized report proposed giving states the dominant role in a radical overhaul of public schools. States would, among other things, assume complete funding of public schools and employ all teachers statewide.[21] But this notion is pie-in-the-sky in the light of how states have failed to provide adequate funding (see chapter 9) and are, as an education journalist noted in summarizing reaction to the report, "reluctant to consider wresting control of K–12 education from local districts."[22] SEAs have also failed to properly regulate teacher-education programs that, as brought to light shortly, have undereducated teachers and administrators.

The impotence of states and their SEAs foreshadows the architecture of a "New Education Federalism" in which SEAs are largely bypassed for all the reasons just enumerated. That doesn't rule out governors or state superintendents who want to shake up the status quo. They can help. But as history shows, they are too few and far between to be a foundation for nationwide reform.

The U.S. Department of Education

Like its state and local counterparts in the education establishment, DOE has been largely dysfunctional. Former DOE official Christopher T. Cross, in his book on the history of federal involvement in K–12 education policy, gives DOE a D grade because of how it has failed to implement federal programs and to build state and local capacity.[23] Finn recounts his days heading the Office of Educational Research and Improvement in DOE in the late 1980s: "While lastingly appreciative of the one-tenth or so of [the Office's] career servants who worked hard, strove to do a good job, and were open to new ideas, I was weary of dealing with the 90 percent who, on good days, just went through the motions, and on bad days sabotaged, leaked, and stonewalled."[24]

Most recently, DOE has drawn blistering rebukes for its weak and inconsistent administration of NCLB. One of NCLB's architects, Democratic Sen. Edward Kennedy, declared, "The [George W. Bush] Administration's implementation of the reforms has been inadequate and ideological."[25] Influential Democratic Rep. George Miller, another staunch supporter, joined Sen. Kennedy in calling for more Congressional oversight of questionable practices that include the approval process for state accountability plans, the distribution of grants, and enforcement steps.[26]

But Democrats aren't the only critics. The report of the bipartisan No Child Left Behind Commission is sprinkled with examples of lax DOE guidelines, technical assistance, and enforcement.[27] The Council of Chief State School Officers has charged DOE with being slow to respond to states' requests and with insufficient documentation of administrative actions.[28]

DOE can justifiably point to mitigating circumstances. First, as examined in detail in chapter 9, the legislative framework of NCLB was rickety and contained unrealistic expectations. Second, as traced earlier, DOE must usually rely on LEAs and SEAs that are hostile to federal regulation and too bureaucratically inept to cooperate effectively even if they wanted to. Third, DOE has been handcuffed by politics. Presidents, Democratic and Republican alike, have politicized the appointment of top DOE administrators, the enforcement of federal regulations, grant-making, and even DOE-sponsored research.[29] Fourth, DOE, like SEAs and LEAs, is short of management capacity for promulgating regulations, technical assistance and enforcement.[30]

How then do we sort out the proper future roles of DOE, SEAs and LEAs? The New Education Federalism, delineated in later chapters, specifies how. Still, departments of education aren't the only parts of the education establishment that require overhaul. We turn next to the establishment breeding grounds: teacher-education programs.

TEACHER-EDUCATION PROGRAMS

Teacher-education programs—about 1200 of them in colleges and universities—have been indicted as "third-tier backwaters" that have low admission standards and are intellectually shallow and out of touch with the day-to-day problems of public schools.[31] The ripple effect is devastating. Undergraduate and graduate courses of study incubate teaching methods and professional norms that do not just land in the classroom, but eventually come home to roost full-grown in the education establishment. The condemnation of teacher-education programs is so rampant that in recent decades, critics include insiders in the Holmes Group, a coalition of deans of graduate schools of education,[32] and the National Commission on Teaching and America's Future.[33]

But their critiques were just a warm-up for the most recent comprehensive—and damning—study led by Arthur Levine, who at the time was the president of the prestigious Teachers College at Columbia University and therefore a supreme insider. The purpose of the Levine study was to "look beyond the usual, untested assertions of education school critics and the defensive posture of the schools."[34] Heads and faculties of education schools and public school principals were surveyed, and twenty-eight diverse education schools were case-studied.

The findings, set forth in a trilogy of reports written by Levine, are scathing across the blackboard. Titled *Educating School Leaders* (2005), *Educating School Teachers* (2006), and *Educating Researchers* (2007), they leave no doubt that the teacher-education sector of the education establishment has ill-served its students and ultimately public schoolchildren.[35]

It is bad enough, according to the Levine reports, that teacher-education students aren't properly taught how to teach. And that training in research is feeble. But the most damaging fallout is their failure to prepare teachers with the skills they need when they move up into leadership positions in the education establishment. To Levine, preparation of school system administrators is "the weakest of all the programs at the nation's education schools."[36] While purporting to train nearly all of the roughly 250,000 administrators currently employed in American public schools, they have "faced a steady stream of criticism, their reputations have declined, and their future has been thrown into doubt."[37] The *Educating Leaders* report catalogues severe deficiencies.

- The programs lack coherent and rigorous curricula specifically designed to prepare principals and superintendents.
- The programs admit nearly everyone who applies. The standardized test scores of applicants are among the lowest in education-related fields and in all academe.
- Faculty are ill-prepared. Only 6 percent have been principals and 2 percent have been superintendents.[38]

Others have joined *Educating Leaders* in a crescendo of condemnation and calls for major reforms.[39] Reacting to talk of possible Congressional cuts in federal aid for teacher-education programs, Linda Darling-Hammond, a prominent scholar who was executive director of the National Commission on Teaching and America's Future, told *Education Week,* "Even if you don't like what [education schools] are doing, you can't get around them. If you think they're broken, then you need to fix them . . . [Policymakers] are not going to change [the] system by ignoring" the colleges.[40]

But few reformers outside of the education establishment are persuaded. Given past experience, there is little confidence that teacher-education schools can shake off their sickly condition. Therefore, most reformers are pressing for bypass surgery. As detailed in later chapters, non-educators are being recruited as superintendents and employed as top managers and outside consultants, alternative certification routes for teachers and principal preparation programs are flourishing, and cadres of classroom mentors and coaches are being employed to fill the training gap.

TEACHERS' UNIONS

Teachers' unions are mighty branches of the education establishment. Their leaders are educators who typically worked their way up the ranks of classroom teachers, and the huge teacher unions—the National Education Association (NEA) and the American Federation of Teachers (AFT)—made the top-ten list in the *Education Week* study of the most influential educational organizations.[41] But how much are they to blame for the failure of public schools? According to conventional wisdom, a lot. They are widely believed to protect incompetent teachers from being fired, to prevent teachers from being assigned to schools where they are most needed, and to resist NCLB and other school reforms. In short, to put their own self-interests ahead of the best interests of students.

There is some truth to these charges. Yet, is this customary portrayal the whole truth? Is there objective research that sheds light on whether collective bargaining agreements have a negative impact on student achievement? Lurking beneath these questions are issues that challenge the very existence of teachers' unions. How can teachers reconcile their professionalism with traditional unionism? Should teachers resort to union organizations and adversarial tactics at all?

These loaded issues are explored next.[42] The conclusion I reach is that the establishment teachers' unions could do more for school reform than they do, but they are often made scapegoats for the failures of others, and on balance, they are good for schoolchildren.

Labor Pains

To political conservatives, teachers' unions are *the* problem with K–12 public schools. Teachers' union-bashing was a centerpiece of Republican Bob Dole's campaign for president in 1996.[43] President George W. Bush's former education secretary Rod Paige compared the NEA to a "terrorist organization."[44] Teachers' unions, Paige has written, are "rich, powerful, politically manipulative, self-aggrandizing organizations that are blocking urgently needed reforms to our struggling public education system."[45] Terry M. Moe, an influential, conservative policy analyst, believes that collective bargaining in public education should be abolished.[46]

Liberals historically have been almost as adamantly pro-teachers' unions. As they see it, before labor activism, teachers, mainly women, were underpaid and unprotected from arbitrary personnel actions. They were without any voice in school policy and still would be, liberals argue, if not for unions. Moreover, teachers' unions have grown into the most muscular lobbying force for school budgets. In particular they are the political lifelines for fiscally and politically impoverished urban school districts.[47]

What's indisputable is that the unions are political giants. NEA has about 3.2 million members and spends over $355 million annually; for the AFT, it's 1.4 million members and about $196 million per year.[48] Their clout has provoked numerous lawsuits by conservatives seeking to curb their partisan politics, but to little avail. NEA and AFT continue to throw their weight around in elective politics as well as on school funding, school board elections and the reform issues of the day like student testing, teacher qualifications, charter schools and vouchers.

With their large campaign treasuries and foot soldiers, it has been a rare Democrat who dares to cross them. But that is changing. In 2004 Democratic presidential nominee John Kerry challenged union dogma on teacher tenure and merit pay.[49] And in the primary run-ups to the 2008 election, some of the major Democratic candidates, including Barack Obama, signaled their willingness to buck the unions on teacher tenure, merit pay, and even vouchers.[50] In doing so, they were cautiously acknowledging the growing discontent among many liberals over the seeming intransigence of the NEA and the AFT.

My model for the correct liberal approach to teachers' unions is Albert Shanker, the president of AFT until his death in 1997. A superb biography of him by Richard D. Kahlenberg chronicles his "stunning transformation."[51] Time and time again, he broke with the education establishment and political liberals. He was open to changes in teacher testing, tenure, and compensation and out-in-front early in support of high academic standards, rigorous student testing, and charter schools. The seeds that Shanker planted are beginning to grow into what is sometimes called a "new unionism."

Toward a More Perfect Teachers' Union

Are teacher unions good or bad for public education? No one knows for sure: the research on the link between teachers' collective bargaining and student academic achievement is scant and suspect. Moe, no fan of teacher unions, concedes that unions can take credit for higher pay, smaller teacher-student ratios and bigger school budgets. But as to the effect on student performance, he writes, "[T]he literature yields mixed findings . . . Some studies say [union contracts] lead to better performance, some say they lead to worse performance, but we cannot be confident that they are telling us anything valid."[52] Jane Hanaway and Andrew J. Rotherham, co-editors of an exemplary balanced volume of papers on collective bargaining in education, observe "how little evidence exists and also how much of what has been put forward as evidence is substantially flawed in one way or the other."[53]

One clear thing, however, is that teacher unions, for all their faults, have not been as obstructionist as commonly pictured. This is particularly true on the most serious indictment against them: that collective bargaining provisions make it near impossible to discipline and fire unsatisfactory teachers. In a national survey, 67 percent of principals thought it difficult but doable to remove a tenured teacher.[54] In a separate survey of teachers, a majority who voiced an opinion believed that it was not that hard in their districts to get rid of bad teachers.[55] Hanaway and Rotherham drive the point home: "The problem is not that the teachers unions enjoy too much power or leverage, it is that other constituencies [including superintendents and principals] exercise too little."[56]

Union contracts are also misrepresented in other aspects, according to an unexpected source. A study in 2008 published by the conservative Thomas B. Fordham Institute analyzed the contracts in the fifty largest school districts using a database collected by the National Council on Teacher Quality, which is also critical of unions as a rule. The study reported that more contracts were rated restrictive or highly restrictive than flexible, but

> the most surprising finding is that labor agreements in a majority of large districts are neither blessedly flexible nor crazily restrictive: they are simply ambiguous, silent on many key areas of management flexibility, neither tying leaders' hands outright nor explicitly conferring authority on them to act. We call this the 'Leadership Limbo.' And we take it as more good than bad, for it means, at least in the short run, that aggressive superintendents and principals could push the envelope and claim authority for any management prerogative not barred outright by the labor agreements. And it means that, for a majority of big districts, the depiction of [collective bargaining agreements] as an all-powerful, insurmountable barrier to reform may be overstated.[57]

In recent years the leaders of some local unions are taking new tacks, as revealed in a 2007 report by the centrist think tank Education Sector. Presidents of thirty NEA and AFT chapters in six states were interviewed. The report characterized the sample of presidents as "the newest generation of local leaders, rather than those . . . whose views were forged three or four decades ago when . . . industrial-style unionism prevailed."[58] As a group, the presidents

> did not fit the traditional stereotype of labor leaders ready to do battle at any cost in order to enhance their members' welfare. In some cases, they fiercely opposed management's proposal or actions with traditional tactics . . . Far more

often, however, they worked together with school officials on a variety of initiatives . . . Those who went well beyond the basic union agenda still absolutely
affirmed the importance of winning better salaries, benefits, and working conditions. Yet they framed those goals within the context of improving schools and
retaining a skilled and committed teaching force.[59]

The "new unionism" is blossoming in local AFT and NEA chapters, including
experiments with merit pay and peer evaluations of teacher competence. Some
locals are sponsoring or promoting charter schools. The Teacher Union Reform
Network (TURN), formed in 1996, encompasses over twenty NEA and AFT
locals with reform-minded leaders.[60] And nationally the NEA has shown signs
of wanting to close the gap between AFT's reform aspirations and its own.[61]

What future turns might teacher unionism take? Kahlenberg and others
are disappointed that the unions have not changed as much as hoped.[62] But
much depends on which ways the policy and political winds blow. Part of
a bi-partisan Congressional deal for an expanded federal role may be directives or incentives for changes to teacher tenure, seniority, and merit pay.
At the local level as highlighted in later chapters, take-charge mayors and
break-the-mold urban superintendents will also push teachers' unions in
the direction of "new unionism." Another reform dynamic is generational
change. Newcomers to teaching are much less wedded to union protections
and more open to reform than veteran teachers who were schooled in and
fought for traditional unionism.

NATIONAL ASSOCIATIONS

Educators, like everybody else, organize to promote their interests.[63] Their
associations inform members about professional happenings, hold con-
ferences, publish reports and practice Politics 101. Although none of the
national associations made the top-ten list of organizations in the *Influences*
study, many are active players on the national and state political scenes.
These include the Council of Great City Schools, a coalition of superintendents and board members from about sixty-five of the largest urban school
districts, the Education Commission of the States, the Council of Chief State
School Officers composed of state superintendents, the National School
Boards Association which represents local boards, and the National Association of State Boards of Education.

Other associations represent particular segments of the profession. Administrators are organized in groups like the American Association of School
Administrators, the National Association of Elementary School Principals,

and the National Association of Secondary School Principals. Groups are also organized along subject matter lines, such as the American Education Research Association, the International Reading Association, the National Council of Teachers of Mathematics, the National Science Teachers Association, and the National Association for the Education of Young Children.

Special education has its own web of organizations. The closest to an umbrella group is the Council for Exceptional Children, self-described as the largest organization in the field.[64] Others include the National Association of Special Education Teachers and the National Association of State Directors of Special Education. And some groups represent particular disabilities, like the Learning Disabilities Association of America, CHADD (Children and Adults with Attention-Deficit/Hyperactivity Disorder), The Arc (whose mission includes mental retardation and other developmental disabilities), and the U.S. Autism and Asperger Association.

Each association proclaims to be working in the best interests of students, of course. And no doubt they think they are. Still, what is in the best interests of students is contentious, and the groups have separate priorities. They combine to push for more federal and state funding, while sometimes disagreeing on issues like accountability, testing, teacher qualifications, and how to divide up the money. Notably, the Council of Great Cities Schools frequently vies against other associations over funding priorities and its support for NCLB.

Some national associations that are most active politically often have non-educators at their helm. And parents and professionals from disciplines other than education (like psychology, human development, and medicine) are dominant in special education and early childhood associations. A richer analysis of the influence of these diverse organizations is beyond the scope of this book. But it seems apparent that whether headed by educators or not, their points of view are shaped by the culture and self-interest of the education profession.

In other words, the education establishment by and large calls the shots for national associations. This parochialism helps to explain why educational associations are losing their political muscle. A scholar on the politics of federal education policy writes that the education establishment has been taking a back seat to non-traditional education interest groups, especially conservative Republican lobbies.[65]

THINK TANKS

Education think tanks, supported primarily by philanthropic foundations, engage in research, policy analysis, advocacy, and public debate. Their leaders are often well-recognized policy intellectuals who write newspaper opinion articles and are television talking heads. In the *Influence* study rankings, four of the top-ten organizations are think tanks: the Education Trust, Achieve, Inc., the Thomas B. Fordham Institute, and the Center on Education Policy.

Think tanks, therefore, are education establishment forces to be reckoned with. But, to their credit, they are rogue nonconformists.[66] They are usually led by non-educators or persons with relatively brief traditional educational careers. They are on the cutting edge of school reform and constantly scorn the professional orthodoxy of the full-fledged establishment.

At the same time, some caution is in order. While it is unfair to pigeonhole them too tightly, most of the heftiest think tanks travel along fairly narrow ideological paths. Several examples follow, going from right/conservative to left/liberal in their orientation. The Fordham Institute is a hub of the large network of conservative think tanks including the American Enterprise Institute, the Heritage Foundation, the Manhattan Institute, and the Hoover Institution. In the middle are the Brookings Institutions and the Urban Institute. And moving to the left slightly are the Education Trust and the Center on Education Policy, and farther left the Center for American Progress, the Century Foundation, and the Economic Policy Institute.

There are many others. The Education Sector aims to find common ground between political liberals and education conservatives. The National Council on Teacher Quality has close ties to education conservatives. Achieve, Inc. was created on a nonpartisan basis by governors and the business community to advance the accountability movement. The National Commission on Education and the Economy has a fairly centrist focus on education policies linked to workforce development.

The question is whether, across this range, they should be suspect because they may be too beholden to the interests of their founders and funders. Professors of education policy Kevin G. Weiner and Alex Molnar think so: "At a time when America's education policymakers have nominally embraced the idea of tying school reform to 'scientifically-based research,' many of the nation's most influential reports are little more than junk science. A hodgepodge of private 'think tanks' at both the state and national levels wield significant and often undeserved influence in policy discussions by cranking out an array of well-funded and slickly produced—yet ideologically driven—research."[67]

Weiner and Molnar mainly pan conservative think tanks, but raise warning flags that apply left and right. The best case for think tanks was made by Christopher DeMuth, the retiring head of one of the nation's most prominent conservative think tanks, the American Enterprise Institute. His observations were self-serving but still hit the mark: "Think tanks are identified in the public mind as agents of a particular political viewpoint . . . Yet their real secret is not that they take orders from, or give orders to, the [George W] Bush administration or anyone else. Rather, they have discovered new methods for organizing intellectual activity—superior in many respects (by no mean all) to those of traditional research universities."[68]

That's the way I view them. Yes, there are some think tanks whose work is intellectually dishonest. Throughout this book, I am critical of the ideological polarization that dominates education policy debates. Still, I find think tanks invaluable to the cause of school reform. Whether nonpartisan or partisan in political outlook, they do innovative policy analyses of the highest order. They write and talk in blunt ways that contrast with educational jargon, and they wade into the policy arena and political process. Most valuable of all, their outspokenness often unmasks the conventional explanations and excuses of the overall education establishment.[69]

This book turns now from diagnosis to prescription, from analyses of bedrock barriers and blame to recommendations for reform. The next set of chapters lays out the architecture of a New Education Federalism that dramatically alters the role of the education establishment.

NOTES

1. E. D. Hirsch, Jr., *The Schools We Need and Why We Don't Have Them* (New York: Doubleday, 1996), 15.

2. Fuller discussion of NCLB is found later in this chapter and in chapters 8 and 9.

3. John Merrow, "A 'Surge' Strategy for No Child Left Behind?" Commentary, *Education Week* (February 14, 2007): 32, 44.

4. National Center on Education and the Economy, *Tough Choices, Tough Times: The Report of the New Commission on the Skills of the American Workforce* (San Francisco: Jossey-Bass, 2007), xxv.

5. Robert Epstein, "Why High School Must Go: An Interview with Leon Botstein," *Phi Delta Kappan,* vol. 88, no. 9 (May 2007): 659–663, 663.

6. Jane C. Owen, "Finding Our Voice, An Educational Call to Arms," Commentary, *Education Week* (April 2, 2007): 28–29.

7. Christopher B. Swanson and Janelle Barlage, *Influence: A Study of the Factors Shaping Education Policy* (Washington, DC: Editorial Projects in Education Research Center, December 2006).

8. Swanson and Barlage, *Influence,* i.

9. Chester E. Finn, Jr. "Archaic architecture, creaky machinery," *The Education Gadfly,* vol. 4, no. 31 (August 26, 2004): 2.

10. Arun K. Ramanathan, "Paved With Good Intentions: The Federal Role in the Oversight and Enforcement of the Individuals with Disabilities Education Act (IDEA)

and the No Child left Behind Act (NCLB)," *TCRecord,* November 15, 2007, www .tcrecord.org/content.asp?contentid=14532.

11. The Institute for a Competitive Workforce, *Leaders and Laggards: A State-by-State Report Card on Educational Effectiveness* (Washington, DC: U.S. Chamber of Commerce, 2007), 7.

12. Thomas Timar, *The Invisible Hand of Ideology* (Denver, CO: Education Commission of the States, 1999), 19.

13. For background on the wobbly performance of SEAs: Susan H. Fuhrman, "Less than Meets the Eye: Standards, Testing, and Fear of Federal Control," in Noel Epstein, ed., *Who's in Charge Here: The Tangled Web of School Governance and Policy* (Washington, DC: Brookings Institution Press, 2004), 147; Susan Follett Lusi, *The Role of State Departments of Education in Complex School Reform* (New York: Teachers College Press, 1997); Michael W. Kirst, "Turning Points: A History of American School Governance," in Epstein, *Who's In Charge Here?;* Gail L. Sunderman and Gary Orfield, "Domesticating a Revolution: No Child Left Behind Reforms and State Administrative Response," *Harvard Educational Review,* vol. 76, no. 4 (2006): 526–556.

14. These lawsuits are discussed in chapter 9.

15. For background on the development of the accountability movement in the states and at the federal level pre-NCLB: Christopher T. Cross, *Political Education: National Policy Comes of Age* (New York: Teachers College Press, 2004); Patrick J. McGuinn, *No Child Left Behind and the Transformation of Federal Education Policy, 1965–2005* (Lawrence, KS: University Press of Kansas, 2006); Diane Ravitch, *National Standards in American Education* (Washington, DC: The Brookings Institution, 1995).

16. Kirst, "Turning Points," 28.

17. NCLB is more fully discussed in chapter 9.

18. Vallas is quoted in Greg Toppo, "How Bush education law has changed our schools," *USA Today,* January 8, 2007.

19. Nancy Zuckerbrod, "National Education Standards Under Review," *Contra Costa Times,* January 14, 2007.

20. There are few efforts underway to strengthen their management capacity or backbone. An exception that proves the rule is the report on the workings of the Massachusetts SEA by the Rennie Center for Education Research and Policy which focuses on public education in Massachusetts. Although Massachusetts is recognized as a national leader in reform policymaking, the report was fairly critical. It found that the Massachusetts department was without "adequate knowledge or staffing capacity to support schools and districts." While increasing aid to local districts, Massachusetts "did not sufficiently invest in developing the infrastructure at the state level to provide leadership" in turning around low-performing districts. Rennie Center for Education Research & Policy, *Reaching Capacity: A Blueprint for the State Role in Improving Low Performing Schools and Districts* (Boston: Rennie Center for Education Research & Policy at MassINC, 2005), 19, 5.

21. National Center on Education and the Economy, *Tough Choices, Tough Times.*

22. Michele McNeil, "School Proposals in 'Tough Choices' Report Could Face Frosty Reception From States," *Education Week* (January 10, 2007): 1, 19.

23. Cross, *Political Education,* 147.

24. Chester E. Finn, Jr., *Troublemaker* (Princeton, NJ: Princeton University Press, 2008), 145.

25. Kennedy is quoted in Michael J. Petrilli, "The Problem with 'Implementation is the Problem': A Short History of No Child Left Behind," paper prepared for the American Enterprise Institute/Thomas B. Fordham Foundation Conference, "Fixing Failing Schools: Is the NCLB Toolkit Working?" November 30, 2006, www.aei .org/event1351.

26. Alyson Klein, "Democratic Congress to Step Up Department Oversight," *Education Week* (December 20, 2006): 22, 24–25.

27. The Commission on No Child Left Behind, *Beyond NCLB: Fulfilling the Promise to Our Nation's Children* (Washington, DC: The Aspen Institute, 2007), for example at 20, 35, 165.

28. David J. Hoff, "Chiefs: Ed. Dept. Getting Stingier on NCLB Flexibility," *Education Week* (December 13, 2006): 19.

29. See chapter 9 on the politicization of research under DOE.

30. Cross, *Public Education.*

31. Matt Miller, *The 2% Solution, Fixing America's Problems in Ways Liberals and Conservatives Can Love* (New York: Public Affairs, 2003), 116.

32. Arthur Levine, *Educating School Teachers* (Washington, D.C: The Education Schools Project, 2006), 19; Chester E. Finn, Jr., "High Hurdles," *Education Next,* vol. 3, no. 2 (Spring 2003): 62–67, 65.

33. National Commission on Teaching & America's Future, *What Matters Most: Teaching for America's Future* (New York: National Commission on Teaching and America's Future, 1996), 31–34.

34. Levine, *Educating School Leaders,* 6.

35. Levine, *Educating School Leaders;* Arthur Levine, *Educating School Teachers* (Washington, DC: The Education Schools Project, 2006), and Arthur Levine, *Educating Researchers* (Washington, DC: The Education Schools Project, 2007).

36. Levine, *Educating Leaders,* 13.

37. Levine, *Educating Leaders,* Executive Summary, 3.

38. Levine, *Educating Leaders,* Executive Summary, 3–4.

39. For example, James W. Guthrie and Theodore Sanders, "Who Will Lead The Public Schools?" Education Section, *The New York Times* January 7, 2001, 46; David S. Spence and Gene Bottoms, "How States Can Build Leadership Systems," Commentary, *Education Week* (December 13, 2007): 25, 36.

40. Alyson Klein, "Teacher Ed. Grants Would Be Slashed Under Pending Bills," *Education Week,* (October 9, 2007): 1, 26. Various recommendations for reform can be found in the Levine, Holmes and National Commission reports and many publications of the National Council on Teacher Quality.

41. Swanson and Barlage, *Influence.*

42. This section draws heavily upon an excellent, balanced collection of papers in Jane Hanaway and Andrew J. Rotherham, eds., *Collective Bargaining in Education – Negotiating Change in Today's Schools* (Cambridge, MA: Harvard Education Press, 2006).

43. Elizabeth Gleick, "'Mad and Mobilized'," *Time,* September 9, 1996: 52–53.

44. Greg Toppo, "Education Chief Calls Teachers Union 'Terrorist Organization,'" *USA Today,* February 23, 2004.

45. Rod Paige, "Three Cheers for Steve Jobs," *The Education Gadfly,* vol. 7, no. 7 (March 10, 2007), 2.

46. Terry M. Moe, "Union Power and the Education of Children" in Hanaway and Rotherham, *Collective Bargaining in Education,* 252.

47. See generally Diane Ravitch, "Why Teachers Unions Are Good for Teachers and the Public," *American Educator,* vol. 30, no. 4 (Winter 06–07); Richard D. Kahlenberg, "The History of Collective Bargaining among Teachers," (7–25) and Leo Casey, "The Educational Value of Democratic Voice," (181–201) in Hanaway and Rotherham, *Collective Bargaining in Education.*

48. Chart, "Teachers' Union Spending," *Education Week* (March 5, 2008): 10.

49. Jonathan Schorr, "Hot For Teachers, John Kerry's Quietly Radical School Reform Plan," *Washington Monthly* (July/August 2004): 21–23.

50. See chapter 14.

51. *Tough Liberal: Albert Shanker and the Battles over Schools, Unions, Race, and Democracy* (New York: Columbia University Press, 2007), 306.

52. Moe, "Union Power and the Education of Children," 241.

53. Hanaway and Rotherham, "Conclusion" in Hanaway and Rotherham, *Collective Bargaining in Education,* 260. In the same volume, for a full discussion of the absence of research on point, see Dan Goldhaber, "Are Teacher Unions Good for Students."

54. Steve Farkas, Jean Johnson and Ann Duffett, *Rolling Up Their Sleeves, Superintendents and Principals Talk About What's Needed to Fix Public Schools* (New York: Public Agenda, 2003), 32. There is abundant evidence that many weak principals use union provisions as an excuse for their own unwillingness to take decisive personnel actions. In the Public Agenda survey, only seven percent of superintendents rated their principals as excellent and only 29 percent rated them as good at moving ineffective teachers out of their building.

55. Steve Farkas, Jean Johnson and Ann Duffett, *Stand By Me, What Teachers Really Think about Unions, Merit Pay and Other Professional Matters* (New York: Public Agenda, 2003), 21.

56. Hanaway and Rotherham, "Conclusion," 263.

57. Foreword by Chester E. Finn, Jr. and Michael J. Petrelli in Frederick M. Hess and Coby Loup, *The Leadership Limbo, Teacher Labor Agreements in America's Fifty Largest School Districts* (Washington, DC: Thomas B. Fordham Institute, 2008), 6.

58. Susan Moore Johnson and others, *Leading the Local: Teachers Union Presidents Speak on Change, Challenges* (Washington, DC: Education Sector, 2007), 1.

59. Johnson, *Leading the Local,* 21.

60. Julia Koppich, "The As-Yet-Unfulfilled Promise of Reform Bargaining," in Hanaway and Rotherham, *Collective Bargaining in Education;* Vaishili Honawar, "Mooney Institute Tries to Blend Unionism, School Reform," *Education Week* (April 9, 2008): 1, 14–15.

61. Bess Keller, "NEA Wants Role in School Improvement Agenda," *Education Week,* (January 24, 2007): 1, 22–23.

62. Kahlenberg, "The History of Collective Bargaining among Teachers," and Koppich, "The As-Yet-Unfulfilled Promise of Reform Bargaining."

63. For lists that appear to cover most of the largest associations, see the Education Advocacy and Lobbying Organizations website, http://politicsol.com/advocacy -directory/advocacy-education.html; and the National Association of State Science and Mathematics Coalitions website, http://www.nassmc.org/archived%20docs/ primer.html.

64. http://cec.sped.org.

65. Elizabeth DeBray-Pelot, "Dismantling Education's 'Iron Triangle'," in Carl F. Kaestle and Alyssa E. Lodewick, *To Educate A Nation: Federal and National Strategies of School Reform* (Lawrence, KS: University of Kansas Press, 2007), 32.

66. For example, Chester E. Finn, Jr. (Fordham Institute), Frederick M. Hess (AEI), Kati Haycock (Education Trust), Jack Jennings (CEP); Andrew Rotherham and Thomas Toch (Education Sector), Kate Walsh (NCTQ), Michael Cohen (Achieve), Marc Tucker (NCEE), Richard Kahlenberg (Century) and Richard Rothstein (EPI). Their careers have been forged almost entirely outside of K–12 teaching and departments of education.

67. Kevin G. Weiner and Alex Molnar, "Truthiness in Education," Commentary, *Education Week* (February 28, 2007): 32, 44. See also Frederick M. Hess, "Conclusion: Education Research and Public Policy," in Hess, ed., *When Research Matters,* (Cambridge, MA: Harvard Education Press, 2008), 246–249.

68. Christopher DeMuth, "Think-Tank Confidential," *Wall Street Journal,* October 11, 2007.

69. Foundations also play an influential role, but by and large, they are dependent on departments of education, and their impact has usually fallen short of expectations. Notable disappointments have been massive initiatives by the Bill and Melinda Gates and the Walter H. Annenberg foundations.

Part IV

A New Education Federalism

Public education is typically viewed as a monolithic and bureaucratic "system." But while bureaucratic it is, monolithic it's not. It's more like a giant jigsaw puzzle in which the pieces don't fit. The pieces of the puzzle include *local* departments of education, school boards and mayors, *state* governors, legislatures and departments of education, and the *federal* White House, Congress, and Department of Education. Which among them is responsible for which education policies and administrative actions?

It's impossible to tell. For example, under NCLB, Congress requires states to adopt academic content standards, tests, and sanctions for failing schools; the U.S. Department of Education promulgates regulations and monitors compliance; state departments of education set the standards and tests and also monitor compliance; and local departments of education decide how to incorporate the standards into curricula and instruction and are subject to sanctions if schools fail to improve significantly. The public is confused and frustrated and for good reason. No one level of government can be held accountable, each points the finger at the other, and school reform flounders.

The way to put the pieces of the puzzle together—to clarify, unify, and strengthen the governance of our public schools—is through what I call a "New Education Federalism." Its foundation is a commanding federal role that reflects both the national interest in high-quality public education and the failure of states and local governments to provide it. It is senseless to have fifty states and over 14,000 school districts going their own separate and unequal ways. At the same time, local governments, especially urban mayors, are better able than school boards to assure that local schools meet national standards and wisely spend federal funds.

Chapter 8

The Folly of Local Control

In 1974 Chief Justice Warren Burger of the U.S. Supreme Court intoned: "No single tradition in public education is more deeply rooted than local control over the operation of schools; local autonomy has long been thought essential for both the maintenance of community concern and support for public schools and to the quality of the educational process."[1] But today local control is a myth. And in my view, it should stay that way.

THE NATIONAL INTEREST IN PUBLIC EDUCATION

The motto E Pluribus Unum—"one out of many" or "from many one"—belongs on the doorway of every schoolhouse. It would signify that public education must play a fundamental role in the development of a cohesive and strong nation.[2] Education, as the Supreme Court stated in outlawing racial segregation in *Brown v. Board of Education,* "is required in the performance of our most basic public responsibilities. It is the very foundation of good citizenship."[3] Yet, inequality of opportunity and the achievement gap between races and economic classes keep us from accomplishing this mission. The losers in school (and in the work force) are alienated from the larger society, creating the kind of inferiority that the Court in the *Brown* decision stated "may affect their hearts and minds in a way unlikely ever to be undone."[4]

The second fundamental mission of public schools has been to keep our economy booming. The *A Nation at Risk* report in 1983 defined the risk in terms of our declining preeminence in the global economy. The evolution of federal involvement in public education since then has been closely linked to the business community's pursuit of a skilled, world-class workforce.

A former schoolteacher named Lyndon B. Johnson embraced both missions when as president he introduced the Elementary and Secondary Education Act, the first landmark federal education law: "[N]othing matters more [than public education] to the future of our country; not our military preparedness, for armed might is worthless if we lack brainpower to build a world of peace; not our productive economy, for we cannot sustain growth without trained manpower; [and] not our democratic system of government, for freedom is fragile if citizens are ignorant."[5]

Still, a national problem doesn't require a federal solution. And Americans have resisted the transfer of governmental power from local and state governments to Washington. Federalism has been "America's endless argument."[6] Today, the federal government is of course mightier than ever, but federal dominance in domestic policy accrued only gradually and grudgingly in response to failures at the state and local levels. The federal government stepped in to provide a floor of protections for Americans in civil rights and in the New Deal and Great Society web of social welfare programs.

Yet on public education, we remain ambivalent and battle endlessly over responsibility for governance of K–12 public schools. As one expert put it: "[W]e Americans are usually a pragmatic and efficient people, yet we prefer a bit of chaos when it comes to the governance of our [public schools]. We are allergic to anything that smacks of central authority, and if there is a civil religion that binds us, then its sacred texts include stern commandments on the dispersion of power."[7] Still, in the last half-century, the preservation of local control has been a losing battle.

THE ONSET OF FEDERAL ENCROACHMENT

In the aftermath of the Civil War, after creating the first federal department of education, Congress considered but did not pass legislation to establish a "national system of education." Under the bill, if states did not provide schools "reasonably for all the children therein," the Commissioner of Education could operate "national schools."[8] The issue of federal responsibility was revived periodically, but nothing much happened. Between 1862 and 1963, Congress considered unrestricted general aid to schools thirty-six times and defeated it every time.[9]

Federal abstinence changed following the 1954 *Brown v. Board of Education* decision. The impact of the ruling went beyond segregated schools in southern states. School districts across the country were forced to recognize the inferior quality of instruction available to Black students. Then in 1957, the Russian launch of the space satellite Sputnik frightened Americans into thinking that we were in danger of losing the cold war because of our deficient public schools. The next year, at the urging of president Dwight D. Eisenhower, Congress enacted the National Defense Education Act to upgrade instruction in math, science, and foreign languages. Eisenhower favored these federal interventions "not so much for their own [academic value] as for creating the scientists and technologists who could keep America ahead in the arms race."[10]

In the 1960s, civil rights and President Johnson's Great Society refocused the federal role. The Elementary and Secondary Education Act of 1965 created the Title I program which distributed federal aid to poor communities. LBJ declared, "I deeply believe no law I have signed or will ever sign means more to the future of America."[11] The same idealism, fueled by unrest over state and local inaction, led to passage in 1974 of the federal Education for All Handicapped Children Act, now known as the Individuals with Disabilities Education Act. The law sought to guarantee children with special learning needs the right to a "free and appropriate education" and linked federal aid to compliance with the law's mandates.

Next came the *A Nation at Risk* report. Local and state governments were in charge of education, but the problem was *national*. The federal government, the report said, should have "the primary responsibility to identify the national interest in education. It should also help fund and support efforts . . . and provide the national leadership."[12] Still, the states and localities were left holding the bookbag and given the assignment of carrying out the report's recommendations.

At that point, governors picked up the challenge. Many states raised academic standards and initiated tests of minimum academic competency. Then in the mid-1980s, the "education governors," as they were known, led by Democrat Bill Clinton from Arkansas and Republican Lamar Alexander from Tennessee, went farther. The National Governors Association crafted a bipartisan agenda that included national content standards, a national board to certify teachers, performance-based pay for teachers, school choice and "academic bankruptcy" for schools not meeting standards.

By 1988, George H. W. Bush was campaigning to be "the education president" on a platform similar to the governors. After taking office, he appointed Alexander as education secretary and, in his State of the Union address in 1990 (with Clinton as his featured guest), announced "National Education Goals." However, Bush's legislation addressing the goals was riddled by political crossfire. Democrats mainly wanted more federal money, Republicans mainly school choice. And both parties withered under the political heat generated by grass-roots communities and the education establishment that wanted to protect local control. The education establishment also feared that educators would be unable to measure up to high standards and their professional judgment would be second-guessed by federal and state bureaucrats.

Bush's bill failed but the issues carried over into the 1992 election campaign. Bush, running for re-election, backtracked and largely campaigned for choice while the Democratic nominee Clinton stuck to the case for national standards and tests. Clinton, after his victory, introduced his own legislation titled Goals 2000. But it too ran into stiff opposition even though the Democrats controlled Congress, and Clinton scaled back on his earlier goals. His education secretary Richard Riley (a former governor) declared education to be a national priority but a "local function" and "a state responsibility."[13]

As eventually signed into law, Goals 2000 also quashed Clinton's attempt to force states to develop "opportunity-to-learn" (OTL) standards that would expose the inequitable funding of schools serving concentrations of poor children. Most Democratic and Republican governors opposed OTL standards, fearing state capitols would have to pick up a hefty check. Still, for all its toothlessness, Goals 2000, as education federalism expert Patrick J. McGuinn writes, was "widely recognized as a watershed moment in the history of American education."[14] In secretary Riley's words, "[F]or the first time in the nation's history, a statutory framework defines the federal role as one of supporting and facilitation to improve all schools for all children."[15]

That framework set the stage for the reauthorization of the Elementary and Secondary Education Act in the same year. As enacted, that bill, titled the Improving America's Schools Act (IASA), dramatically raised the federal stakes. IASA conditioned sizable federal funding for disadvantaged students on adoption by the states of academic standards. In effect, voluntary standards under Goals 2000 became mandatory under IASA. IASA also tied further strings on federal aid. States were required to develop student tests, set benchmarks for "adequate yearly progress," publish test results that separated out the performance of students by race, and required local departments to take "corrective actions" for failing schools.

These provisions were similar to those that emerged seven years later in NCLB. But IASA never achieved its promise. The federal and state education establishments lagged in enforcement. Student performance improved very little. And the public stayed dissatisfied. On the political right, the Newt Gingrich-led Republican majority that took control of Congress in 1994 sought to roll back IASA as a heretical intrusion on local control. Nonetheless, after passage of several relatively minor amendments, the political center—led by Clinton and backed by most Congressional Democrats and Republican moderates, governors and business leaders—held ranks.

Clinton put education at the center of his comeback against the Gingrich forces. It became a pivotal issue in his winning re-election campaign in 1996 against Republican nominee Robert Dole who railed against federal involvement. In his second term, Clinton was unable to enlarge the scope of federal involvement but did sweeten the pot with "the most dramatic increases in federal K–12 spending since the 1960s."[16]

Education policy stayed front and center in the 2000 presidential election between George W. Bush, who as governor of Texas championed accountability reform, and Albert Gore, Clinton's vice-president. George W. and Gore offered "remarkably similar education platforms."[17] Both were willing for the federal government to force state and local educators to be more accountable for the academic achievement of all students. And groundwork was laid for the passage of the most radical assault on local control in the nation's history: NCLB.

In the next chapter, the remarkable story of NCLB is told in more detail. But its revolutionary impact cannot be grasped without further understanding of the nation's enduring obsession with local control.

THE MYTH AND FALLACY OF LOCAL CONTROL

Each of the over 14,000 local school districts in forty-nine states is vested with substantial legal power to determine what will be taught in its public schools and how it will be taught.[18] As summarized by a scholar on education governance, "Historically, American education has been rooted in local policy, local management, and local financial control, traditions deeply embedded in our political culture."[19] But what is left of local control after a half a century of mounting federal and state regulation? And should we want to restore it to the pedestal of K–12 public school policymaking?

The Myth

Local control ain't what it used to be. As we have seen, states, as well as the federal government, have severely eroded the power of local districts. In addition, there are other nationalizing influences that diminish what little local control is left. A relatively small number of vendors of textbooks and tests control the market and homogenize instruction nationwide. As education journalist Jay Matthews described it, "No matter how steadfastly school boards and their congressional allies defend local decision-making, schools actually offer a fairly steady diet of curricular Big Macs and Cokes."[20]

National associations of educators, teachers' unions, think tanks, foundations, the business community, research centers, and the internet also exert considerable nationwide influence.

Nonetheless passion for local control persists. And not just among conservatives who fervently oppose big government. Liberals too are drawn to the theory that school governance closest to parents, students, and teachers is ideal. Localism, says progressive educator Theodore R. Sizer, shows respect for "the assumption that those close to the children ultimately know what is best for them . . . centralized government is an inept and inappropriate tool to set and shape the substance and standards of school policy and practice."[21] Deborah Meier, a liberal education icon, says that "individual schools and families must have more, not less, power to decide not only how to teach, but also what is to be taught . . . schools must be able to respond to local circumstances."[22]

And so the fight continues, with the political left and right using the controversy over NCLB as fresh ammunition. Education professor Milton W. Kirst summarizes and sympathizes with their cause: "[State and federal] officials increasingly have been driving education policy in recent decades, with modest results to show. On the other hand, while local school board members, as well as superintendents . . . have less and less say over education, the public still holds them accountable for school results. In terms of democracy and accountability, then, it is local school districts, with all their imperfections, that would appear to be the superior governance choice."[23]

But there is no evidence that they are the best choice, and countless empirical reasons why they are not.

The Fallacy

Take accountability standards for example. It is nonsensical for 14,000 school districts, or even the largest ones, or even fifty states to go their own way in deciding what to teach and test. What is the difference between what should be learned in reading, math and other subjects in districts that are large or small, rich or poor, or in a blue or red state? The duplication, waste of effort, and diffusion of accountability are obvious.

Less obvious but also daunting are other inescapable realities. One is the incapacity of local school boards to make wise policy on their own. Appointed or elected local boards comprised of part-time volunteers don't have the time or knowledge to assess education research and practice, even if school systems were more inclined to be transparent than they are. (In chapter 10, I make the case for abolishing school boards and putting mayors in charge as part of the New Education Federalism.) Another is the fact of life that poor school districts with scarce resources don't have all that much to control locally. The gap between the ideal and real degree of local decision-making is especially vast in poor neighborhoods where parental and community participation is difficult to mobilize.

What is not in dispute is that the U.S. stands relatively alone among developed nations in its devotion to local control. Our foreign competitors, for example, almost invariably have national standards and curricula.[24] Kirst, while a devotee of local control, recognizes the reality: "[I]t appears likely that traditional local governance structures will be overwhelmed by the trend toward increased nonlocal power over schools."[25] That is of course what has happened when NCLB, which we now turn to, sealed the coffin of local control.

NOTES

1. *Milliken v. Bradley,* 418 U.S. 717, 741–742 (1974).

2. Americans have long recognized this national imperative. Education historian Lawrence A. Cremin points out that the abiding characteristics of American education have included "the tendency to make education widely available...to diverse peoples...and the effort to solve certain problems indirectly through education rather than directly through politics." Cremin, *Popular Education and Its Discontents* (New York: Harper & Row, 1989), viii. Diane Ravitch writes that Americans "long ago decided, without too much discussion of the matter, that education would be the best vehicle with which to change society." Diane Ravitch, *The Troubled Crusade, American Education 1945–80* (New York: Basic Books, 1983), 323.

3. *Brown v. Board of Education,* 347 U.S. 483, 493 (1954).

4. *Brown v. Board of Education,* 483.

5. Johnson is quoted in Patrick J. McGuinn, *No Child Left Behind and the Transformation of Federal Education Policy, 1965–2005* (Lawrence, KS: University Press of Kansas, 2006), 29.

6. John D. Donahue is quoted in Richard B. Freeman and Joel Rogers, "The Promise of Progressive Federalism," in Joe Soss, Jacob S. Hacker, and Suzanne Mettler, eds., *Remaking American: Democracy and Public Policy in an Age of Inequality* (New York: Russell Sage Foundation, 2007), 207.

7. Michael J. Feuer, "Moderation: A Radical Approach to Education Policy," Commentary, *Education Week* (June 14, 2006): 36. For rich accounts of the origins, development and tensions inherent in the federal role in education: Christopher T. Cross, *Political Education: National Policy Comes of Age* (New York: Teachers College Press, 2004); Goodwin Liu, "Education, Equality, and National Citizenship," *The Yale Law Journal,* vol. 116, vol. 2 (2006): 330–411; Paul Manna, *School's In: Federalism and the National Education Agenda* (Washington, DC: Georgetown

Press, 2007); McGuinn, *No Child Left Behind and the Transformation of Federal Education Policy.*

8. Lui, "Education, Equality, and National Citizenship," 371–395.

9. Michael W. Kirst, "Turning Points: A History of American School Governance," in Noel Epstein, ed., *Who's in Charge Here: The Tangled Web of School Governance and Policy* (Washington, DC: Brookings Institution Press, 2004), 22.

10. Historian Stephen E. Ambrose is quoted in E. J. Dionne, Jr., *Why Americans Hate Politics* (New York: Simon & Schuster, 1991), 171.

11. McGuinn, *No Child Left Behind and the Transformation of Federal Education Policy,* 31.

12. The National Commission on Excellence in Education, *A Nation At Risk: The Imperative for Educational Reform* (Washington, DC: U.S. Government Printing Office, 1983), 5.

13. McGuinn, *No Child Left Behind and the Transformation of Federal Education Policy,* 91.

14. McGuinn, *No Child Left Behind and the Transformation of Federal Education Policy,* 91.

15. McGuinn, *No Child Left Behind and the Transformation of Federal Education Policy,* 91.

16. McGuinn, *No Child Left Behind and the Transformation of Federal Education Policy,* 144.

17. McGuinn, *No Child Left Behind and the Transformation of Federal Education Policy,* 145.

18. The exception is Hawaii which is one statewide school district.

19. Kirst, "Turning Points," 14. For an excellent short history, see Matt Miller, *Nationalize the schools (. . . A Little)!* (Washington, DC: Center for American Progress, 2008), 8–10.

20. Jay Mathews, "Curricular Big Macs," *The Washington Post,* December 10, 1997.

21. Theodore R. Sizer, *Horace's Hope: What Works for the American High School* (Boston: Houghton Mifflin Company, 1996), 141.

22. Deborah Meier and Diane Ravitch, "Bridging Differences: A Dialogue Between Deborah Meier and Diane Ravitch, Commentary, *Education Week* (May 24, 2006): 36–37, 36.

23. Kirst, "Turning Points," 39.

24. Chester E. Finn, Jr., Liam Julian, and Michael J. Petrilli, *To Dream the Impossible Dream: Four Approaches to National Standards and Tests for America's Schools* (Washington, DC: Thomas B. Fordham Foundation, 2006), 10; Nancy Kober, *A Public Education Primer* (Washington, DC: Center on Education Policy, 2006), 14.

25. Kirst, "Turning Points," 15.

Chapter 9

A Federal Takeover

The future of NCLB is uncertain. Its reauthorization, pending since 2007, has been politically stalemated, and the 2008 presidential and congressional elections did little to reconcile public opinion between those who want to revise it and those who want to scrap it altogether. What both groups have in common, however, is the belief that NCLB goes too far in the direction of federal interference with state and local control.

I disagree: *NCLB doesn't give the federal government too much power, but too little.* In this chapter, I spell out why that's true and how the federal government must assume much greater responsibility through a single set of mandated national standards and tests, a guarantee of adequate funding for low-income school districts, and powerful research and development that drives reform. The chapter also explains why, contrary to conventional political wisdom, a federal takeover is politically possible.

A POLITICAL MIRACLE

For all its faults, NCLB lays a remarkable foundation for a New Education Federalism. It was unquestionably the most revolutionary intrusion ever by the federal government into public schools. Yet, it was championed by a president and enacted by a Congress controlled by conservative Republicans long wedded in principle to retrenchment of big government. Many liberal Democrats too were wary of its major components. Nonetheless, against these political odds, it passed in 2001 by astounding bipartisan majorities in the House (381–41) and Senate (87–10).

In the light of President George W. Bush's bitter partisan warfare with Democrats on virtually every other policy front, its passage seems miraculous. And in some respects it was. As surveyed earlier, some groundwork was laid during the elder Bush and Clinton presidencies, and the younger Bush and Al Gore did not differ much in their education platforms during the 2000 election campaign. Still, there were deep disagreements to be overcome between Republicans and Democrats, a task further complicated because each party had its own internal divisions between moderates and ideologues.

Compromise became possible first because of George W.'s unswerving commitment. He believed (like his father) in the necessity of federal action to improve public education, and sought a national version of the state accountability law he had trumpeted as governor of Texas.[1] His goals were clear: academic standards and tests in all fifty states that would disclose which students in which school districts and schools were performing far below their capabilities—that is, which students were suffering, in his famous phrase, from "the soft bigotry of low expectations."

In a Nixon-goes-to-China historical moment, he confronted head-on the Republican party's abhorrence of a federal role in public schools. "[C]hange will not come," he declared, "by disdaining or dismantling the federal role in education. Educational excellence for all is a national issue and at this moment is a presidential priority."[2]

Democrats had their own reasons to cut a deal, not least of all fear that Bush and Republicans would steal their ownership of public education as a political selling point. In the end, moderates of both parties carried the day. A leading historian of NCLB observed: "The final version of the legislation was a compromise bill in every sense of the word—there was plenty for politicians of every persuasion to like and dislike about it, and its reforms went too far for some and not far enough for others."[3] The liberal Education Trust rendered a similar verdict: "NCLB was a defeat for liberals on the left and conservatives on the right—it was a bill that was always designed to run straight down the middle so neither extreme won the day."[4]

Major concessions were made. Republicans dropped their quest for vouchers and accepted minor step-ups in local flexibility over federal aid. Democrats accepted federal mandates on testing and unbinding promises of greater federal funding. And both parties, in order to mute criticism of a federal takeover, approved vague language that papered over differences in how the law's major mandates were to be defined and implemented. The steep costs of these compromises lay ahead.[5]

THE LAW'S NUTS AND (LIGHTNING) BOLTS

As enacted, the bill's major components were:[6]

- *Standards and testing.* Each state must implement its own curriculum standards and annually test all students—with modest exceptions for students with disabilities (SWD) and English as Second Language learners (ESL)—in reading and math in grades 3–8 and once in grades 10–12. Science was to be added in the 2007–2008 school year. In addition, states must administer the same national tests, the National Assessment of Educational Progress, every other year in reading and math to a sample of students in grades four and eight.
- *Public disclosure of test scores and failing schools.* Annual state test results must be reported annually and broken down by school, race, gender, poverty level, and SWD and ESL students.
- *Performance benchmarks.* Each state must set its own targets for "annual yearly progress" (AYP) provided that all students, with minor allowances for SWD and ESL students, achieve proficiency in reading and math by the 2013–2014 school year.
- *Escalating sanctions for failing schools.* Schools that do not make AYP for two consecutive years must receive technical assistance, and students in those schools must be offered the option to transfer to another public school in the district. After three consecutive years of not making AYP, students in failing schools are entitled to tutoring services provided by the school district or by private companies. After four years, failing schools must take corrective action like replacing staff or adopting new curricula. After five years, the school must be restructured with the options including conversion to a charter school or turnover to a private company.
- *Highly qualified teachers.* All new teachers hired with the largest pot of federal funds (Title I funds) must be "highly qualified teachers" (HQTs). By the school year 2005–2006 (extended later to 2006–2007), each class where a core subject is taught must have a HQT. "Highly qualified" requires full state certification or licensing, at least a bachelors degree and expertise in subject knowledge and teaching skills.
- *Flexibility in use of federal funds.* States were given modest latitude to consolidate various funding streams under the Elementary and Secondary Education Act, and pilot projects to expand consolidation were authorized.
- *Funding.* Authorized were a 20 percent increase in Title I funds, expanded funding for charter schools, and new grants programs in reading, math and science.

But these provisions were easier said than done, and a backlash erupted immediately once implementation began.

"RACE TO THE BOTTOM"

The fault lines in the law ran through the fifty states. States could set their own academic standards, tests, measures of AYP, and sanctions. They also had wide wiggle room in administration of the requirements for HQTs. And state and local education officials meant well at the outset. Reporters at *Education Week* concluded from interviews shortly after NCLB's passage that most state officials generally supported it.[7] But they were up against what were generally regarded as unrealistic timelines and compliance targets, particularly on AYP and HQTs. They knew they lacked the management capacity to administer the complicated requirements and the know-how—proven reform models—for turning around failing schools. And so they feared that they couldn't comply with the law and would be embarrassed and censured for low achievement levels.

It did not take long for the appearance of a chorus of critics demanding go-easy enforcement or repeal of the law. The National Council of State Legislators and the National Governors Conference blasted it as an unwarranted intrusion and un-funded mandate. Various states passed resolutions that expressed defiance. The NEA teachers' union and the state of Connecticut filed suits challenging the law.[8] The Council of Chief State School Officers pleaded for waivers. Arne Duncan, then the reform-minded CEO of the Chicago school system (later president Obama's secretary of education), worried that NCLB was a "complex and impractical mandate that sets overly-ambitious yearly improvement standards."[9]

Special education presented its own array of conflicts. Advocates and educators expressed alarm over what were considered unreasonable expectations for many students with disabilities. The Council for Exceptional Children, a leading advocacy group in special education, reported "overriding sentiment" that NCLB makes no sense for students with disabilities.[10] In a national opinion poll in 2007, 78 percent of parents with children in public schools opposed holding students in special education to the same academic standards as other students.[11] Disapproval mounted when many schools that made giant academic strides overall were still labeled as failing because a small population of students with disabilities did not meet AYP.

Bipartisan support in Congress unraveled. Conservative lawmakers crowed, we told you so, the feds would make a mess of things. Liberals bitterly attacked the president for reneging on funding. Moderates of both parties wavered. Still the president and Congressional leaders held firm. States, unwilling to opt out because they would lose federal funds, went along. But they used every means they could think of to blunt or subvert the intent of the law.

The "laboratories of democracy" discovered ingenious ways to inflate test results and to manipulate calculation of AYP. After NCLB, student performance on state tests rose, but, as summarized in chapter 2, the big gap between those results and the much lower student performance on the nationwide National Assessment of Educational Performance (NAEP) tests widened. States also gamed qualifications for HQTs. And worst of all in the eyes of conservative school choice advocates, states stalled on sanctions with relatively few students from failing schools receiving transfers or tutoring and with school privatization hardly happening at all.[12]

The backlash reflected NCLB's many liabilities. But the law also has many undervalued assets. And, to continue the financial metaphor, though NAEP test scores haven't risen significantly, NCLB represents investment capital that can pay big dividends in the future. No one disputes that the public attention surrounding NCLB has deeply etched into our national consciousness the persistent, dire straits of public schools.

There is now a "wealth of data, sunlight, and transparency" on the achievement gap.[13] As expressed by Michael Casserly, executive director of the association of big city school districts: "Although [NCLB] has proved complicated to implement and cumbersome to administer, it has helped America's urban schools direct attention to students who, for too long, were out of sight and out of mind. That alone has made NCLB worth the effort."[14] Others note that NCLB has "created political cover for state, district, or school officials to take bolder [reform] actions than they otherwise might."[15]

MEND IT OR END IT?

Most mend-it advocates want to leave the basic structure intact with modifications. Typical of their views are a lengthy set of prescriptions offered by the bipartisan National Commission on No Child Left Behind.[16] The Commission recommends changing measures of annual student progress (AYP) to better reflect growth in student test scores, a position widely accepted and piloted by DOE beginning in 2007. It also proposes rule changes to ease how students with disabilities are tested and counted in AYP calculations. On sanctions, the Commission calls for strengthening students' access to transfers and tutoring and for more aggressive interventions and restructuring of failing schools. On "highly qualified teachers," it wants less emphasis on teacher qualifications when they enter the classroom and more on their effectiveness as teachers.

Overall, the mend-it ranks have dwindled. In 2008 most of the presidential candidates from both parties—feeling political heat from conservative and liberal ideologues, suburban parents, and the education establishment—expressed considerable or outright opposition to reauthorization. On the other hand, Barack Obama was more supportive than most. And other liberal stalwarts remain in line, including Rep. Miller and Sen. Kennedy, the Council of Great Cities Schools, the Congressional Black Caucus, and civil rights groups. William L. Taylor, a legendary hero of the civil rights movement for the past fifty years, says, "I can't think of any other issues on which I agree with [George W.] Bush."[17]

Many education conservatives also favor reauthorization, although some call for a more radical overhaul. Conservative opinion-makers Chester E. Finn, Jr. and Frederick M. Hess are mostly disillusioned with the federal failure under NCLB to push states harder on choice remedies. "After a certain trigger point is reached . . . when schools have gone several years without sufficient improvement," they write, "the interventions that follow should be draconian."[18] Failing schools should be closed and turned over to outside operators. They believe state and local educators can be better trusted than federal officials to make this happen.

While I usually agree with education conservatives on accountability, I find this position puzzling. Hess and Finn refer to the sanctions in NCLB as federal "cookie-cutter prescriptions."[19] But only the *kinds* of sanctions to be imposed on staggered timelines are prescribed. The reality is that state and local educators have all the room they need to impose flexible and, where necessary, draconian remedies, if they choose to. But the great majority haven't chosen to, before or since NCLB.[20]

The end-it advocates include an expedient alliance of political conservatives, liberal teachers' unions, and education progressives. The hostility to reauthorization from the political right is not surprising. Rep. Peter Hoekstra voiced the opposition widely shared among anti-big-government Republicans in the House and Senate: "We have clearly moved on the road to . . . federal government schools . . . People are going home and listening to their school boards and listening to their parents saying 'We want our schools back.'"[21]

The shocker is the opposition on the left, since liberals have historically been on the side of federal action to address the problems of low-income and minority Americans, from civil rights to anti-poverty programs. But the NEA, the largest teachers' union and a liberal powerhouse in Democratic politics, has fought NCLB from the start, while the AFT has recently taken a similar hostile position.[22] The unions are aided and abetted by other liberals, particularly educational progressives, who have long favored local control of schools as an expression of grass-roots democracy. Deborah Meier fears that NCLB is breeding "the growth of a sense of powerlessness and alienation from public life . . . [that] is a more potent danger to democracy than any real or imagined loss of academic purity."[23]

To many liberals, moreover, that's not the worst of it. NCLB, they allege, is a Trojan horse for conservatives who want to end public education as we know it and then privatize it. A book *Many Children Left Behind—How the No Child Left Behind Act is Damaging Our Children and Our Schools* contains articles written by leading education progressives who argue that even if various problems are fixed, "*NCLB cannot, will not, and perhaps was even not intended to deliver on its promises* (italics in the original)."[24]

Richard Rothstein adds another frequent liberal grievance. He believes that NCLB holds out the false hope that "schools alone can enable all children to reach high levels of proficiency," regardless of their social and economic disadvantages.[25] Students and schools are unfairly stigmatized, he says, and attention is diverted from issues of poverty and race.

But mend-it liberals differ. In a published exchange with Rothstein, Robert Gordon, then connected to the liberal Center for American Progress and now in a prominent job in the Obama administration, stated, "If we throw NCLB out the window . . . [p]oor children will not suddenly have universal preschool or health care. They will simply have the status quo minus NCLB."[26] Liberals should also realize that NCLB, by revealing how far we have to go to improve student performance, builds up, not relieves, pressure for more federal and state funding for school reform. NCLB has been legally challenged as an un-funded mandate. And the imposition of high standards and tests is driving lawsuits in the states seeking more money to enable students to pass the tests.

All told, I think end-it liberals are on the wrong track. Federal intervention, through NCLB, is a powerful vehicle on the right track towards equal educational opportunity for American children. If anything, it needs to carry more reform freight.

NCLB ON STEROIDS: NATIONAL STANDARDS AND TESTS

Education federalism scholar Paul Manna offers a telling perspective: "[W]ithout a major revolution in educational governance in this country, federal and local officials will continue relying heavily upon state policy and leadership . . . Put another way, the persistence of state power in education means that NCLB's ambition and federal officials' promises to enforce the law strictly will continue to collide head-on with the primary institutions that control American schools."[27] Exhibit I is the absurdity of fifty states with different content standards and tests. It's not just that states have abused their unbridled authority under NCLB to write their own and have galloped off in a "race to the bottom." It's simply that there's no sensible rationale, in the first place, for fifty different world-class versions of what students need to know in reading, math, science, and history.

But can the nation be brought to its senses? Are national standards and tests politically feasible? A report published by the Thomas B. Fordham Foundation has incisively framed the issues and options.[28] In 2006 it sent questionnaires to twelve experts, "left, right, and center," asking their opinions on different approaches. The toughest was a single mandatory set of standards and tests. A step down were voluntary national standards and tests with incentives, such as more federal money or fewer federal regulations, for states that adopted them.

In either approach, the standards and tests would be *national not federal,* meaning that they would be set by an independent body as far removed from the political control of the Congress (and education ideologues) as possible. The most frequently mentioned candidate for the job is the National Assessment Governing Board, which runs the National Assessment of Educational Progress (NAEP) testing program.[29]

The two weakest models would encourage states to voluntarily decide upon common standards and tests or require that state standards and tests be compared against national benchmarks like the NAEP tests.

In my judgment, the most persuasive approaches are the toughest: national standards and tests that are developed by an independent body and mandated or linked to federal aid that states could not afford to forego. Anything less, that is, any voluntary system, is likely to mirror the states' weaving-and-dodging now under NCLB. The argument for a tough stand is so compelling that William J. Bennett and Rod Paige, former conservative secretaries of education, jointly wrote that "right-thinking Republicans should think long and hard before opposing national standards and tests."[30] In doing so, they echoed the longstanding advocacy of education conservatives like Finn and Diane Ravitch.[31] And the circle of support is widening to include urban school leaders and influential Democrats.[32]

Still, to some mend-it and all end-it adherents, national standards and tests are NCLB on steroids. Even George W. Bush's last secretary of education Margaret Spelling, while staunchly standing by NCLB, opposes them on the grounds (ironic for a NCLB stalwart) that "Neighborhood schools deserve neighborhood leadership, not dictates from bureaucrats thousands of miles away."[33] The experts surveyed for the Fordham Institute study mainly agreed that the mandatory model, while best, was politically taboo: the title of the study was *To Dream the Impossible Dream*.[34] Yet, the nationalization of academic standards and tests isn't as pie-in-the-sky as some politicians and educators would have us believe, and political prospects are surging.

In a national opinion survey in 2007, 73 percent of respondents favored national standards and tests.[35] Most remarkably, in that survey 77 percent of Republicans were in favor, compared to 69 percent of Democrats.[36] In another 2007 national poll, when the question highlighted the loss of local control if national standards and tests were enacted, 51 percent still favored them.[37] The same phenomenon is reflected in public opinion on NCLB. In the face of the battering NCLB has taken from many conservative and liberal politicians and the education establishment, popular support has eroded. But it still remains substantial. In a 2008 poll, respondents were about equally divided between those who wanted it renewed with minimal changes and those who wanted it renewed with major changes or not at all.[38]

Most astonishing, the American public appears willing to go even further and endorse not just national standards and tests but national curricula that detail instructional content and methods. In a 2002 poll, two-thirds were willing to go that far.[39] Our global economic competitors have national curricula as well as national standards and tests.[40]

The Obama administration has signaled its support for voluntary national standards. Secretary of education Duncan says, "If we accomplish one thing in the coming years, it should be to eliminate the extreme variations in standards across America."[41] He has emphasized that higher standards will be a criteria for states that want to grab a share of the sizable discretionary funds under the American Recovery and Reinvestment Act, as well as part of the Obama platform for reauthorization of NCLB. The states are getting the message. In June 2009 under the co-sponsorship of the National Governors Association and the Council of Chief State School Officers, forty-six states announced a plan to craft common standards.[42]

I am skeptical, as earlier noted, that such a voluntary joint effort will surmount the lingering localism, entrenched pride of authorship, and different viewpoints among state educators and politicians. Even more worrisome, while the idea of national academic standards is picking up steam, little is being said or done about national tests. National standards by themselves won't tell us whether students are achieving them; national tests will. Nonetheless, it seems only a matter of time before the inherent logic of a federal takeover of standards and tests, as well as public outcry, wins out. Bear in mind that national standards and tests would only lay down a floor of *what* children should know; localities could still dictate *how* children should be taught.

But do local school systems now know the best ways to teach, and do they, particularly urban districts, have the resources to support effective classroom teaching? The answer to both questions is no. And that's not about to change without other major federal investments, beginning with more robust research and development (R&D).

THE ABC'S OF R&D

To paraphrase Mark Twain's quip about quitting smoking, it's easy to reform education: we've done it a thousand times. But we haven't gotten it right, and while there are many reasons and many wrongdoers, a paramount reason is the deplorable state of education R&D. R&D is taken for granted in medicine, science, technology, engineering, industry, and other fields. But it is largely absent in public education, and its absence hinders almost every step towards school reform.

The good news is that R&D doesn't arouse the partisanship that plagues other school policy debates. Even diehard local-control liberals and conservatives agree that it must be a federal responsibility and upgraded. The bad news is that R&D draws yawns from the public, political officials, and, most tellingly, the education establishment. It's been woefully neglected, and research functions under the U.S. Department of Education (DOE) have been historically inept. But it's a critical necessity for school reform, and its status and science must change as a pillar of the New Education Federalism.

Lack of Rigor and Relevance

Two decades ago, the Consortium on Productivity in the Schools—a nonpartisan panel that included business leaders, economists, systems analysts, and educators—found that the "education sector is heavily politicized in part because . . . [t]he system suffers from too much scattered and unevaluated change."[43] The Consortium quoted one observer: "A grocery shopper can find out more from a label on a box of cereal than an educator . . . can about a set of educational tools—textbooks, activity guides, computer programs, films, etc.—that cost millions of dollars to develop and market."[44] RAND Corporation analysts found that, unlike research conducted by the National Institutes of Health (NIH), education R&D "has almost no scientifically structured clinical trials, has relatively few major longitudinal surveys, and has no equivalents of teaching hospitals or schools of public health that combine research with practice."[45]

Rigor is lacking and subject to controversy. How much should education R&D rely on the scientific "gold standard" of randomized trials, common in medicine research in which patients are randomly assigned to treatment or control groups? Many experts think that's the way to go in education research. NCLB leans in that direction. And its proponents include Grover "Russ" Whitehurst, director of DOE's research Institute for Education Sciences from its creation in 2002 through 2008.

But others contend that randomized trials are difficult, expensive, and not much superior to other methods. The executive director of the National Research Council cautions that the quest should be for R&D that produces "*reasonably good solutions to inordinately complex and dynamic problems* (emphasis in the original)."[46] The problems involve difficulties in isolating and measuring innumerable variables like teacher adherence to the research design and funding.[47]

Another major complication is how to bridge the gulf between research scientists and school practitioners. The "ivory tower" syndrome is worse in education than in other fields, as the National Research Council has underscored. In 2005 the Council spearheaded the creation of a new organization, the Strategic Education Research Partnership Institute (SERP). SERP's charge is "to build a coherent, 'use-inspired' program of research and development focused on the problems of classroom practice, and school and district management."[48] Its projects embed university researchers from different disciplines in school district operations.

A promising model is the Consortium on Chicago School Research (CCSR). Founded in 1990 at the University of Chicago, CCSR's credo is, "if research is to build capacity, the role of the researcher and the product of research must change from outside evaluator or expert to engaged and interactive participant in building knowledge of what matters."[49] CCSR has produced high-quality, influential policy research, and its director, John Q. Easton, was selected by secretary of education Duncan, former head of the Chicago public schools, to head the Institute for Education Sciences.

Such laudable partnership attempts to bridge research and practice, however, pose a tricky question. Can researchers call the shots with scientific integrity and not be rejected or marginalized by school bureaucracies that are notoriously defensive? CCSR seems to have pulled off such a tightrope walk, but it remains to be done elsewhere.

Supply and Demand

The underlying problem in education R&D is quality not quantity. According to professors Dan D. Goldhaber and Dominic J. Brewer, the American Educational Research Association has more members than ever before (14,000 researchers and observers attended its annual conference in 2007), journals are sprouting, and the number of education doctorates has increased.[50] But the output suffers from shoddy research producers and disinterested consumers.

Schools of education within universities are the largest producers of education research and the worst offenders. In part, as glimpsed in chapter 7, that's because their graduate programs are inferior training grounds for researchers. The pressure on faculty and graduate students to churn out publications and earn tenure as fast as possible tends to compromise the worth of the work. The quality also suffers because schools of education are dependent on good relationships with local school systems for enrollments, intern placements, and research sites, so, according to Goldhaber and Brewer, they "have relatively little incentive to want to critically study issues of productivity and costs."[51]

Beyond schools of education, there is a sprawling web of producers of education research. The Institute for Education Sciences (IES) is, by far, the largest enterprise, and a later section of this chapter is devoted to its role. But there are other major players, featuring think tanks which, as surveyed in chapter 7, are prolific and influential. Frederick M. Hess, editor of an enlightening volume on education R&D, has coined the term "democratization of dissemination" to describe the "emergence of a more entrepreneurial and freewheeling" research environment in which think tanks are prominent.[52] Almost all their work is policy-relevant since, to survive fiscally, they, more than universities, must compete for "soft money" grants and contracts, primarily from foundations.

On the other hand, their research is not subject to peer review and runs the risk of being rushed and "spun" for public release. Also their ideological affiliations, Goldhaber and Brewer say, enhance "the likelihood that the research they conduct is designed to buttress a particular ideology rather than to be truly independent."[53] Nonetheless, as a general rule, the ability of think tanks—right, left and center—to bring complex issues into sharp policy focus and their willingness to engage in the give-and-take of public debate makes them invaluable contributors to R&D.

Private companies are also important producers of research that is generally regarded as being of relatively high quality and independence. The companies span non-profits like the RAND Corporation and the American Institutes for Research and for-profits like Mathematica Policy Research, Inc. and Abt Associates. Like think tanks, they have more flexibility than tenure-tethered universities to deploy researchers as need be. Together, think tanks and private research companies appear to be ahead of academic researchers in garnering IES as well as foundation grants.[54]

Reluctant Consumers

The problems with the supply of education research, as big as they are, are fewer than the problems with the demand for it. Rather the lack of demand for it. The extent to which educators—who should value learning as well as teaching—don't appreciate and utilize research is alarming. Richard F. Elmore, a scholar in school management and R&D, has put it simply: educators as a general rule "don't believe that . . . problems can be solved by inquiry, by evidence, and by science."[55] Whitehurst, before he became head of IES, stated: "Education has not relied very much on evidence, whether in regard to how to train teachers, what sort of curriculum to use, or what sort of teaching methods to use. The decisions have been based on professional wisdom or the spirit of the moment rather than on research."[56]

Why such resistance to research? To start with, it's hard to figure which is the chicken and which is the egg between the low quality of research and educators' resistance to it. Which came first? Poor supply, caused because educators fail to appreciate and manage effectively the R&D process? Or poor demand, since educators experience research as divorced from the reality of the classroom and riddled with politics? Undoubtedly it's a mixture of both, but either way, educators are under the sway of a professional culture that prefers, in Whitehurst's words, "folk wisdom" over science.[57]

This culture has many origins. One, previously mentioned, is that educators learn in schools of education to undervalue research. Another, and more pernicious, is the ethic of individualism that dominates the education profession. Elmore refers to teachers as "solo practitioners."[58] They cherish their professional autonomy and regard teaching as more art than science.

Through many years in government and non-profit agencies, I have never seen an environment like public education in which administrators and teachers exchanged so little information and showed such little curiosity about innovative practices outside their narrow environs. In a meeting in which school staff were to write a services plan for a student with learning disabilities, I, as the pro-bono attorney for the student, asked the staff to consider the recommendations in a book by a national expert on dyslexia. The counsel for the school system bristled and said that *writing the service plan for the student had nothing to do with research.* This indifference to research is rarely stated so bluntly, but it's commonplace.

The "D" in R&D

Educators as a rule are not just indifferent consumers of research. They are also weak managers of the "D" (development) part of the R&D process.

The development stages include fidelity of implementation (are the research designs being implemented as intended?), continuous improvement (is feedback incorporated in upgrades in the instructional model?), and scale-up (how can research-proven programs be adopted or adapted on a large scale within a school district or even nationwide?).[59] Particular challenges are posed when the R&D seeks to change "the instructional core of schools."[60]

Absent close attention to these issues, many innovations are not implemented the way they are supposed to be, and it is impossible to tell whether negative or inconclusive outcomes are due to the design or to lax implementation. Elmore again gets to the heart of the matter: "The pathology of American schools is that they know how to change. They know how to change promiscuously and at the drop of a hat. What schools do not know how to do is to improve, to engage in sustained and continuous progress toward a performance goal over time."[61]

But public school systems seldom have the skills or patience for continuous improvement. Researchers and practitioners generally agree that it takes around five years for any reform program to be fairly judged. School reforms—like innovations in science, medicine, and industry—rarely lend themselves to thumbs-up or –down verdicts based on their original designs. But education suffers from what I diagnose as "institutional attention deficit disorder." Innovations are planted but, as the saying goes, educators and politicians keep pulling up the roots to see if they're growing fast enough.

This attention disorder is caused, first, because superintendents and school boards (especially elected ones) feel under the gun to create quick fixes. They believe, with some justification, that parents and the public will not allow them the luxury of long gestation periods before they give birth to significant boosts in academic test scores.[62] Second, superintendents and members of school boards turn over rapidly. Each transition brings the temptation for fresh starts and signature imprints. Third, beyond school officials and politicians, there are multitudes of wannabe reformers—among them ideologues, entrepreneurs, and researchers competing for scarce dollars—who relentlessly prod school officials to switch innovation horses in midstream.

If a reform gets over all these hurdles—if, as researchers Carolyn A. Denton and Jack M. Fletcher write, it "is found to be sufficiently robust and generalizable"[63]—it still has a way to go to reach the R&D summit destination: scale-up. Scale-up is the widespread adoption and adaptation of research-proven models in schools and school systems across the country. But the larger the attempted scale-up, the larger the opportunities for educator resistance and poor management, and so it rarely succeeds. Hess comments on the "deep, systemic incapacity of U.S. schools, and the practitioners who work in them, to develop, incorporate, and extend new ideas about teaching and learning in anything but a small fraction of schools and classrooms . . . Innovations that require large changes in the core of educational practice seldom penetrate more than a fraction of schools, and seldom last for very long when they do."[64]

It is hard to predict how quickly these R&D obstacles can be overcome. But a lot will depend on the pace at which politics is taken out and more money is put in.

Politics, Money and IES

Politics has too often contaminated what's been researched, who receives federal funds to do the research, and how the research is disseminated. Goldhaber and Brewer observe that because "political cycles are short and politicians fickle," research topics may have a short life span and be subject to shifting political winds.[65] Politics also drives funding, or more precisely under-funding. The overwhelming portion is appropriated by Congress through DOE and is a drop in the bucket compared to other federal R&D expenditures. In federal fiscal year 2007, the DOE budget for R&D was $327 million compared to billions elsewhere: for instance, Defense $78 billion, Health and Human Services $29 billion (most of which goes to NIH), and Agriculture $2 billion.[66] Altogether only about four cents of every federal R&D dollar go to DOE.[67]

No doubt the education lobby lacks the political clout of others such as the military-defense and health-care industries. But the paltry funding also reflects Congressional lack of confidence that DOE would spend the money well.[68] Prior to 2002, many institutional rearrangements and initiatives for research within DOE came and went. Two celebrated heads of research at DOE during this period were Chester E. Finn, Jr. and Diane Ravitch. Yet, they were unable to make much of a dent in DOE's cemented ways. Finn recalls, "After three years [on the DOE research job], I had made modest headway with my reforms, which of course crumbled soon after I was gone."[69]

Congressional frustration prompted requirements in NCLB, enacted in 2001, for research-based instruction. The word "research" appears in the law 216 times and is amplified by the words "scientifically based" over half of the time.[70] The next year, to complement NCLB, Congress passed the Education Sciences Reform Act of 2002 creating IES within DOE. At long last, its sponsors and supporters thought, education R&D would be brought up to the standards of other agencies like NIH and the National Science Foundation.

And the appointment of Whitehurst as the first director was widely regarded as an auspicious sign. Still, IES got off to a slow and uncertain start. An article in *Education Week* in 2006, headlined "IES Gets Mixed Grades as It Comes of Age," summarized many of the overhauls taking place and divided opinion on its progress.[71] Yet, by the time of its report to Congress in 2007, IES claimed a litany of accomplishments.[72] And outside experts also began to toot IES's horn. In answer to the question "Has anything really changed?," scholar Andrew Rudalevige writes, "The short answer is 'yes,' which might best be witnessed by the nervous complaints issued by those in the education community most skeptical about the applicability of 'science' to education research."[73] Rudalevige also applauded IES's "impressive independence vis-a-vis the Department of Education and the [George W. Bush] administration generally."[74] In 2007 IES won a prized "effective rating" from the U.S. Office of Management and Budget.[75]

Still, the jury is still deliberating on whether IES will grow to the stature of NIH. Resistance persists. At the end of 2008, when Whitehurst departed from IES, its reauthorization was pending, and some matters were unsettled. Lurking too is the effort by some organizations to nullify the language in NCLB calling for research-based practices by igniting a debate over whether the language was a mandate or just guidance.[76] But most observers are cautiously optimistic and particularly upbeat about the strong backing of the Obama administration. A big boost in funding for education R&D has been promised, and secretary Duncan has emphasized that states and local districts seeking a big slice of the discretionary fiscal stimulus pie under the American Recovery and Reinvestment Act of 2009 had better show that their applications are steeped in research.

As we turn next to the case for a federal takeover of the role of guarantor of adequate school funding, the link between R&D and money warrants emphasis. The nation's willingness to spend what it takes for school reform depends in large measure on whether the public trusts educators to spend the money wisely, and that trust can only be fulfilled if there is credible R&D.

WHO'S GOING TO PAY THE BILL FOR EQUALITY?

Do urban and other low-wealth school districts have enough money to buy a high-quality, R&D-driven education for their students? Conservatives think they do, if current resources were spent more efficiently. Liberals counter that "savage inequalities" in funding, more than anything else, perpetuate the achievement gap. But even liberals, paralyzed by their distrust of federal power over local schools, have been slow to wake up to the political reality that if the feds don't pay the bill for educational equality, no one else will. States haven't and, as history shows, never will.

In this light, I propose a federal takeover of the guarantor role of equal opportunity funding for poor schools and students. Such a leap has almost never been discussed in political and policy circles, and it is controversial. But it is as indispensable to school reform as it is contrarian. Sure, money isn't all that matters. Sure, school budgets must be managed better. But there are vast disparities in resources between school districts in different states and within states, and it will be expensive to bring children from poverty into the educational mainstream.

The task, as formulated throughout this book, is to convince the president and Congress that more money, if forthcoming, will be focused in the right places (in the classroom), spent on the proper things (R&D-based programs), and managed in the right way (through the revolution in management proposed in subsequent chapters.)[77]

Money Trials and Tribulations

The legal struggle over school funding began in the early 1970s by focusing on disparities in per-pupil spending among local school districts within states (intrastate disparities). Poor school districts spend much less per pupil than wealthier districts, even though the poorer districts tax themselves at higher rates. Nonetheless, in 1973 in *San Antonio Independent School District v. Rodriguez,* the Supreme Court held, in a 5–4 decision, that states were not mandated under the U.S. Constitution to remedy the huge disparities. The Court acknowledged the critical importance of education to the nation, but ruled that judicial relief would have to come, if at all, through litigation under state laws.[78] The U. S. Constitution contains no explicit right to education, but virtually every state constitution does. So lawsuits proliferated in over forty-five state courts.[79]

The first wave of lawsuits resulted in victories for plaintiffs (school finance reformers) in California, New Jersey and Texas. The tide shifted in the 1980s, and plaintiffs lost more cases than they won. Then, following the accountability groundswell in the states to raise academic standards, the tide turned again. Ever since, reformers have prevailed in the majority of suits, with state courts typically holding that students in low-wealth districts were not receiving an "adequate" education that would enable them to meet the rising standards. Adequacy, the courts stated, meant that low-income students and others with "special needs" required more than equal per-pupil spending to overcome their disadvantages.

NCLB has piled on more pressure. Rudalevige concludes that "As NCLB continues to produce more data, and more schools are deemed to be failing, even states where adequacy judgments have already been pursued may be revisited. That might apply both to states where adequacy claims were once rejected and to those where earlier remedies now appear insufficient."[80] A strong argument can be made that if NCLB had been in existence in 1973, the Supreme Court would not have rejected (by 5–4) the existence of a right to equal education under the U. S. Constitution.

But what does an "adequate" shopping cart filled with school system supplies—teachers, extra instruction for struggling learners, school security, decent facilities, and so on—cost? And how much good will it do? We have seen throughout this book that no one is able with certainty to put a sticker price on the educational goods and services that might dramatically lift academic achievement. What's more, even assuming that specific inputs of money could be linked to specific outcomes of academic achievement, do school systems already have enough money to go around?

The School Finance Redesign Project, supported by the Gates Foundation, found in 2008 that "after five years and more than thirty sponsored studies . . . that money is used so loosely in public education . . . that no one can say how much money, if used optimally, would be enough."[81] Bureaucratic mismanagement and waste are parts of the problem. On top of that, states and local districts have tended to spend willy-nilly, and can't pinpoint measurable results.

Should school systems be getting better results? The findings of the famed Coleman report—that school resources were less important determinants of school success than the family background of students—set off two chain reactions. The first is the view that school reform is doomed unless economic and social forces that depress student achievement are overcome. In chapter 6, I rejected this single-minded explanation for student failure. Improved schools can make a big difference, and such improvement will require more money (among other things).

The second chain reaction set off research efforts intended to zero in on which school resources mattered most. According to a National Research Council report in 1999, hundreds of "input-output studies" were conducted to measure the relationship between school spending and student performance.[82] But the pursuit degenerated into slugfests between researchers.[83] Economist Eric A. Hanushek, the heavyweight champ for conservatives, asserted in the mid-1990s: "The unfortunate truth is, Washington and the states have spent literally tens of billions of dollars on school reforms over the past fifteen years with virtually nothing to show for it."[84] The National Research Council observed that Hanushek "probably had an impact second only to the original

Coleman report itself in persuading people that money (or school) doesn't matter in efforts to improve education."[85]

Liberals counter-punched, contending that the money supposedly available to buy higher student achievement had been far less than advertised, and had been eaten up by mandated cost hikes in non-instructional programs.[86] This view was supported by consultants who sprouted up and were employed by judges and legislative committees to try to figure out what "adequate" meant in actual dollars.[87] Some of the consultants used a methodology in which they attached costs to a small but growing body of research that vouched, they said, for the payoff from higher spending: for example, on smaller class size, higher teacher pay, extended school time including more days, longer days and summer school, and professional development.

The National Bottom Line

What is certain is that, despite decades of litigation, enormous inequities in per-pupil spending among school districts remain. The Education Trust think tank (an advocate for more funding) publishes frequent reports on "The Funding Gap." In its 2008 report, using the most recent data available (for 2005) and after adjustments for geographical differences in costs, the gaps in spending of state and local funds between the highest 25 percent and the lowest 25 percent districts were as high as $3,068 per pupil per year in New York State, $2,235 in Illinois and $1,629 in Minnesota.[88]

Moreover, between 1999 and 2005 the gaps between the highest and lowest poverty districts narrowed in ten states but widened in sixteen.[89] For the nation as a whole in 2005, the equity gap was $938 per pupil (or about $25,000 per classroom).[90] There's no doubt, writes law professor Goodwin Lui, a scholar on school finance, "The burden of such disparities tends to fall most heavily on disadvantaged children with the greatest educational needs."[91]

States generally lack the political will to eliminate these disparities because the school districts that would benefit most are politically as well as fiscally downtrodden. States are also under pressure to hold down taxes because of competition with neighboring states to attract industries and taxpayers.[92] And state revenues are more vulnerable to fluctuations in the economy than federal ones; states, unlike the federal government, can't run deficits. In addition, there are vast differences in the fiscal wealth of states. Based on the 2001–2002 data used by Lui, "The fiscal capacity of the top quintile of states is over 57 percent greater than the capacity of the bottom quintile."[93]

This stark picture portrays a *national* failure. In retrospect the Supreme Court decision in 1973 that tolerated school finance inequities has been likened to a "Dred Scott decision for the underclass."[94] Since the states won't, and poor school districts can't, pay for adequate educational opportunity, the lack of a federal guarantee has consigned generations of children to inferior and dismal academic futures.[95]

The Federal Price Tag

How can this inferiority and inequality be ended? Federal aid to K–12 public schools has inched up over the years, particularly funds for low-income children under the Title I of the Elementary and Secondary Education Act and under the Individual with Disabilities Act (IDEA). And hundreds of other federal grant programs have proliferated. But all of these funds only total around $60 billion per year, or about 10 percent of all spending for public schools.[96] That is, they did until the earth-shaking American Recovery and Reinvestment Act of 2009 that nearly doubles that amount over two years.

President Obama's earmarking of $100 billion in fiscal stimulus funding for education, whatever it will do for the economy, could transform the federal role in funding public schools. Or it could not. It depends on whether the money is just a temporary two-year boost as the legislation intends.[97] That seems the likely fate for the largest pot, the State Stabilization Fund, that is intended to keep school systems from having to lose teachers because of state and local budget cutbacks. But the outlook is brighter for the additional funds—over $20 billion over two years—under Title I and IDEA. Title I and IDEA have large national constituencies and pent-up demands, and the president and Congress will be under great pressure not to pull the plug on the stimulus injections.

In any event, the stimulus bonanza can't be counted on to solve the school finance problem entirely and permanently. Other options must be pursued.[98] Lui, building on the work of school finance expert Allan R. Odden and others, favors "a national foundation aid plan" that is "power-equalizing."[99] A base amount representing an adequate floor of funding would be set, adjusted for geographic differences in costs, and the federal government would pay a percentage of the costs in each state depending on the state's fiscal effort.[100] In other words, for equal taxing effort, richer states would get less federal aid, poorer states more.

But how would the cost of the federal "adequate floor" of funding be determined? Not easily based on the stormy course of adequacy litigation in the states. But the average per-pupil costs in the states could be a starting point supplemented by extra expenditures for students with special needs. Some state finance formulas and some local districts in their distribution of federal and state dollars already weight the costs of students who are poor, who have disabilities, and for whom English is a second language. The Education Trust points out that "[s]chool finance scholars, the U.S. Department of Education, and the U.S. General Accounting Office use a 40 percent cost adjustment for low-income students."[101]

No doubt, any adequacy accounting is going to be controversial. As Lui puts it, "In sketching the basic contours of a national foundation program, I recognize that, in the hands of Congress, all of the parameters—pupil weights, cost adjustments, minimum state effort, federal matching rate, and the foundation level itself—would be informed by a complex mix of research, expert judgment, and politics."[102] So it will not be easy to establish the credibility of any federal adequacy standards.

But one way to establish trust would be to follow the same route recommended for the creation of national academic standards and tests: an entity as independent of politics as possible, such as the Governing Board of the National Assessment of Educational Progress (NAEP). To get the ball rolling, a national bipartisan commission could be convened to consider national adequacy benchmarks, in the tradition of the commission on Social Security years ago that unknotted seemingly unsolvable political issues in that program.[103] A more potent and credible federal R&D program could itself advance the state of knowledge about the best ways to cost out adequacy.

The national foundation plan could be augmented (if necessary, depending upon the exact foundation formula) with federal categorical grants, the most logical candidates being increased funding under Title I and IDEA. At the least, the Title I allocation formula should be corrected to allocate aid in proportion to each state's percentage of poor children.[104] Numerous other categorical grants could be added to the mix, such as the proposal for a "Marshall Plan for Teaching."[105]

Whether federal aid is packaged as part of a national foundation plan or as categorical grants, it should come tied with strings that require states to eliminate intrastate inequities and to achieve adequate levels of funding for all school districts. Federal aid formulas that require state matching funds (with each state's percentage varying according to its fiscal capacity and effort) are common.

At the same time, the amount of federal aid that is available with or without state match must be large enough so that states, which would prefer to keep the feds out of their hair, can't afford to turn it down. States have whined and threatened to reject Title I grants tied to the conditions imposed under NCLB, but, because big bucks would be lost, not a single state has pulled out.[106] Federal aid should also require *local* school systems to join Baltimore and a few other school districts in abolishing the common practice whereby low-performing schools in low-income neighborhoods often receive fewer state and local dollars than higher-performing schools in better-off neighborhoods.[107]

The exact amount of direct federal aid necessary to achieve adequate educational opportunity will depend upon the matching ratio that the states are mandated to pay. Lui explores various scenarios for a national foundation plan that would cost about $30 billion dollars in additional federal funds, close, he says, to several other expert estimates.[108] Policy analyst Matt Miller suggests raising the federal share of total expenditures for public schools from the current 10 percent to 20 percent.[109] That would boost federal aid, exclusive of the fiscal stimulus funds, to about $90 billion per year.

Federal aid in such doses doesn't seem as forbidding as it did before the election of president Obama and the fiscal stimulus bill. $90 billion annually would constitute only 2 percent of the total federal budget in 2008 and less than one-half of one percent of gross domestic product.[110] That seems a bargain if it buys equal educational opportunity that will close the achievement gap and enhance our nation's workforce and social well-being.

And it's consistent with polls that show public support for aggressive federal action on funding (as well as national standards, tests, and curricula). In a large national poll in 2008, the need for more money was rated for the sixth straight year as the biggest problem facing schools.[111] As to where the additional money should come from, those polled thought federal taxes were preferable to state or local taxes.[112] In a national poll in 2002, respondents were told that two and one-half cents of every federal budget dollar were spent on public schools and then asked whether they supported doubling it to five cents; 54 percent were in favor, and 30 percent thought even more than five cents should be spent.[113]

The stage is set for a federal guarantee of equal educational opportunity. It's been a long time coming. But whoa . . . let's not forget that more money and other elements of the federal takeover aren't the whole solution either. We look next at how local governance must change too as part of a New Education Federalism.

NOTES

1. The test results in Texas turned out to be exaggerated. See chapter 13. Nonetheless, the Texas standards and testing regimens were in the forefront of the accountability movement in the states.

2. Patrick J. McGuinn, *No Child Left Behind and the Transformation of Federal Education Policy,* 1965–2005 (Lawrence, KS: University Press of Kansas, 2006), 166.

3. McGuinn, *No Child Left Behind and the Transformation of Federal Education Policy,* 177.

4. McGuinn, *No Child Left Behind and the Transformation of Federal Education Policy,* 177.

5. The story of NCLB has been the subject of countless publications and endless arguments. Among the literature across a range of points of view: Frederick M. Hess and Chester E. Finn, Jr., *No Remedy Left Behind* (Washington, DC: American Enterprise Institute, 2007); Paul Manna, *School's In: Federalism and the National Education Agenda* (Washington, DC: Georgetown Press, 2007); McGuinn, *No Child Left Behind and the Transformation of Federal Education Policy;* Deborah Meier and George Wood, eds., *Many Children Left Behind* (Boston: Beacon Press, 2004); a collection of articles "Assessing NCLB—Perspectives and Prescriptions," *Harvard Educational Review,* vol. 76, no. 4 (2006); Gail L. Sunderman, James S. Kim and Gary Orfield, *NCLB Meets School Realities: Lessons From the Field* (Thousand Oaks, CA: Corwin Press, 2004).

6. Concise summaries are found at Manna, *School's In,* 128; and McGuinn, *No Child Left Behind and the Transformation of Federal Education Policy,* 180.

7. Lynn Olson, "States gear up for new federal law," *Education Week* (January 16, 2002).

8. McGuinn, *No Child Left Behind and the Transformation of Federal Education Policy,"* 187; Richard Blumenthal, "Why Connecticut Sued the Federal Government over No Child Left Behind," in "Assessing NCLB—Perspectives and Prescriptions," 564–569.

9. Duncan is quoted in Gail L. Sunderman and James S. Kim, "The Expansion of Federal Power and the Politics of Implementing the No Child Left Behind Act," *TC Record,* 2007, http:www.tcrecord.org/Content.asp?ContentID=12227, 6.

10. Council for Exceptional Children, "CEC Members Speak Out Against No Child Left Behind," http://www.cec.sped.org/AM/Template.cfm?Section=search&template=/CM/HTMLdisplay.cfm&ContentID=6267.

11. Lowell C. Rose and Alec M. Gallup, "The 39th Annual Phi Delta Kappa/Gallup Poll of the Public's Attitude Toward The Public Schools," *Phi Delta Kappan,* vol. 89, no. 1 (September 2007): 34–45, 36.

12. Frederick M. Hess and Chester E. Finn, Jr., "Conclusion: Can This Law Be Fixed? A Hard Look at the NCLB Remedies," in Hess and Finn, *No Remedy Left Behind,* 319–322.

13. Hess and Finn, "Conclusion," 316.

14. Michael Casserly, "America's Great City Schools: Moving in the Right Direction," in Hess and Finn, *No Remedy Left Behind,* 65.

15. Hess and Finn, "Conclusion," 313.

16. The Commission on No Child Left Behind, *Beyond NCLB* (Washington, DC: Aspen Institute, 2007). See also Lynn Olson and David J. Hoff, "Framing the Debate," *Education Week* (December 13, 2006): 22, 24, 26–27, 29–30.

17. Taylor is quoted in Samuel G. Freedman, "Parting Liberal Waters Over 'No Child Left Behind'," *New York Times,* January 4, 2006.

18. Hess and Finn, "Conclusion," 320.

19. Frederick M. Hess and Chester E. Finn, Jr., "Crash Course: NCLB is driven by education politics," *Education Next,* vol. 7, no. 4 (Fall 2007): 38–45, 45.

20. Hess and Finn think that new leadership—from "governors, mayors, nonprofit organizations, for-profit firms, regional authorities, and other such entities"— could shake up the system and encourage or impose more privatized takeovers. Hess and Finn, "Conclusion," 320. It's possible. It's happening in some "turnaround" local districts (see chapter 13), and the call for such leadership is a recurring theme of this book. But relieving the federal pressure put on them by NCLB seems more likely to slow down than speed up the process.

21. David J. Hoff, "Conservative Plan Would Shift Accountability to the States," *Education Week* (March 14, 2007): 22.

22. See chapter 7.

23. Deborah Meier and Diane Ravitch, "Bridging Differences: A Dialogue Between Deborah Meier and Diane Ravitch, Commentary, *Education Week* (May 24, 2006): 36–37, 36. In addition, progressive teaching methods have a better chance of prevailing against traditionalist pedagogy if instructional policies are left in the hands of individual school districts, as described in chapter 5.

24. George Wood, "Introduction," in Meier and Wood, *Many Children Left Behind,* xi.

25. Robert Gordon and Richard Rothstein, *Point Counterpoint: Should We Repair 'No Child Left Behind' or Trade It In?* (Washington, DC: Center for American Progress, 2006), 11.

26. Gordon and Rothstein, *Point Counterpoint,* 11.

27. Paul Manna, "NCLB in the States: Fragmented Governance, Uneven Implementation," in Hess and Finn, *No Remedy Left Behind,* 41.

28. Chester E. Finn, Jr., Liam Julian, and Michael J. Petrilli, *To Dream the Impossible Dream: Four Approaches to National Standards and Tests for America's Schools* (Washington, DC: Thomas B. Fordham Foundation, 2006).

29. Finn, Julian and Petrilli, *To Dream the Impossible Dream,* 22. The Governing Board is an independent, bipartisan group created by Congress. Its 26 members, appointed by the U. S. secretary of education, include governors, state legislators, local and state school officials, educators, business representatives and members of the general public. http://www.naeg.org/cella.html.

30. William J. Bennett and Rod Paige, "Why We Need a National School Test," Opinion, *The Washington Post,* September 21, 2006.

31. Chester E. Finn, Jr. and Diane Ravitch, "A Yardstick for American Students," Opinion, *The Washington Post,* February 25, 1997. And more recently, Ravitch, "Every State Left Behind," Opinion, *The New York Times,* November 7, 2005.

32. Rudolph Crew, Paul Vallas and Michael Casserly, "The Case for National Standards in American Education," Commentary, *Education Week,* March 5, 2007; Cindy Brown and Elena Rocha, *The Case for National Standards, Accountability, and Fiscal Equity* (Washington, DC: Center for American Progress, 2005); Richard D. Kahlenberg, "What to Do With No Child Left Behind?," Commentary, *Education Week* (October 28, 2008): 34, 40.

33. Margaret Spellings, "A National Test We Don't Need," Opinion, *The Washington Post,"* June 9, 2007, A17.

34. Finn, Julian and Petrilli, *To Dream the Impossible Dream.*
35. William G. Howell, Martin R. West and Paul E. Peterson, "What Americans Think About Their Schools," *Education Next,* vol. 7, no. 4 (Fall 2007): 13–26, 15.
36. Michael J. Petrilli, "Conservatives love national testing," *The Education Gadfly,* vol. 7, no. 41 (October 25, 2007): 2.
37. Rose and Gallup, "The 39th Annual Phi Delta Kappa/Gallup Poll Of the Public's Attitudes Toward The Public Schools," 42.
38. Will G. Howell, Martin R. West and Paul E. Peterson, "The 2008 Education Next-PEPG Survey of Public Opinion," *Education Next,* vol. 8, no. 4 (Fall 2008): 13–26, 17.
39. Michael W. Kirst, "Turning Points: A History of American School Governance," in Noel Epstein, ed., *Who's in Charge Here: The Tangled Web of School Governance and Policy* (Washington, DC: Brookings Institution Press, 2004), 15.
40. Diane Ravitch, *National Standards in American Education,* (Washington, DC: The Brookings Institution, 1995), 14; Nancy Kober, *A Public Education Primer* (Washington, DC: Center on Education Policy, 2006), 14.
41. Duncan is quoted in Walter Isaacson, "How to Raise the Standard in American's Schools," *Time CNN,* April 15, 2009, http:www.time.com/nation/article/0,8599,1891468,00.html, 3.
42. Maria Glod, "46 States, DC. Plan to Draft Common Education Standards," *The Washington Post,* June 1, 2009.
43. Consortium on Productivity in the Schools, *Using What We have to Get the Schools We Need* (New York: Consortium on Productivity in the Schools, Teachers College, Columbia University, 1995), 82.
44. Consortium on Productivity in the Schools, *Using What We have to Get the Schools We Need,* 22.
45. Ann Flanagan and David Grissmer, "The Role of Federal Resources in Closing the Achievement Gap," in John E. Chubb and Tom Loveless, eds., *Bridging the Achievement Gap* (Washington, DC: The Brookings Institution, 2002), 220.
46. Michael J. Feuer, "Moderation: A Radical Approach to Education Policy," Commentary, *Education Week* (June 14, 2006): 36.
47. Frederick M. Hess and Jeffrey R. Henig, "'Scientific Research' and Policymaking," Commentary, *Education Week* (February 5, 2008): 25, 36.
48. www.serpinstitute.org/content/page.php?cat=4.
49. Melissa Roderick and John Q. Easton, "Developing new roles for research in new policy environments: The Consortium on Chicago School Research," http://nycresearchpartnership.ssrc.org/Paper2%202.pdf, 5.
50. Dan D. Goldhaber and Dominic J. Brewer, "What Gets Studied and Why: Examining the Incentives That Drive Education Research," in Frederick M. Hess, *When Research Matters* (Cambridge, MA: Harvard Education Press, 2008), 198.
51. Goldhaber and Brewer, "What Gets Studied and Why," 206.
52. Frederick M. Hess, "Conclusion: Education Research and Public Policy," in Hess, *When Research Matters,* 242.

53. Goldhaber and Brewer, "What Gets Studied and Why," 206.

54. Jeffrey R. Henig, "The Evolving Relationship between Researchers and Public Policy," in Hess, *When Research Matters,* 54. For-profit research companies are not to be confused with for-profit educational companies that peddle questionable evidence of the effectiveness of their commercial textbooks, technology and other products. In the competitive scramble to be considered research-based under NCLB, these companies sometimes put forth their own in-house data and analyses. See Todd Oppenheimer, "Selling Software: How vendors manipulate research and cheat students," *Education Next,* vol. 7, no. 2 (Spring 2007): 22–29. Widespread mistrust has forced private education vendors to more and more switch to external evaluations. Nonetheless, concerns remain about conflicts of interest that tempt company-sponsored researchers to puff up or bury unfavorable results. Kathleen Kennedy Manzo, "Surge in Company-Sponsored Studies Sparks Concern," *Education Week* (December 6, 2006): 12–13.

55. Richard F. Elmore, "The Limits of 'Change'," *Harvard Education Letter,* January/February 2002, http://www.edletter.org/past/issues/2002-jf/limitsofchange.shtml, 2.

56. Whiteurst is quoted in James Traub, "No Child Left Behind: Does It Work," *Education Life, The New York Times,* November 10, 2002, 24.

57. Whitehurst is quoted in Maria Glod, "Searching for Science to Guide Good Teaching," *The Washington Post,* April 28, 2008, B2.

58. Richard F. Elmore, "Getting to Scale with Good Educational Practice," *Harvard Educational Review,* vol. 66, no. 1 (Spring 1996): 1–26, 2.

59. Exemplary guidance is offered in recent companion volumes: Barbara Schneider and Sarah-Kathryn McDonald, eds., *Scale-Up in Education, Volume I, Issues in Principle and Scale Up in Education, Volume II, Issues in Practice* (Lanham, MD: Rowman & Littlefield, 2007).

60. Mark Berends, "Overview: Scaling Up Promising Educational Interventions," in Schneider and McDonald, *Scale Up in Education, Volume II,* 21.

61. Elmore, "The Limits of 'Change'," 1.

62. See Frederick M. Hess, *Spinning Wheels: The Politics of Urban School Reform* (Washington, DC: Brookings Institution Press, 1999), 52.

63. Carolyn A. Denton and Jack M. Fletcher, "Scaling Reading Interventions," in Barbara R. Foorman, ed., *Preventing and Remediating Reading Difficulties* (Baltimore: York Press, 2003), 455.

64. Hess, *Spinning Wheels,* 151.

65. Goldhaber and Brewer, "What Gets Studied and Why," 211.

66. See chart of expenditures in Debra Viadero, "U.S. Position on Research Seen in Flux," *Education Week,* March 5, 2007, 14.

67. Henig, "The Evolving Relationship between Researchers and Public Policy," 55.

68. Foundations don't come close to making up the slack. They shy away from education R&D for much the same reasons as the Congress does. Henig, "The Evolving Relationship between Researchers and Public Policy," 57.

69. Chester E. Finn, Jr., *Troublemaker* (Princeton, NJ: Princeton University Press, 2008), 144.

70. Paul Manna and Michael J. Petrilli, "Double Standard? 'Scientifically Based Research' and the No Child Left Behind Act," in Hess, *When Research Matters,* 69.

71. Debrah Viadero, "IES Gets Mixed Grades as It Comes of Age," *Education Week* (September 27, 2006): 1, 8–9.

72. Institute for Education Sciences, *Toward a Learning Society: Director's Biennial Report to Congress* (Washington, DC: U.S. Department of Education, 2007).

73. Andrew Rudalevige, "Structure and Science in Federal Education Research," in Hess, *When Research Matters,* 35.

74. Rudalevige, "Structure and Science in Federal Education Research," 36.

75. Deborah Viadero, "Report Card Time for Research Arm of Education Dept.," *Education Week* (October 24, 2007): 25.

76. Debra Viadero, "Call for 'Scientifically Based' Programs Debated," *Education Week* (March 24, 2004): 10.

77. This section draws upon Kalman R. Hettleman, "The Time Has Come: A Federal Guarantee of Adequate Educational Opportunity," in *Passing the Test: The National Interest in Good Schools For All* (Washington, DC: Center for National Policy, 2000). It also relies heavily on two brilliant articles by law professor Goodwin Liu. Unfortunately, the articles are entombed in law journals and have not received the policy attention they merit. Liu, "Interstate Inequality in Educational Opportunity," *New York University Law Review,* vol. 81, no. 6 (2006): 2044–2128; Liu, "Education, Equality, and National Citizenship," in *The Yale Law Journal,* vol. 116, no. 2 (November 2006): 330–411.

78. *San Antonio Independent School District v. Rodriguez,* 411 U.S. 1, 1973.

79. For a recent state-by-state compilation of suits and capsule "Outcome" comments, see Martin R. West and Paul E. Peterson, eds., *School Money Trials: The Pursuit of Educational Adequacy* (Washington, DC: Brookings Institution Press, 2007), "Appendix: Significant School Finance Judgments, 1971–2005," 345–358. For other accounts of equity and adequacy litigation, see: Eric A. Hanushek, ed., *Courting Failure* (Stanford, CA: Hoover Institution Press, 2008); Peter Schrag, *Final Test: The Battle for Adequacy in America's Schools* (New York: The New Press, 2003); Richard Rothstein, "Equalizing Educational Resources on Behalf of Disadvantaged Children," in Richard D. Kahlenberg, ed., *A Notion at Risk: Preserving Public Education as an Engine for Social Mobility* (New York: The Century Foundation Press, 2000).

80. Andrew Rudalevige, "Adequacy, Accountability, and the Impact of the No Child Left Behind Act," in West and Peterson, *School Money Trials,* 250. The claim that NCLB is an un-funded mandate has taken on a legal life of its own. John W. Borkowski and Marie Sneed, "Will NCLB Improve or Harm Public Education?" *Harvard Education Review,* vol. 76, no. 4 (2006): 503–525.

81. Paul T. Hill and Marguerite Roza, "The End of School Finance As We Know It," Commentary, *Education Week* (April 30, 2008): 32, 36.

82. National Research Council, *Making Money Matter: Financing America's Schools* (Washington, DC: National Academy Press, 1999), 140–147.

83. See, for example, Gary Burtless, "Introduction and Summary," in Burtless, ed., *Does Money Matter? The Effect of School Resources on Student Achievement and Adult Success* (Washington, DC: Brookings Institution Press, 1996), 43–73.

84. Eric A. Hanushek, "Remedial Math," *The New Democrat,* vol. 7, no. 6 (November/December, 1995): 26.

85. National Research Council, *Making Money Matter,* 142.

86. Richard Rothstein and Karen Hawley Miles, *Where's the Money Gone? Changes in the Level and Composition of Education Spending* (Washington, DC: Economic Policy Institute, 1995), 3, 7–8. See also Richard Rothstein, *Where's the Money Going? Changes in the Level and Composition of Education Spending* (Washington, DC: Economic Policy Institute, 1997).

87. For reviews of the various methodologies, see Michael A. Rebell, "Professional Rigor, Public Engagement and Judicial Review: A Proposal for Enhancing the Validity of Education Adequacy Studies," *TCRecord,* http:www.tcrcord.org/PrintContent.asp?ContentID=12742; Matthew G. Springer and James W. Guthrie, "The Politicization of the School Finance Legal Process," in West and Peterson, *School Money Trials,* 102–130; Thomas A. Downes and Leanna Stiefel, "Measuring Equity and Adequacy in School Finance," in Helen F. Ladd and Edward B. Fiske, eds., *Handbook of Research in Education Finance and Policy* (New York: Routledge, 2008), 222–237.

88. Carmen G. Arroyo, *The Funding Gap* (Washington, DC.: The Education Trust, 2008), 6.

89. Arroyo, *The Funding Gap,* 2, 3.

90. Arroyo, *The Funding Gap,* 4.

91. Lui, "Education, Equality and National Citizenship," 333.

92. Thus, the lure of lotteries and other forms of gambling that are regressive sources of revenue but, to make them politically palatable, are earmarked for school funding or made to appear that way. An example is the 2008 Maryland referendum on slot machines. Philp Rucker, "Teachers Union Gives Backing to Slot Machine Initiative," *The Washington Post,* March 16, 2008.

93. Lui, "Interstate Inequality in Educational Opportunity," 2085–2086.

94. Hettleman, "The Time Has Come," 57.

95. Although a federal guarantee of adequacy appears necessary, this does not mean that adequacy lawsuits in the states should be abandoned. Conservatives disparage their effect. Martin R. West and Paul E. Peterson, "The Adequacy Lawsuit: A Critical Appraisal," in Martin and Peterson, *School Money Trials,"* 8. Yet, in some states, they pay off in increased funding. In all the states, they keep the adequacy issue alive and build up pressure on the president and Congress to bail out the states. And, pending a national guarantee, there's Murphy's Law to keep in mind: no matter how bad the present inequities, without the litigation they would surely be worse.

96. U.S. Census Bureau News, "Public Schools Spent $9,138 Per Student in 2006," http://www.census.gov/Press-Release/www/releases/archives/education/011747.html.

97. For further discussion of the possible impact of the stimulus funds, see chapter 14.

98. See generally Lui, "Interstate Inequality in Educational Opportunity," and an earlier report, Stephen M. Barro, *Federal Policy Options for Improving the Education of Low-Income Students: Volume III, Countering Inequity in School Finance* (Santa Monica, CA: RAND, 1994).

99. Lui, "Interstate Inequality in Educational Opportunity," 2117–2118.

100. Lui, "Interstate Inequality in Educational Opportunity," 2104, 2119.

101. Arroyo, *The Funding Gap,* 10 (footnote 5).

102. Lui, "Interstate Inequality in Educational Opportunity," 2121.

103. *Report of the National Commission on Social Security Reform* (1983), http://www.ssa.gov/history/reports/gspan.html.

104. Lui, "Interstate Inequality in Educational Opportunity," 2116–2117.

105. Linda Darling-Hammond, "Evaluating No Child Left Behind," *The Nation,* May 21, 2007, 11–18.

106. Law professor Lui offers another intriguing path towards a national guarantee. His scholarly argument is that the clause of the Fourteenth Amendment to the U. S. Constitution affording the right to national citizenship is more fertile ground for a national guarantee of equal educational opportunity than the equal protection clause relied upon by the plaintiffs in the *Rodriguez* case. Lui, "Education, Equality, and National Citizenship." Several other unlikely vehicles for getting to a national guarantee have been proposed. One is a constitutional amendment introduced by Representative Jesse Jackson, Jr. in 2003 (http://www/house.gov/jackson/EducationAmendment.shtml). Another is The Equal Protection School Finance Act, introduced in 1997 by Representative Chaka Fattah (News Release, "The Equal Protection School Finance Act Gets Its Day in Congress," http://www.house.gov/fattah/pr_dc_archive-2002-2000/euityhering.html). Neither has made any headway.

107. Thomas B. Fordham Institute, *Fund the Child: Tackling Inequity & Antiquity in School Finance* (Washington, DC: Thomas B. Fordham Institute, 2006); Mike Petko, *Weighted Student Formula (WSF): What Is It and How Does It Impact Educational Programs in Large Urban Districts* (Washington, DC: National Education Association, 2005).

108. Lui, "Interstate Inequality in Educational Opportunity," 2122–2124.

109. Matt Miller, *Nationalize the Schools (...A Little)!* (Washington, DC: Center for American Progress, 2008), 24.

110. Office of Management and Budget, *Mid-Session Review, Budget of the U.S. Government, Fiscal Year 2009,* http://www.gpoaccess.gov/usbudget/fy09/pdf/09msr.pdf, 21.

111. William J. Bushaw and Alec M. Gallup, "Americans Speak Out – Are Educators and Policy Makers Listening?" *Phi Delta Kappan,* vol. 90, no. 1 (2008): 8–20, 8, 12.

112. Bushaw and Gallup, "Americans Speak Out," 11.

113. Ruy Teixeira, *What the public really wants on education,* (Washington, DC: The Century Foundation and Center for American Progress, 2006), 5.

Chapter 10

Mayors In, School Boards Out

Under the New Education Federalism, the federal government will give local school districts greater wherewithal—strengthened governance, better research, and more money—to improve student achievement. Still, such leaps in federal responsibility by themselves will only go so far. Who, thereafter, is to exercise executive authority and assure *how* the money is spent and managed so that local schools and students meet national standards? I am convinced that role must be played by the heads of local governments, not local school boards. In particular, since low-performing students and schools are concentrated in large urban districts, mayors have to step up and assume more authority and accountability.[1]

Part of the appeal of mayors and other elected local government executives is by default. As documented throughout this book, state departments of education can't be counted on. They can contribute technical assistance, oversight, and support for adequate funding. But they have severe management shortcomings of their own. And they will always be diverted from a focus on poor urban students because they have so many diverse districts, including rural and suburban ones, to tend to.

But haven't we already seen also that local departments of education lack the capacity to carry out their part of a new federalism bargain? Right now, that's true. And it will stay that way as long as local departments mismanage classroom instruction and remain wedded to the status quo. But bold city mayors could lead the overthrow of the local establishment. They are better positioned than anyone else, including school boards and superintendents, to provide muscular executive authority that can uproot old management ways and implant new ones.

THE WAY IT WAS

The premise of mayoral leadership turns upside down a century of conventional wisdom that politics needs to be taken out of public education and city hall kept at arm's length. Beginning in the early 1900s, school reform meant eliminating the political machinations of city hall. School systems were sources of mayoral patronage and rife with graft. To remove these influences, reformers instituted school boards led by business elites and professional administrators who were independent of city government. As further insulation, school board elections were usually held at different times than general elections.

Many mayors didn't mind being relieved of direct control, especially after the 1960s as cities deteriorated and the middle class (African-American as well as white) fled to the suburbs. Student learning and behavior fell apart, and mayors were quick to claim that they weren't to blame. Their hands were tied, mayors said, by independent school boards. Mayors were also eager to point the finger at state governments, as a wave of lawsuits sought to force states to put up a much larger share of school funding. Baltimore's William Donald Schaefer, often publicized as the best mayor in America during his tenure in office from 1971–1986, distanced himself as much as he could from education policy.[2]

Of course mayoral detachment hasn't worked. Witness the plight of urban schools. Children suffer and so do cities. The so-called urban renaissance in large cities across the country has typically stopped at the borders of downtown renewal, rarely spreading to poor neighborhoods with poor schools. Yet, the link between better schools and urban revitalization is obvious. Businesses migrate in search of a well-prepared work force. Youth violence, fanned by school dropouts, diminishes the quality of life throughout the city. Mayors now realize they can't afford to keep their hands off the governance and management of public schools.

OBSOLETE SCHOOL BOARDS

Mayors who step up will be stepping on the toes of local school boards. Through most of the history of American public education, local boards have been in charge of local schools. They are supposed to represent the voices of parents and the community and to act as bulwarks against political interference.[3] Urban boards have been mainly elected. And they still are, notwithstanding the numerous switches in recent years from elected to appointed boards and the virtual abolition of boards in New

York City and the District of Columbia. Does it matter whether boards
are appointed or elected? Or did mayors Michael R. Bloomberg in New
York and Adrian M. Fenty in D.C. have a better idea which was to get rid
of them altogether?[4]

The crescendo of criticism of urban boards has been around for a long time.
Mark Twain said, "In the first place, God made idiots. That was for practice.
Then he made school boards."[5] Today critics characterize them as chaotic and
dysfunctional.[6] They say history speaks for itself: urban schools wouldn't be
failures if school boards had governed more effectively.

But defenders say that is an unfair verdict. It doesn't take into account the
economic and social barriers to school learning and state and federal usurpa-
tion of local policymaking. Moreover, defenders aver, public schools are so
vital to families and communities that direct democratic governance must be
paramount, particularly as a safeguard for racial minorities.[7]

Sarah C. Glover, director of a Houston-based group that promotes school
board leadership, acknowledges the many missteps that boards have taken.
Still, in her view, while somebody has to shake up the bureaucracy, mayors,
who are already overburdened and subject to re-elections and term limits,
aren't superior to boards as the ones to do it. "If the democratic process is
yielding poorly-qualified school board members," she comments, "then we
should all pay attention to recruiting and supporting talented people to run
for school board."[8]

Yet, there is no credible evidence that local school boards govern effectively. Research doesn't say. Frederick M. Hess finds that "[e]xisting
research yields no firm answers."[9] Sam Stringfield, an educational researcher
and a former Baltimore school board member, notes, "The shallowness of
research on school boards almost defies belief."[10] Nonetheless, basic management principles and common sense reveal the inherent and insurmountable
weaknesses of boards (even if they regained the policymaking authority lost
over the years to federal and state officials).

Despite the lofty rhetoric about citizen boards, board members simply
lack the time and the knowledge to do their jobs well. As a member of the
Baltimore board during 2005–2008, I spent at least 20–25 hours per week
in committee and board sessions, reviewing policy proposals and contracts
(ranging from the approval of curricula and charter schools to complicated
procurements of information technology and school construction), visiting
schools, and communicating with parents and other stakeholders.

But time isn't the only constraint. Education gospel holds that the board
sets policy and the superintendent administers it. But as a practical matter,
volunteer part-time board members, who almost invariably are not professional educators, are dependent on staff for policy information and options.

Yet, education establishment bureaucracies usually present boards with scant information slanted to support their policy recommendations.

As a result, boards tend to be captives of the bureaucracy or, if they strike out on their own, uninformed and prone to engage in micromanagement and political squabbling. A study by the Harvard Public Education Leadership Project on how to improve management of urban school districts pointed out that "[u]rban superintendents often point to their school boards as sources of constant misery that require them to spend an enormous amount of time on issues unrelated to student performance."[11]

These tendencies are worse when boards are elected. In theory, elected boards enfranchise parents, especially minorities, increase accountability, and isolate schools from political influences. However, in practice, parents turn out to vote in low numbers, teachers' unions tend to dominate the campaigns, and elected members engage frequently in overtly political conduct. Hess conducted a study of school boards nationwide for the National School Boards Association in 2002. "The most striking conclusion," he wrote, "is that large-district boards are fundamentally different from their smaller, more plentiful counterparts. In large districts . . . school boards are relatively political bodies, with more costly campaigns, more attentive interest groups, more politically oriented candidates, and more hotly contested elections."[12]

Hess has also noted that school board candidates are frequently looking for stepping stones to other political offices, and in sparsely attended elections, "the central issues are often undefined and the candidates' positions unclear."[13] Several of the last decade's most reform-minded urban superintendents were undercut and eventually driven out by elected boards in San Diego, Los Angeles, and Miami.

A fitting epitaph for school boards was written by an expert on them, Professor Thomas E. Glass. He concluded that elected urban board members by and large "are not accountable to the public, seemingly possess modest skills, are very conflict prone, politicized, and demonstrate they often cannot work successfully in tandem with superintendents."[14] I agree. It is time for elected and appointed boards to go and for mayors to take the reins. Many mayors are doing just that.

HANDS-OFF TO HANDS-ON

The new era of mayoral involvement is generally traced to Boston mayors Raymond Flynn and Thomas M. Menino as early as 1989 and Chicago mayor Richard M. Daley in 1995. Daley, when president of the U.S. Conference of Mayors, declared that "education is the greatest challenge facing our cities today."[15] He sought and got authority from the Illinois legislature to appoint a five-member board and CEO (superintendent). In Boston a thirteen-member elected board was replaced by a seven-member mayor-appointed board; Menino proclaimed: "[W]hen it comes to educating our kids, *the buck stops in the mayor's office* (emphasis in the original)."[16]

The movement has spread in one form or another to Cleveland, Detroit, Oakland, Providence, Los Angeles, Philadelphia, New York, the District of Columbia, and elsewhere. In some cities, mayors—without gaining more legal control—have used the bully pulpit and other means at their disposal to exert influence. In other cities, elected school boards have been replaced by mayor-appointed boards. And Bloomberg in New York City and Fenty in D.C. have aggressively taken full control, spearheading the elimination of school boards, appointing school superintendents, and thrusting themselves into policymaking.

Most of these mayors seem willing to take on the education establishment and to imprint their own leadership. But what kind of marks have they earned so far? The mayoral movement is in its early stages, solid data is scarce, and meaningful reform takes time. But there are hopeful signs that it is succeeding.

Education policy professor Kenneth K. Wong and colleagues, as reported in their 2007 book, *The Education Mayor, Improving America's Schools,* undertook an unprecedented "large-scale, cross-district empirical analysis" of mayoral involvement in 104 large-city school districts across the country.[17] Among their findings:

- Mayors can make a significant, positive difference in raising achievement levels in elementary and high school reading and mathematics.
- There is no evidence that local expenditures rise, but there are "increased resources for instructional purposes and less spending on general administration."[18]
- There is more focus on accountability and academic performance.

The Wong study states the "strong conclusion" that "the first wave of mayoral control has been a success."[19] And secretary of education Duncan has strongly endorsed the trend.[20] But not everyone shares this viewpoint.

The doubters include the editors of the series of articles titled "Mayoral Leadership in Education: Current Trends and Future Directions" in the *Harvard Educational Review* (published in 2006 prior to the Wong study). Citing Boston and Chicago in particular, they point out that "although mayors have won some important initial victories after assuming control of school districts, the record suggests that the long-term benefits of takeovers are more elusive, especially when it comes to improving student achievement."[21] They and Michael Casserly, executive director of the organization that represents large-city school districts, lament the loss of citizen input as local school boards, elected or appointed, are diminished or abolished.[22]

Mayoral takeovers don't always take hold. In Detroit, an elected school board was replaced by a mayor-appointed board, but five years later, a public referendum restored the elected board.[23] In D.C., mayoral control prior to the incumbent Fenty had its ups and downs. Most at-risk children in Boston and Chicago, despite gains in test scores, are still left behind academically. The extent of academic gains in New York is hotly disputed.[24]

Some naysayers also warn that mayors might play the wrong kind of education politics. Mayors could, like in the old days, trade school system appointments and contracts for political benefits. They could favor the interests of working- and middle-class families that vote in higher percentages than poor families (equity competes with excellence even within urban districts). They also could bend too far in the direction of politically powerful teachers' unions.[25] But so far there's little evidence that any of this has happened following recent takeovers.

More substantial concerns are the obstacles mayors face in getting control and sustaining reform. On the front end, governors and state legislatures usually must approve mayoral authority. Down the line, reform takes time, but mayors must get re-elected and may be up against term limits. All the while, local and state legislators and the public must be won over.

According to a national poll in 2007, 59 percent opposed mayoral takeovers. But the opposition dropped from 67 percent in 2006, and parents of children in public schools were more favorable than persons with no children in school.[26] Polling in New York City shows voter support for Bloomberg's takeover.[27] African-Americans appear less supportive than whites, which may represent unease over any disruption in the status of their "source of solid middle class jobs."[28] But overall Black as well as White mayors have sought to expand mayoral influence, and Black as well as White citizens are divided in their approval or disapproval.[29]

Despite the arguments for keeping local boards, the advantages of mayoral takeovers seem overwhelming. Mayors have more ways to shake up the local education establishment than boards do. One person at the top is more effective and efficient than a board of diverse members. Mayors are used to wielding executive authority, and successful mayors, unlike insular school systems, are attuned to bringing in outside management and shaking things up. A first step often is to hire a non-traditional superintendent/CEO as occurred in Chicago, New York, Philadelphia, and D.C.

Mayors also are more deft in politics and know how to stir up public support and act as buffers for change-agent superintendents. They are better able to mobilize parental and community support behind the school system and to strengthen intergovernmental relationships. And with their necks on the line, mayors will be more disposed than in the past to provide essential management assistance in non-educational areas like finance, building operations, and information technology. They will also be more motivated to promote "community schools"—that is, neighborhood schools with on-site or close links to health, mental health, recreation, social, employment, and other municipal services for children and parents.

This potential may be blossoming. In addition to the promising results in the Wong study, the experience in New York and D.C. is shaping up as a beacon for turning around urban school systems across the country (see chapter 13).

The biggest test, however, is still to come. Remember, it's the classroom, stupid: school reform will ultimately succeed or fail on the ground in the classroom. So can the most determined and empowered mayors, together with the other elements of the New Education Federalism, provide the ways and means for vast improvement in the design and delivery of classroom instruction? As revealed next, policy-makers and even educators, themselves, have failed to grasp what it will take to make this happen.

NOTES

1. This chapter is indebted to: Kenneth K. Wong and others, *The Education Mayor: Improving America's Schools* (Washington, D.C.: Georgetown University Press, 2007); a collection of articles, From the Editors, "Mayoral Leadership in Education: Current Trends and Future Directions," *Harvard Educational Review,* vol. 76, no. 2 (Summer 2006): 141–200; and Frederick M. Hess, "Looking for Leadership: Assessing the Case for Mayoral Control of Urban School Systems," *American Journal of Education,* vol. 114, no. 3 (May 2008): 218–245. It is also informed by my experience as a deputy mayor or top aide for education (and other social programs) to mayors of Baltimore City in the years 1967–1970 and 1987–1989.

2. During most of my first term on the Baltimore school board in 1970–1973, Schaefer was the mayor.

3. For excellent historical perspective, see Deborah Land, *Local School Boards Under Review: Their Role and Effectiveness in Relation to Students' Academic Achievement* (Baltimore: Johns Hopkins University and Howard University Center for Research on the Education of Students Placed at Risk, Report No. 56, January 2002).

4. School reform in New York under Bloomberg and in D.C. under Fenty is examined in more detail in chapter 13.

5. Twain is quoted in Matt Miller, *Nationalize the Schools (. . . A Little)!,* (Washington, DC: Center for American Progress, 2008), 20.

6. See for example: Hess, "Looking for Leadership," 230–232; Land, *Local School Boards Under Review,* 13; Chester E. Finn, Jr. and Lisa G. Keegan, "The Future of School Boards: Lost at Sea," *Education Next,* vol. 4, no. 1 (Summer 2004): 15–17.

7. See generally: Sarah Glover, "The Future of School Boards: Steering a True Course," *Education Next,* vol. 4, no. 1 (Summer 2004): 11–13; Wong, *The Education Mayor,* 5–6; From the Editors, "Mayoral Takeovers in Education," 5.

8. Glover, "The Future of School Boards," 13.

9. Hess, "Looking for Leadership," 225.

10. Sam Stringfield, "School Boards and Raising Student Outcomes, Reflections (Confessions?) of a Former Urban School Board Member," in T. Alsbury, ed., *The Future of School Board Governance: Relevancy and Revelation* (Lanham, MD: Rowman & Littlefield Education, 2008), 287.

11. Stacey Childress, Richard Elmore and Allen Grossman, "How to Manage Urban School Districts," *Harvard Business Review* (November 2006): 55–68, 67. For similar reasons, state school boards should be eliminated.

12. Frederick M. Hess, *School Boards at the Dawn of the 21st Century* (Washington, DC: National School Boards Association, 2002), 3.

13. Hess is quoted in Wong, *The Education Mayor,* 20.

14. Glass is quoted in Jay Mathews, "Playing Politics in Urban City Schools," *The Washington Post,* September 10, 2002.

15. Wong, *The Education Mayor,* 1.

16, Wong, *The Education Mayor,* 1.

17. Wong, *The Education Mayor,* xii–xiii.

18. Wong, *The Education Mayor,* 198.

19. Wong, *The Education Mayor,* 198. See also Hess, "Looking for Leadership," 221–223.

20. News in Brief, "U.S. Education Secretary to Push for Mayoral Control of Schools," *Education Week* (April 8, 2009): 5.

21. From the Editors, "Mayoral Leadership in Education," 143.

22. Michael Casserly, "Why the Mayor Shouldn't Take Over D.C.'s Schools," Opinion, *The Washington Post,* November 26, 2006, B7. See also Anne L. Bryant, "Should the Mayor Be in Charge?," Commentary, *Education Week* (December 12, 2007): 26–27.

23. Wong, *The Education Mayor,* 45.

24. See chapter 14.

25. On the other hand, a union critic suggests that unions generally oppose mayoral takeovers, since, in his opinion, they prefer weak school boards. Myron Lieberman, "School Board Weakness: The Reform Issue That Can't Be Faced," Commentary, *Education Week* (September 19, 2007): 24–25.

26. Lowell C. Rose and Alec M. Gallup, "The 39th Annual Phi Delta Kappa/Gallup Poll of the Public's Attitude Toward The Public Schools," Phi Delta Kappan, vol. 89, no. 1 (September 2007): 34–45, 38. See also Wong, *The Education Mayor,* 50, 172, 173.

27. Peter Meyer, "New York City's Education Battles," *Education Next,* vol. 8, no. 2 (Spring 2008): 11–20, 20.

28. Wong, *The Education Mayor,* 174.

29. Wong, *The Education Mayor,* 21–32, 174.

Part V

Better Weapons of Mass Instruction

The mismanagement of classroom instruction is the ugly secret and fatal flaw of school failure. Everyone knows that school systems are horrendously mismanaged. The media keep us fully informed and outraged at bureaucratic foul-ups. Like when principals can't get timely maintenance or supplies for their schools. When applicants for teacher positions are told their paperwork has been misplaced. When textbooks are left in cartons and lost. When heating and air-conditioning systems don't work right. When computer glitches are rampant, and report cards and test scores are late. When fiscal crises erupt as in recent years in Baltimore, Detroit, Philadelphia, Oakland, St. Louis, Seattle, and elsewhere. And so on.

But these management failings, as serious as they are, tell only a small part of the story. They only recite the *non-instructional* mismanagement. There is of course fallout from them on the classroom. Teachers and students are distracted and impeded. Even so, the damage pales in comparison to the harm caused by management malfunctions in the design, professional training, delivery, monitoring, and supervision of classroom instruction. Parents and the public rarely glimpse these breakdowns, and some people may glaze over them as too much educational "inside baseball." But they are the ones that most depress student achievement and demoralize teachers.

Chapter 11

Below the Radar

School reformers of all stripes recognize the paramount importance of good teaching. The NCLB mandate of a "highly qualified teacher" in every classroom is an accepted goal. But the most dedicated and accomplished teachers must be able to rely on support from an instructional infrastructure that is soundly constructed and competently managed. Highly qualified managers are needed too.

The Public Education Leadership Project studied the management practices of fifteen urban districts. As summarized in an article in the *Harvard Business Review,* "Achieving excellence on a broad scale requires a district-wide strategy for improving instruction in the classroom and an organization that can implement it."[1] But things don't happen that way. The authors state that knowledge about how to manage urban districts "is amazingly sparse . . . There is no management model."[2]

Educators James W. Guthrie, chairman of the Vanderbilt University Department of Leadership and Organizations, and Theodore Sanders, CEO of the Education Commission of the States, come to the same conclusion. They lament the void in public education of the "sophisticated management strategies used by American business, medicine or the military for addressing complex challenges."[3]

This absence of management competence is particularly glaring when it comes to the design and implementation of instruction. The design includes the planning and selection of what is to be taught and how it is to be taught. What core curricula should be chosen? Poor choices result from inattention to research and subservience to commercial publishers. As one analyst put it, "[S]chool systems are notoriously poor purchasers who generally don't understand their needs well, have protracted and expensive sales cycles, rely

139

too much on personal vendor relationships, and use under-informed cross-functional committees to make key buying decisions."[4]

Then, regardless of which curricula are selected, what training is offered or mandated for teachers and supervisors, including sequence and pacing of lesson plans? What tools are provided for gathering and analyzing data that can drive classroom and individualized instruction? Is there a realistic alignment between what is to be taught and the capacity of teachers to teach it successfully? In particular, is there sufficient instructional time and is the pupil-teacher ratio low enough to enable teachers to address the normal continuum of slow-to-fast learners and students with mild learning difficulties? Without these instructional supports, expectations for teachers and students are unrealistic, and the system is set up for failure.

Finally, is there a plan that will yield not just data on student outcomes but also information on how faithfully and effectively the design has been implemented? Deficient implementation is the notorious downfall of the best-designed instructional initiatives. Have the instructional materials gotten to the classroom and the training to the teachers on time and intact? Are teachers following the prescribed curriculum, especially veterans who are prone to do things their own way? Are pupil-teacher ratios and time allocations being adhered to? Are supervision, monitoring and feedback loops being carried out as intended, leading to course-corrections if warranted?

Most of these questions about implementation are rarely asked, much less answered. Implementation evaluations (sometimes referred to as qualitative evaluations to distinguish them from quantitative measures of student achievement) are few and far between, leaving policymakers and educators in the dark about what's going right or wrong in the trenches. Andres A. Alonso, CEO of the Baltimore City public schools, uses the words "invention" and "execution" in discussing the management of instruction. Invention corresponds to design, execution to implementation. His view, which I share, is that in the overall scheme of school reform, execution is more important than invention.

Teachers are well aware of the instructional support that is absent from class. In a California study that asked teachers their reasons for leaving the profession, teachers cited "inadequate system supports" and "bureaucratic impediments" more than pay and benefits. They lamented daily facts of life like inadequate "time for planning and professional development, textbooks for their students, and reliable assistance from the district office" as well as "excessive paperwork, too many unnecessary classroom interruptions, or too many restrictions on teaching itself." [5]

A glimmer of hope that recognition and corrective action may be on their way is found in the management audits being undertaken by two large national educational organizations. The Council of Great City Schools, an association of urban school districts, has conducted several, and its summary of one includes a diagnosis of the "substantial challenges" common more or less to all:

> The instructional program lacks cohesion and forward momentum. The district has put into place a number of strategies to improve instruction, but these strategies often lack quality, are poorly conceived, are weakly implemented, and fail to connect in any systemic fashion. No one is really accountable for results. Staff members have been locked in pitched battles about how to proceed . . . The school system lacks an effective way of monitoring program implementation or using its abundant data to make good policy or program decisions.[6]

The Council has made similar findings in other districts it has audited. But the findings have not led to substantial, institutionalized management reforms.

Phi Delta Kappa International, a mammoth K–12 education association, has established a Curriculum Management Audit Center to "focus on the main business of schools: teaching, curriculum, and learning."[7] While most of the audits have been in small or suburban districts, one of the large city school systems it audited was Baltimore.[8] In 2002 the auditors found:

- The lack of a "comprehensive curriculum management" system that provides for "design, delivery, and evaluation," including curriculum guides for teachers and periodic review of the curriculum.[9]
- An unsound organizational design, with an absence of clear delineation of administrative role relationships, including span of control, chain of command, separation of line and staff functions, and lack of job descriptions.
- A proliferation of over 1000 initiatives in the schools without a "system-wide plan for piloting interventions, determining the most successful practices, or for replicating effective programs based on student assessment data."[10]

Despite these devastating findings, there was little follow-up by the Baltimore school system leadership between the audit's completion in 2002 and the advent of a new CEO in 2007. One anecdote from my experience illustrates the institutional culture of mismanagement. A highly-respected administrator was recruited personally by the then-Baltimore City CEO to head the central department on "curriculum and instruction." Yet from the start the administrator got the bureaucratic runaround, was unable to hire an executive assistant or secretary even though funds were in the budget, and encountered resistance from regional superintendents. She was the instruction chief: imagine how the instructional Indians are left to fend for themselves.

It's a minor example but school reform in urban districts suffers death from thousands of such self-inflicted managerial wounds that never show up in the media. Frederick M. Hess, an astute analyst of school management, concludes that these problems seem "nearly insoluble."[11] They appear insoluble because educators, as a profession, are prone to management dysfunctions that exceed those of other large public or private organizations.

THE NATURE AND NURTURE OF EDUCATORS

No one would expect public school systems to be better managed than other large bureaucracies, and they aren't. Education managers resist change, suffer from inertia, protect their turf and colleagues, and hide behind red tape of their own making. They tend to be blind to their own managerial shortcomings, particularly in the design and implementation of instruction. But if they're no better than other bureaucracies, are they, generally speaking, worse?

The answer seems to be "yes" for three main reasons. First, predisposition: The personal temperament of educators and their professional culture of insularity predisposes them to be weak managers. Second, lack of management skills: Educators don't learn management skills in education courses in college or graduate school or on the job, and managerial appointments are often based on personal relationships rather than merit. And third, the nature of the beast: Urban school systems, because of their complex problems, are as tough to manage as any public or private organization. The nature of the beast is well understood, but predisposition and woeful instructional management skills are not.

Predisposition

People who go into the education profession may be ideally fit to become outstanding teachers. But do they have the right temperament to be effective managers? And equally important, do they have the right personal disposition and professional norms to be good followers of strong management leaders? Even a great leader can't overcome the rank and file's deeply ingrained inertia or resistance.

Unfortunately, educators are as a rule ill-suited to be effective managers. Richard M. Ingersoll, a scholar on teacher attributes, has found that "the motives, values, and aspirations of those entering the teaching occupation differ dramatically from those entering many other occupations."[12] A defining characteristic, he writes, is altruism.[13] Most educators are drawn to the profession of teaching by the opportunity to cultivate the growth of children. Further, they are more at ease with informal than formal managerial relationships, more facilitators than decision-makers, more collegial than hierarchical. They resist competition and are reluctant risk-takers. According to another expert, they are disposed to be disorganized and to resist planning.[14]

Many teachers, for these reasons as well as others, shy away from the pursuit of administrative positions, including the job of principal.[15] And those who opt to move up the ladder resist being squeezed into a corporate management mold. For instance, focus groups of school administrators were ambivalent "about whether corporate-type training is beneficial or not;" naysayers thought that "Education isn't along profit and production lines . . . Education is about [children's] growth and development."[16] But this is a false dichotomy. The intrinsic values and goals of teachers will be better satisfied if classroom teaching is supported by vastly upgraded management systems and managers.

To bring this about, reformers must overcome the professional culture that conditions educators to be insular in outlook and practice. I have coined the term "ethic of individualism" as a defining concept of teacher insularity. It is close to the notion of professional autonomy and refers to the fact that most experienced teachers (and principals) want to close their classroom doors and do their own thing in their own way. I heard someone describe a school as a series of autonomous classrooms connected by a common parking lot.

Recall education management expert Richard F. Elmore's reference to teachers as "solo practitioners."[17] In a national survey, about a third of teachers thought that they didn't need more professional training.[18] A professor of education at a university in Baltimore criticized the desire of the state board of education to spend more money on training: "I am sorry," she wrote, "that the board doesn't seem to recognize that our teachers are educated professionals, not 'trained' laborers."[19]

The same culture is implicit in the common assertion that teaching is more art than science. Teachers must be given extensive professional latitude to exercise creativity and judgment. But they should exercise their art within the boundaries staked out by scientific evidence. As noted in the earlier discussion of R&D, in other professions like medicine, if scientific evidence is not followed, it's called malpractice. Yet, many educators think directives to use research-based instructional practices undercut their professional expertise and independence.[20] According to a report by the National Council on Teacher Quality, teacher-education colleges cast the decision about how best to teach reading "as a personal one, to be decided by the aspiring teachers."[21]

Another dimension to teacher insularity is rejection of advice from outsiders. A "we-versus-they" mindset prevails. "They" include parents, advocacy groups, policymakers, politicians, researchers, and management experts who are not education insiders. Educators perceive outsiders in general as grandstand quarterbacks who constantly second-guess their expertise.

In fairness, micro-management by outsiders resembles a national pastime. Multitudes of people who wouldn't dare challenge their doctors, lawyers, electricians or plumbers have little hesitation in criticizing and offering unsolicited advice to superintendents, principals, and teachers. Consciously or unconsciously, parents, political officials, and the public draw upon their personal experience as students, and parents think they know better than teachers what it takes to reach and teach their own children. So there is some justification for educators feeling "dissed" and closing ranks.

But the circle-the-wagons culture goes too far when it repels management norms and reforms, resulting in "overwhelming resistance to bringing in leaders from outside education."[22] The prevalent sentiment is rarely blurted out like one teacher did: "We get sick and tired of these [outside] bozos trying to come into the schools and tell us our jobs. We're the experts. We know what works. I wish all these noneducators would just shut up, take care of their own jobs, and let us take care of ours."[23]

Lack of Management Skills

Many educators are reluctant to seek management positions because the jobs are tough and thankless, and because they simply want to keep doing what they love most—nurturing and teaching children in the classroom. Still, many are motivated to climb the administrative ladder for various reasons, including respite from the classroom, higher pay and status, and a platform to help children on a larger scale. But if those who move up have the will, they too often lack the skill to be effective superintendents, middle managers, or principals. And no wonder. They haven't learned in undergraduate and graduate education courses how to manage. And they don't receive good on-the-job training.

This lack of management preparation is hardly surprising, given the overwhelming evidence that undergraduate and graduate teacher-education programs are deficient even at teaching teachers to teach. Yet, for training of quality managers, education schools are worse, as revealed in chapter 7. The Public Education Leadership Project reports that "even bright, highly motivated [educators] generally lack the training needed to perform well in district office jobs. Schools of education and state certification programs rarely require proof of leadership and management skills."[24] Guthrie and Sanders are rare luminaries of the education establishment who have been blunt about the failure of university training for school administrators:

Over the past quarter-century, university preparation of educational administrators has fallen into a downward spiral dominated by low-prestige institutions, diploma mills, outmoded instruction, and low expectations. Many of these sub-par training programs have virtually no entrance requirements, save an applicant's ability to pay tuition . . . To make matters worse, most of America's elite universities have fled the field. There are few analogues to great business schools or to military academies for providing intellectual nourishment in education management.[25]

Front-line educators voice similar concerns. In a national survey in 2003, 72 percent of superintendents and 67 percent of principals agreed that "typical leadership programs in graduate schools of education are out of touch with the realities of what it takes to run today's school district . . . As one principal put it, 'Graduate school— that's probably the worst way of learning what it is that you need to do in order to be a principal.'"[26]

Nor do teachers receive on-the-job management training as they work their way up the instructional chain of command, typically from assistant principal to principal to regional and central administrative offices. Too often, job promotions reflect collegial relationships more than merit, and supervisors themselves lack management competence. Personnel evaluations are non-existent or perfunctory, and administrators who fall short on the job are recycled in the infamous "dance of the lemons."

This inbreeding and favoritism is customary in large bureaucracies, but it appears more prevalent in public education than in other public agencies and the corporate world. In school systems, it's less the "old boys" and more the "old girls" network. But it works the same. Teachers and administrators have frequently gone to teachers' colleges or worked together. Sometimes they belong to the same sorority or fraternity or are otherwise social friends. Other bonds may be ethnic, religious, or racial. As a result, central offices, as Alonso wrote in his doctoral dissertation before becoming CEO in Baltimore, "contain a myriad of personal and political relationships that are often used to sabotage, delay, or dilute a superintendent's initiatives."[27]

Nothing I did as an occasional renegade school board member was resented as much by top school executives as my public comments, after two years of rubber-stamping personnel appointments, that too many top-level appointments were influenced more by chummy personal relationships than merit. (On the other hand, many administrators and teachers thanked me privately for telling it like it is, although they would not say so publicly for fear of retribution.) Still, I was unable to stop the steady stream of dubious appointments or the practice of golden-parachuting deficient managers into make-work positions with fewer responsibilities but comparable salaries.

Complacency becomes an occupational disease. Reforms and reformers, including superintendents, come and go, but the system's managers wait them out, while seeking to deflect the blame for failure elsewhere. Of course, some administrators are not defensive. Some are informed critics and passionate advocates of reform, and a few are whistle-blowers. But they are a distinct minority. The silent majority hunkers down in their offices, unaware of or indifferent to management shortcomings and fearful of making waves. That doesn't mean that they don't care deeply about schoolchildren and take pride in their educational calling. They do. But they are captives of the professional predispositions and culture and resigned consciously or sub-consciously to the status quo.

To get leadership that will break the cycle of mismanagement in the design and delivery of classroom instruction, the system must undergo a form of shock treatment. The boldest reformers have given up hope that management-training programs and administrative bureaucracies can reform themselves. Instead, they are looking to import non-educators and outside management systems and managers into leadership and upper-rank positions. The most hopeful sight on the horizon of school reform is that this is beginning to occur, as highlighted next.

NOTES

1. Stacey Childress, Richard Elmore and Allen Grossman, "How to Manage Urban School Districts," *Harvard Business Review* (November 2006): 55–68, 55.

2. Childress, Elmore and Grossman, "How to Manage Urban School Districts," 56.

3. James W. Guthrie and Theodore Sanders, "Who Will Lead The Public Schools?" Education Life, *The New York Times,* January 7, 2001, 46.

4. Joanne Weiss, *Conditions for Student Success: The Cycle of Continuous Instructional Improvement* (Seattle, WA: University of Washington Center on Reinventing Public Education, Working Paper 4, 2007), 13.

5. Ken Futernick, *A Possible Dream: Retaining California Teachers So All Students Learn* (Sacramento, CA: The Center for Teacher Quality, California State University, 2007), 2, 7, 58–59.

6. Council of the Great City Schools, *Review of the Instructional Program, Operations and Business Services of the Kansas City (Missouri) School District* (Washington, DC: Council of the Great City Schools, 2006), 5.

7. International Curriculum Management Audit Center, Phi Delta Kappa International, *A Curriculum Management Audit of the Baltimore County Public Schools District* (Bloomington, IN: Phi Delta Kappa International, 2007), 4.

8. International Curriculum Management Audit Center, Phi Delta Kappa International, *A Curriculum Management Audit of the Baltimore City Public Schools System* (Bloomington, IN: Phi Delta Kappa International, 2002).

9. International Curriculum Management Audit Center, *A Curriculum Management Audit of the Baltimore City Public Schools System,* 60.

10. International Curriculum Management Audit Center, *A Curriculum Management Audit of the Baltimore City Public Schools System,* 213.

11. Frederick M. Hess, *Spinning Wheels: The Politics of Urban School Reform* (Washington, DC: Brookings Institution Press, 1999), 154.

12. Richard M. Ingersoll, *Who Controls Teachers' Work? Power and Accountability in America's Schools* (Cambridge, MA: Harvard University Press, 2003), 168

13. Ingersoll, *Who Controls Teachers' Work?,* 168.

14. Mary Kennedy, *Inside Teaching: How Classroom Life Undermines Reform* (Cambridge, MA: Harvard University Press, 2005), 186–190.

15. Aimee Howley, Solange Andrianaivo and Jessica Perry, "The Pain Outweighs the Gain: Why Teachers Don't Want to Become Principals," *TCRecord,* vol. 107, no. 4, 2005, http://www.tcrecord.org/PrintContent.asp?ContentID=11819.

16. Steve Farkas, Jean Johnson and Ann Duffett, *Rolling Up Their Sleeves: Superintendents and Principals Talk About What's Needed to Fix Public Schools* (New York: Public Agenda, 2003), 40.

17. Richard F. Elmore, "Getting to Scale with Good Educational Practice," *Harvard Educational Review,* vol. 66, no. 1 (Spring 1996): 1–26, 20.

18. Brian K. Perkins, *Where We Teach: The CUBE Survey of Urban School Climate* (Alexandria, VA: National School Boards Association, 2007), 60.

19. Nancy Rankie Shelton, "Training isn't what our teachers need," Letter to the Editor, *The Baltimore Sun,* February 10, 2007.

20. The ethic of individualism is particularly associated with progressive pedagogy. E. D. Hirsch, Jr., *The Schools We Need and Why We Don't Have Them* (New York: Doubleday, 1996), 99–106.

21. Kate Walsh, Deborah Glaser and Danielle Dunne Wilcox, *What Education Schools Aren't Teaching about Reading and What Elementary Teachers Aren't Learning* (Washington, DC: National Council on Teacher Quality, 2006), Executive Summary, 30.

22. Steve Farkas and others, *Trying to Stay Ahead of the Game: Superintendents and Principals Talk about School Leadership* (New York: Public Agenda, 2001), 29.

23. Quoted in Frederick M. Hess, *Common Sense School Reform* (New York: Palgrave Macmillan, 2004), 45.

24. Childress, Elmore and Grossman, "How to Manage Urban School Districts," 58.

25. Guthrie and Sanders, "Who Will Lead the Public Schools?" 46.

26. Farkas, Johnson and Duffett, *Rolling Up Their Sleeves,* 39.

27. Andres A. Alonso, "Leadership in the Superintendency: Influence and Instruction in a Context of Standards-Based Reform," an unpublished paper, Graduate School of Education of Harvard University, 2006, 53.

Chapter 12

A New Breed of Education Leaders

If war is too important to be left to generals, is education leadership too important to be left to educators? My answer is an unequivocal "yes." The preceding chapter itemized reasons why traditional educators make poor managers. This chapter spells out what leadership characteristics are missing and how to find them, bearing in mind that public school leaders must address, most of all, mismanagement of classroom instruction.

It's easy to recognize the generic leadership skills that are prized in the public and private sectors: clear vision and high expectations; willingness to make and be held accountable for controversial decisions; specialized knowledge of the organization's "business"; the ability to spot talent, supervise, and, if necessary, fire subordinates; political savvy; and the right stuff to inspire employees and mobilize stakeholders. But these attributes are easier to list than to find in any one person anywhere, much less in the applicant pool for top leadership in the grueling business of public education.

Are traditional educational leaders up to the job? Should new leaders, like almost all old ones, be drawn from teachers who work their way up the ranks, have hands-on experience in curriculum and teaching, and meet traditional certification requirements? Or should they be recruited among persons who lack training and experience as educators but appear superior on other leadership criteria?

The trade-offs between choosing insiders or outsiders to lead school system reform were confronted squarely in 2003 when the Thomas B. Fordham Institute and the Broad Foundation pulled off the unlikely feat of getting a cross-section of well-known liberals, conservatives, educational progressives and traditionalists to sign on to a report "Better Leaders for America's Schools: A Manifesto."[1] The Manifesto didn't mince words:

The mantra of those hiring school and school-system leaders should be simple: *Recruit for essential skills and attributes first.* Supply the specialized knowledge later. More specifically, school boards should seek people with manifest leadership capabilities bolstered by a solid track record of leadership success. School-specific knowledge and skills can follow. When hiring superintendents or principals, the foremost task is to identify potential leaders from the widest pool of possibilities (emphasis in the original).[2]

Frederick M. Hess, who signed the Manifesto, has noted, "The problem with the notion of instructional leadership is not its healthy focus on teaching and learning but its presumption that this means *only* former teachers are suited to be education leaders (emphasis in the original)."[3] Hess also edited a book titled *Educational Entrepreneurship* that paints a picture of traditional education managers as the antithesis of entrepreneurs.[4] Entrepreneurs take risks and innovate. Educators cling to the safe status quo.

Needless to say, the education establishment is not happy with the prospect of outsiders busting up its leadership monopoly. But that's happening. Winds of reform are blowing through many school system headquarters, generated in most instances by non-educators hired as superintendents.

THE JOB-LIKE JOB OF URBAN SUPERINTENDENT

James H. Van Sickle, a superintendent in Baltimore City, was supposed to reform the system. Instead he ran into political and union resistance and wound up getting sacked. That was in 1911.[5] And not much has changed. Across the country, the job of urban school superintendent is regarded as being among the hardest and shortest on the planet. Urban superintendents come and go as quickly as football coaches and television reality-show winners. Their average tenure is slightly over three years.[6]

Over the past decade Baltimore City has had five superintendents, and the District of Columbia has had six. One D. C. superintendent who quit, a retired general who fought in three wars and earned numerous combat citations, later commented that trying to reform the schools "has been the toughest job that I've ever had."[7] An article in the *New York Times* put it, "Superintendents must be leaders, teachers, managers, punching bags. Nice job, if you can keep it."[8]

Many factors are beyond the superintendent's control: impoverished home and community environments that adversely impact student learning; lack of funds to pay for even the most research-proven classroom necessities and to secure decrepit school buildings; layers of restrictions imposed by school boards and federal and state regulators; and resistance from the permanent bureaucracy. None of these constraints deters the same ruling authorities plus parents, advocates, community groups, and pundits from putting superintendents under pressure to produce quick, dramatic progress. Experience shows that school reform takes around five years to take hold. But superintendents are seldom given it. Instead, they are asked to produce detailed plans in 100 days and soaring student test scores in a year or two.

Such expectations are unrealistic and self-defeating. Superintendents looking for a quick fix may be afraid to upset the bureaucratic applecart. They may settle for shallow analyses of deep problems, "pursue the latest hot ideas . . . and make decisions that are politically expedient rather than managerially sound."[9] And while they need to be upbeat to rally staff, parents, and stakeholders, they must be careful not to beat the drums too loudly about how much they can accomplish in a short period of time.

It's not that simple, of course. But it's not as hard as many superintendents—schooled in the profession's insular ways—make it. While there is widespread dissatisfaction and anger at the shortcomings of school systems, even the most demanding critics are frequently willing, in off-camera moments, to be realistic in their expectations. They know, beneath the surface of their frustrations, that the superintendent must overcome daunting social, bureaucratic and fiscal problems.

Still, even if these communication skills are mastered, being a school superintendent remains a super-difficult job. Can such leaders be found?

Non-Traditional School Chiefs

The search has led a growing number of mayors and school boards to look in unconventional places, and a trend towards hiring non-educators as superintendents, and sometimes re-naming them "chief executive officers," is underway. They are being recruited from the military, law, finance, and business, and landing in cities including New York, Chicago, Los Angeles, Philadelphia, Seattle, San Diego, Denver, D. C., and Baltimore.[10] School boards and mayors are buying into the argument that managerial aptitude outweighs experience in public education. It seems easier for a non-traditional superintendent to employ a deputy and other top administrators who know pedagogy than for a superintendent whose whole career has been in public schools to pull off transformational leadership.

There are, predictably, doubters among the education establishment. A national survey of superintendents and principals revealed "overwhelming resistance to bringing in leaders from outside education."[11] And the jury is still out on how well the new breed of superintendents is doing. Some, like Paul Vallas who has moved around from Chicago to Philadelphia and now to New Orleans, Arne Duncan in Chicago for seven years prior to his appointment by president Obama as U.S. secretary of education, Joel I. Klein in New York, Roy Romer in Los Angeles, Alan Bersin in San Diego, and Michael Bennett in Denver (before his recent appointment by the governor of Colorado to fill a vacant seat in the U.S. Senate), have earned generally high marks, though encountering varying degrees of resistance. Despite national applause for their reform style and substance, Bersin, a former U.S. Attorney, and Romer, a former governor of Colorado, were stymied and eventually chased out by hostile unions and school boards.[12]

On the other hand, some non-traditional superintendents have flopped on their own, including one in Baltimore. Ironically Vallas, who had been the budget chief for the Illinois state legislature and was at one point the brightest star in the non-traditional constellation, took a meteoric fall in Philadelphia because of a budget deficit on his watch.[13] Similarly in Seattle, Joseph Olchefske, who had a background in investment banking and was the district's chief financial officer before being elevated to superintendent, resigned in the wake of a fiscal crisis.[14]

The chances of success for non-traditional superintendents are being increased by several training programs. A forerunner is the Broad Foundation Superintendents Academy that enables senior executives from private and non-profit organizations to make the transition to K–12 superintendencies. Another Broad Foundation program, Residency in Urban Education. recruits and places "talented, emerging executives" from education and other fields in two-year residencies in public school systems, including charter school organizations.[15] Later I profile the urban school districts that have fashioned the most promising "turnaround" strategies. Almost all are led by non-traditional superintendents.

MANAGERS IN THE MIDDLE

Middle managers can make or break superintendents and the quality of instruction, but too little attention is paid to them. Mostly, they are indiscriminately lumped, disparaged, and targeted as the first "fat" to be cut when the school district's budget is under the knife. They make a convenient target because their functions are not as easily definable as those of teachers, principals, and executive officers. They have no direct constituency except executive superiors who are sometimes hard pressed to justify their own existence.

Yet, they need to function like the managers of efficient army supply trains. Schools can't run and education reform will never fly without able middle managers behind the lines who support classroom instruction.[16] Vallas once reflected, "In order to change the [Chicago] system, you really needed to not only change department heads, but you needed to go three, four deep."[17]

Using Baltimore as an example, middle managers on the instruction side are an array of assistant superintendents, officers, directors, specialists, and assistants. Many specialize in academic subjects like reading, math, science, social studies, and career and technology education. Others are specialists for early childhood and elementary, middle, and high schools, special education for students with disabilities (which also requires a battalion of technical compliance staff), English as a second language programs, extended learning programs including summer school and after-school, assessment and evaluation, staff training, coordination of federal grant programs, suspension, attendance and truancy, parent involvement, and student admission to specialized schools.

The administrators in these offices are typically responsible for knowing the research on their specialties, for selecting curricula and writing teacher guides, for monitoring implementation and analyzing data, and for developing and sometimes delivering training for teachers and principals. They must also be budget managers who juggle numerous federal and state funding streams. And not least of all, they must be diplomats who can calm the troubled waters that frequently flow between central administrators and school-based staff. The evasion of central mandates is an art form among experienced school-based principals and teachers.

The number of middle managers fluctuates depending on the school system's budget situation, which is often a roller-coaster ride, and the devolution of authority to school principals. In Baltimore in 2008, after increases in school-based autonomy and decreases in the budget, the number of middle managers in curriculum and instruction was at an all-time low within recent memory. Nonetheless, several hundred of them were left.

That still seems like a lot and maybe it is. The Public Education Leadership Project found that "[central] offices are often dumping grounds for administrators and teachers who performed poorly in the schools."[18] Hess makes the same point: "[M]ost districts staff many of these positions with former teachers and principals. In many cases this is to comply with state regulations and contractual agreements; in others it is a painless way to move mediocre educators out of the schools."[19]

That said, it is still premature to conclude that middle management ranks are overstaffed. As heretical as it sounds, they may be understaffed to carry out reforms in the design and implementation of instruction. It's easy to rhetorically inflate what critics call the "administrative blob." But there are few studies one way or the other. Moreover, comparisons of the administrative costs of school districts are unreliable because of different budgeting systems and the lack of benchmark measures for managerial functions.

One of the causes of the calamitous fiscal crisis in Baltimore's school system six years ago was lack of sufficient fiscal controls. Yet, the fiscal recovery plan involved a fairly indiscriminate 40 percent reduction in middle managers including fiscal staff. That spared any cuts in the classroom, a worthy goal. But it left the system vulnerable to later management meltdowns. Dispassionate, outside management analyses are needed, therefore, to determine whether more capacity is needed and, if so, whether the functions can be more efficiently done in-house or through outside contracts.

MANAGEMENT PRINCIPALS

The superintendent, top executives, and middle managers set the stage for student achievement. But principals must be featured actors. The rub, of course, is the difficulty in finding enough of them who can perform well given all the role demands. In many ways, the principal is called upon to be no less a super-hero than the superintendent.

Principals are expected to manage, first and foremost, the duties of "instructional leader." This means, depending on the degree of school autonomy, everything from selecting the curriculum design and overseeing its implementation to controlling the school's budget and hiring, supervising, coaching, mentoring, and, if necessary, firing teachers and other staff. Principals can attract or lose good teachers depending on how they set the school climate, back up the teachers on discipline matters, and involve faculty in decision-making. All the while, principals must engage closely with parent-teacher associations and community groups.[20]

So much to be done, yet so little management preparation for doing it. As previously examined, teacher-education programs teach next to nothing about the everyday challenges of school leadership. Licensing credentials for principals mandate little management training or experience. And on the job, principals receive limited supervision and guidance from regional or central superiors who are themselves management underachievers.

No wonder many principals fall short. In one national survey, only about one in three superintendents said they were "happy" with their district's principals when it came to recruiting talented teachers, knowing how to make tough decisions, delegating responsibility, and spending money effectively; 60 percent of superintendents agreed they must "take what you can get" when filling a principal's position.[21] According to another national survey, only

11 percent of superintendents rate principals as excellent at holding teachers accountable for instruction and student achievement, and only 7 percent rate principals as excellent at moving ineffective teachers out of their building.[22]

At the same time, the pool of applicants appears to be drying up. The title of a 2005 journal article is "The Pain Outweighs the Gain: Why Teachers Don't Want to Become Principals." The prospects "of more power, better opportunities for personal and professional development, and more money," write the authors, are outweighed by the "perceived difficulties and frustrations associated with the job."[23] Education journalists Barbara Kantrowitz and Jay Mathews wrote in 2007 that recruiting principals is harder than ever; they cite estimates that "in some areas, 60 percent of principals will leave their positions in the next five years."[24]

An uncertain factor in the recruitment of principals is the trend towards school autonomy (or school-based management as it's commonly called) that places higher demands and expectations on them. Charter schools epitomize the movement. Moreover, the turnaround strategies in two pace-setting school districts, New York City and Baltimore, rely heavily on giving maximum authority to individual principals. Baltimore CEO Andres A. Alonso says that he wants all schools to have charter-like autonomy. But are principals en masse up to the task, and will maximum autonomy help or hurt the search for strong principals?

The prevailing view is that it will help. There's no question that principals should have more authority than they now do over staff hiring and discipline and other school operations. But I venture outside the consensus that would also give principals the responsibility to decide their own *instructional programs and priorities*. This issue is not well understood and its effect on management of classroom instruction is under-appreciated. It involves not just the most feasible sphere of duties of principals. More than that, it goes to the heart of the larger question of how improvement in the management of classroom instruction is affected by the age-old debate over centralization versus decentralization of policymaking.

ONE SIZE FITS MOST

No slogan is more ingrained in the vocabulary of educators than "one size doesn't fit all." Schools and students are diverse. Therefore, the mantra goes, there should be maximum discretion for principals (and teachers) at the individual school level. Alonso is fond of saying that parents don't send their children to the school system, but to the specific school their child attends. Another source of school-based management's popularity is that for reformers and policymakers, it's a safe call. It has such idealistic grass-roots appeal that its advocates can avoid being pinned down about policy particulars.

It also can be used to justify the crowd-pleasing downsizing of central administrators. It is so popular that liberals and conservatives alike sing its praises. A current guru is William G. Ouchi, a professor of management at the University of California at Los Angeles. In a well received book, he all but guarantees that schools will be successful if principals are given full autonomy.[25]

But suffice to say, nothing in public education is that simple. An old adage fits: For every complex problem there is a simple answer, and it's usually wrong. In fact the decentralization of power has been contentious for decades and plagued by disappointing results. Taken to its extreme, the notion of decentralized authority has given rise to elected community school boards, especially experiments that failed infamously in New York and to a lesser degree in Chicago.[26]

Still, milder forms of decentralization remained in vogue through the late 1980s and 1990s when the accountability movement burst on the scene. NCLB in particular pressured local school systems to adopt system-wide research-based instructional programs, and central administrators tightened their grip. But now sentiment is turning again as disillusionment with NCLB sets in and charter schools with their ample autonomy gain popularity.

Why the back and forth? In part, because the issue is ideologically misrepresented as an all-or-nothing proposition. The conundrum, too often ignored, is how to finely calibrate what specific decisions at which centralized or decentralized level will best support good teaching and learning in the classroom. As a practical matter, certain decisions can only be made on the ground by the principal and other school-based staff: setting the school climate, supervising staff, troubleshooting the multitude of daily operations, and interacting with parents and community representatives.

But controversy arises over decisions about *instruction* that can be made centrally or at the school level, such as:

- The design of instruction—including textbooks, teaching methods, sequence and pacing of lesson plans, classroom time allotments and class size.
- Budget priorities among instructional elements—for example, the allocation of scarce resources among classroom teachers (class size), paraprofessionals, instructional coaches and intervention specialists like tutors, staff training, and supplemental programs like after-school and summer school.
- Personnel decisions about teachers.

The last mentioned—how much authority the principal should have over school-based staff—is the easiest to resolve in policy terms. It seems indisputable that school boards and superintendents should give principals maximum authority to hire, discipline, and, if necessary, fire teachers. They also should send a clear message that principals are expected to take full advantage of it, especially with reference to weeding out unsatisfactory teachers. But where to draw the line on instructional programs and budget priorities is more complicated.

The case for giving principals full or near-full autonomy over instructional decisions draws, as we have seen, on popular opinion behind decentralized government in general and local control of public education in particular. "One cannot impose real change from above," writes Deborah Meier, a progressive icon.[27] Ouchi puts it thus: "Every school has a unique collection of students, with different proportions of gifted, special education, arts-oriented, and at-risk students. As a result, each school should have the ability to custom-design a varied curriculum that will reach each and every student."[28] Devolutionists emphasize that centrally imposed instructional programs devalue the expertise and ownership of principals and teachers, and make it impossible to hold them accountable for instructional performance.

Given all the arguments for decentralization and the deservedly bad reputation of most school bureaucracies, it seems counter-intuitive to strengthen the hand of central administrators. Top-down leadership has become an epithet in most educational circles. Yet, for the design of instructional programs and budget priorities, there are strong reasons why the principal's autonomy should be curtailed.

In the first place, centralizers can point to research on the disappointing record of past versions of school-based management that usually included considerable authority over instructional policies. An analysis of the research in 2008 concluded that "the outcomes range from the insignificant to modestly positive."[29] In 2004 researcher Larry Cuban found that "in the best cases of SBM [school-based management] in United States, Canadian, and Australian districts, school-based governance has yet to show a direct causal link to improved school quality and student academic performance."[30]

Another compelling rationale for limiting the principal's autonomy in the instructional realm is what might be termed the science or research imperative. As the discussion on R&D underscored, teaching is in many respects an art, but it also should be a science when empirical evidence points to instructional models that are more effective than others. But doesn't this logic for centralizing instructional policy decisions lead down the slippery slope to nationalization of curricula and scientifically-based instructional models? Yes it does, but why not? The scientific imperative should govern nationally, as addressed in the New Education Federalism.

Another compelling argument for centralized instructional mandates is the staggering frequency with which students change schools. The United States has the highest mobility rate of all developed countries, with as many as 45 percent of all Americans changing their residence each year. A larger percentage of inner-city students transfer in and out of schools at least once per year.[31] According to a landmark study, a quarter of low-income students attend at least three schools per year.[32]

Because of smaller attendance zones, the mobility rate is highest in elementary schools, where educational futures are molded and, therefore, the educational consequences are most severe. Transient students suffer high rates of academic failure in reading, math, behavioral problems, and retention in grade, and they drag down the pace of instruction for classmates. Yet, according to education scientist E. D. Hirsch, Jr., "this big fact of student mobility is generally ignored in discussions of school reform. It is as if that elephant in the middle of the parlor is less relevant or important than other concerns, such as the supposed dangers of encouraging uniformity."[33] The effects of mobility are offset, he adds, where "there is greater commonality of the curriculum."[34]

Centrally prescribed instruction also offers economies of scale in training of staff, supervision, monitoring and evaluation. Teachers switch schools frequently (though much less so than students). For school system managers who are already over their heads, it makes sense that the fewer the number of complex programs to support, the better.

Most principals, themselves, are ambivalent over how much authority they want over instructional polities. In a major study, they rank decision-making on instructional models at or near the bottom of the skills that they need to be effective school leaders.[35] Hiring and firing of staff is far more important to them.[36] Surprisingly, many charter school principals were of a similar mind.[37]

No doubt many principals shy away from decision-making on curricula and budget priorities for one of the reasons some superintendents want to decentralize them: let someone else take the responsibility and heat. Still, some advocates of maximum principal autonomy think it will attract stronger candidates. They are encouraged by the surge of applications for New Leaders for New Schools, which recruits and trains principals in many large urban districts, and the Knowledge is Power Program (KIPP) charter schools. On the other hand, applicants may be scared off if principals feel less empowered and more overpowered by the responsibility to choose instructional programs and priorities on top of their other heavy duties.

Teachers, like principals, are less interested in autonomy than commonly thought. Many complain at one time or another of having their hands tied over what and how they teach, the loudest being those with the most experience. Yet, teachers overall draw clear distinctions when describing what really angers them and causes a large percentage to leave the profession. In a survey of nearly 2000 teachers in California, most teachers bemoaned "bureaucratic constraints." But on closer examination, they meant such facts of everyday school life as inadequate time for planning and professional development, not enough textbooks for their students, excessive paperwork and classroom interruptions and unreliable assistance from the district office.

It seems they'll live in peace with central control over instructional policies if the bureaucracy provides "sensible policies and procedures to maintain a level of order, efficiency, and fairness."[38] The survey turned up the unexpected finding that, while charter schools are regarded as the mecca of deregulation, many teachers "working in the most autonomous charter schools were, surprisingly, *less* satisfied with their jobs than those working in schools with moderate regulations. In some instances, those teachers were simply overwhelmed by the stress and fatigue from being involved in constant decision-making (emphasis in the original)."[39]

The generational dimension to teacher attitudes is powerful. Experienced teachers chafe more at centrally imposed restrictions on their teaching than less experienced teachers. But in urban districts, inexperienced teachers are a large percentage, sometimes a majority, of the teaching force in low-performing schools. In Baltimore, about one-quarter of teachers have three or less years of any teaching experience, and about one-third have three or less years of teaching experience within the Baltimore City system.[40] As the author of the California study put it, "It's not reasonable to expect that a school staffed largely by novices and newcomers will be capable of making sound professional decisions on curriculum . . ."[41]

For all these reasons, despite the general tide towards decentralization, instructional policies often continue to be an exception. The Fordham Institute's Chester E. Finn, Jr. and Michael J. Petrilli favor all schools being treated like charter schools; yet, they concede that "more and more reform-minded districts now embrace managed instruction, under which key curricular and instructional decisions are made centrally. In those settings, the principal's job is to ensure teacher fidelity to, and successful implementation of, the mandated program."[42]

That's the way it should be, in my judgment. Principals are still left with control of personnel decisions. And waivers—granting them control of instructional programs and budget priorities—could be granted under special circumstances, including the concept of "differentiated autonomy" in which principals with good results can earn more control.[43] In the final analysis, whatever the degree of autonomy, it is imperative that principals and other administrators be much more efficient managers than they are. In the next section, we get down to business about how to speed up that process.

BULLS AND BEARS IN THE EDUCATION MARKETPLACE

In New York City, Mayor Michael R. Bloomberg and chancellor (superintendent) Joel I. Klein have mobilized so many outside philanthropic and corporate players that they have been accused of the "corporatization" of public education.[44] Thomas Sobol, the former New York State education commissioner, snapped, "The arrogance, my God, of saying because we know how to run Kmart, we know how to educate children. It represents a giant defeat of democracy."[45]

Few issues are more controversial these days than efforts to push public school systems to become more business-like. The school choice movement, as we have seen, is grounded in the belief that school reform requires marketplace competition. Privatization is happening all over, from for-profit and non-profit entities that directly operate charter or other schools to outsourced management functions, including the design of instruction. A new buzz word in school policy conversations is "entrepreneurship." These trends go hand in hand with the hiring of non-educators as school system CEOs.

Will an outside-in, corporate and entrepreneurial approach work? Should public schools continue down the road towards privatization of classroom instruction itself? Over the past decade or so, the most aggressive form of privatization has been "education management organizations" (EMOs). EMOs are usually defined as for-profit companies that operate public schools as charter schools or under other contractual relationships.[46] Many are key components in the "turnaround" strategies of school districts in New York, Chicago, Philadelphia, New Orleans, Baltimore, and several other cities, as highlighted in chapter 13.

According to one account, in 2006–2007 there were nearly fifty EMOs operating 493 schools enrolling about 228,000 students in thirty-one states, quadruple the number of EMOs in 1998–1999.[47] In addition to running schools, EMOs have other burgeoning businesses. Hundreds of million dollars are available for tutoring services that students in low-performing schools are entitled to under NCLB, and the U.S. Department of Education, under President George W. Bush, went out of its way to favor private companies over public school systems as providers. EMOs have also branched out into other markets, such as online "virtual schools," testing, teacher training, summer school programs, special education, and curriculum development.

Beyond EMOs, public school systems are employing a widening array of for-profit and non-profit companies. Non-profit charter management organizations (sometimes called CMOs) operate more charter and contract schools than EMOs. The gold-medal winner among CMOs so far is the well-publicized

Knowledge is Power Program (KIPP), a franchise-like network of charter schools, almost all in urban school districts. The first KIPP academy opened in Houston in 1994 and by 2008, there were fifty-seven of them in seventeen states and the District of Columbia, serving over 14,000 students.[48]

Public school systems are also hiring more and more management consultants to analyze and re-plan everything from information technology to personnel operations to classroom instruction. Consultants have even been hired to manage an entire school system, including a "big-name New York bankruptcy firm" that has fashioned itself as a public education turnaround specialist.[49]

The most well-known and successful example is Teach for America (TFA) founded in 1989 by Wendy Kopp, then twenty-one years of age. TFA's mission is to recruit in Peace Corps-style the best and brightest college graduates who didn't major in education and prepare them to teach in low-performing schools for a minimum of two years. In the 2007 school year, around 19,000 applicants, including 10 percent of the graduating seniors at Yale and Dartmouth, competed for 2,000 slots.[50] There are now about 14,000 TFA alumni.[51] The New Teacher Project is another national non-profit organization that works hand-in-hand with school districts to find and prepare teachers—28,000 of them between its inception in 1997 and 2008—to work in "hard-to-staff" schools.[52] And New Leaders for New Schools is working on a national scale to recruit and train school principals.[53]

Private-public enterprise in K–12 education is building a name for itself. A course at the Harvard Business School, "Entrepreneurship in Education Reform," has been described as "a breeding ground for the next generation of educational risk-takers."[54] Stanford University and other business schools are offering joint degrees in business and education.

Synergy of ideas and informal networks are also in the works. KIPP originated when two young college graduates in the TFA program met in 1992. Now KIPP, TFA and other non-establishment organizations are cross-fertilizing ideas and growing coalitions.[55] The new crop might be nearing a critical mass, and some of its leaders appear poised to become top executives within the education establishment itself. A forerunner is Michelle Rhee, who in 1997, after three years as a TFA teacher, founded the New Teachers Project. Though without any prior experience in school administration, in 2007 at age thirty-seven she was chosen by D. C. mayor Adrian N. Fenty to be chancellor (superintendent) of the D.C. school system.[56]

So private ventures in public education are on the rise, but are they producing higher student achievement? Evidence is scarce or, as on the extensive privatization initiative in Philadelphia, disputed.[57] And no surprise, liberals and conservatives are trying to put their own spin on developments.

Alex Molnar, a liberal professor and director of the Commercialism in Education Research Unit center at Arizona State University, writes that "there is no clear demonstrated link between a successful education management business model and high student academic performance."[58] Molnar and colleagues note the scarcity of research that they attribute to the tendency of private companies to shield data from public scrutiny. Some liberals go so far as invoking the specter that privatization and other forms of business influence are part of a conservative plot to convert public schools into a private commodity.

Conservatives vehemently disagree. The recent book *Educational Entrepreneurship* includes chapters by Molnar and Larry Cuban, another critic, but its main body of opinion is as optimistic about the potential of for-profit EMOs and other business-like approaches to school reform as liberals are pessimistic. Hess, the editor of the book, writes that EMOs are particularly attractive because of their market-oriented capacity to attract capital investment, to be cost-efficient and to serve the "consumer demands" of parents and students.[59]

In one of the articles, John Chubb, co-author in 1990 of the founding text for the choice movement, *Politics, Markets, and America's Schools,* deplores what he sees as the biases of educators against profit and scale in the operation of schools.[60] In another article, Steven Wilson—a Senior Fellow at the Harvard John F. Kennedy School of Government and founder of a charter school management company—asserts that EMOs are hamstrung by defensive school system officials and teachers' unions. Private operators, he writes, could wield more influence beyond the confines of their own programs—that is, they could rock the institutional boat more—if they were not afraid of retribution from the education establishment.[61]

Cuban has devoted an entire book to the subject. Its title *The Blackboard and the Bottom Line: Why Schools Can't be Businesses* attests to his distrust. In it he shares a tale of a corporate CEO, Jamie Vollmer, who preached the private-market gospel to an audience of teachers. As the CEO later recalled, one teacher raised her hand:

> She began quietly. 'We are told, sir, that you manage a company that makes good ice cream.
>
> I smugly replied, 'Best ice cream in America, ma'am.'
>
> 'How nice,' she said. 'Is it rich and smooth?'
>
> 'Sixteen percent butterfat' I crowed.
>
> 'Premium ingredients?' she inquired.
>
> 'Super-premium! Nothing but the triple-A.' I was on a roll. I never saw the next line coming.

'Mr. Vollmer,' she said, leaning forward with a wicked eyebrow raised to the sky, 'when you are standing on your receiving dock and you see an inferior shipment of blueberries arrive, what do you do?'

In the silence of that room, I could hear the trap snap. I knew I was dead meat, but I wasn't going to lie.

'I send them back.'

'That's right!' she barked, 'and we can never send back our blueberries. We take them big, small, rich, poor, gifted, exceptional, abused, frightened, confident, homeless, rude, and brilliant. We take them with attention deficit disorder, junior rheumatoid arthritis, and English as their second language. We take them all! Every one! And that, Mr. Vollmer, is why it's not a business. It's a school.[62]

That was an epiphany, Vollmer later said. "I have learned that a school is not a business. Schools are unable to control the quality of their raw material, they are dependent upon the vagaries of politics for a reliable funding stream, and they are constantly mauled by a howling horde of disparate, competing customer groups that would send the best CEO screaming into the night."[63]

The story is not fully fair to many business ventures in education, such as charter schools, that are required to serve any eligible children and select through lotteries if oversubscribed. Still, others join Cuban in the opinion that a wholesale turnover of public education to the private market is unworkable and risky. These skeptics include experts at the business-oriented Harvard Public Education Leadership Project who write: "As some corporate executives are beginning to realize, urban school systems are vastly more complex than businesses, yet the knowledge about how to manage them is amazingly sparse."[64] A 2008 scholarly summary of the research concludes: "While data limitations preclude hard and fast conclusions, the existing research on student achievement in privately managed public schools casts doubt on privatization advocates' claims that introducing the discipline of the bottom line to education will lead to improved effectiveness."[65] Similarly, Johns Hopkins University researchers find the evidence of effectiveness to be mixed at best.[66]

My own path through this ideologically overgrown policy underbrush is pragmatic. The mainly liberal education establishment has been too inclined to close the window and keep fresh management breezes out of stuffy bureaucracies. At the same time, education conservatives oversell privatization as the all-or-nothing savior of public education. For-profit (and non-profit) school operators have yet to turn around the academic performance of low-income students on a large scale or, for that matter, to turn a profit for investors.

The bottom line, as I figure it, is that public school systems should encourage the importation of outside talent and corporate management know-how, while closely monitoring and evaluating their effectiveness. There seems little to lose and a lot to gain from experiments since management of instruction is now so deficient. Some students will benefit, and lessons learned can be incubated and transplanted into other schools. Toward this end, EMOs and CMOs can be more helpful than they have been. While school systems tend to give them a hard time for ideological or bureaucratic reasons, some private operators, as noted earlier, tend to withhold information. This may be a matter of trade secrets among the for-profits. But some non-profit charter schools also are button-lipped. As a result, when EMOs and CMOs succeed, it is usually hard to fathom their instructional infrastructure and the costs of different components of it.

This is my experience with two deservedly acclaimed charter middle schools in Baltimore. As good as they are, no one knows how much of their success is due to the enthusiasm and other intangibles characteristics of their founders. Or how much is due to their specific instructional policies. Or how much is due to their outside funding over and above the budgets of other charter and regular schools. The Abell Foundation probed these questions in a unique study in 2006 of these two schools: one, a KIPP school and the other, a local start-up.[67]

The study isolated variables that other analysts of KIPP have examined, such as possible "creaming" of applications to get better enrollees. But it went farther, analyzing, for example, how principal's autonomy, curriculum, teaching methods, and spending patterns were different in the two schools from those in regular Baltimore City schools. Still, no firm judgments were reached: "[I]t is unknown whether extracting certain components from the total education model at these schools will produce improved outcomes."[68]

More such objective analyses of charter schools and other privately run public schools are needed.[69] And there are lessons to be learned from several urban districts that are relying heavily on outside-in management and private initiatives as a core reform strategy. In the next chapter, these and several other trailblazing "turnaround" districts are further examined.

NOTES

1. *Better Leaders for America's Schools: A Manifesto* (Washington, DC: Thomas B. Fordham Foundation, 2003).

2. *Better Leaders for America's Schools*, 15.

3. Frederick M. Hess, *Common Sense School Reform* (New York: Palgrave Macmillan, 2004), 140.

4. Frederick M. Hess, ed., *Educational Entrepreneurship: Realities, Challenges, Possibilities* (Cambridge, MA: Harvard Education Press, 2006).

5. David B. Tyack, *The One Best System: A History of American Urban Education* (Cambridge, MA: Harvard University Press, 1974), 174.

6. Council of the Great City Schools, *Urban School Superintendents: Characteristics, Tenure, and Salary* (Washington, DC: Council of the Great City Schools, 2009).

7. The former superintendent, retired Army Lt. Gen. Juliius W. Becton, Jr., is quoted in April Witt, "Worn Down by Waves of Change," *The Washington Post,* June 11, 2007, A1.

8. Sol Hurwitz, "The Super Bowl," Education Life, *The New York Times,* August 4, 2002, 15.

9. Stacey Childress, Richard Elmore and Allen Grossman, "How to Manage Urban School Districts," *Harvard Business Review* (November 2006): 55–68, 58.

10. For a listing of many of them, see Chester E. Finn, Jr., *Troublemaker* (Princeton, NJ: Princeton University Press, 2008), 278–279.

11. *Better Leaders for America's Schools,* 8.

12. On Bersin, see Frederick M. Hess, ed., *Urban School Reform: Lessons from San Diego* (Cambridge, MA: Harvard Education Press, 2005). On Romer, see Helen Gao, "Romer's losing battle, LAUSD's leader beset by hostile board, " *L.A. Daily News,* September 15, 2003.

13. Susan Snyder, "School district assailed for poor financial steps," *The Philadelphia Inquirer,* June 5, 2007.

14. Jon Fullerton, "Mounting Debt," *Education Next,* vol., no. 1 (Winter 2004): 11–19, 11.

15. www.broadresidency.org. Self-reported "results" and "experience" are positive.

16. See generally: Patricia Burch and James Spillane, *Leading From the Middle: Mid-Level District Staff and Instructional Improvement* (Chicago IL: Cross City Campaign for Urban School Reform, 2004); Allan Odden and others, *Moving From Good to Great in Wisconsin: Funding Schools Adequately and Doubling Student Performance* (Madison, WI: Consortium on Policy Research in Education, Wisconsin Center for Education Research, 2007), 112–113.

17. Vallas is quoted in Kenneth K. Wong and others, *The Education Mayor: Improving America's Schools* (Washington, DC: Georgetown University Press, 2007), 158.

18. Childress, Elmore and Grossman, "Managing Urban School Districts," 58.

19. *Hess, Common Sense in School Reform,* 139.

20. See generally: Steven Adamowski, Susan Bowles Therriault, and Anthony P. Cavanna, *The Autonomy Gap: Barriers to Effective School Leadership* (Washington, DC: American Institutes for Research and Thomas B. Fordham Institute, 2007); *Better Leaders for America's Schools.*

21. Steve Farkas and others, *Trying to Stay Ahead of the Game: Superintendents and Principals Talk about School Leadership* (New York: Public Agenda, 2001), 23.

22. Steve Farkas, Jean Johnson and Ann Duffett, *Rolling Up Their Sleeves: Superintendents and Principals Talk About What's Needed to Fix Public Schools* (New York: Public Agenda, 2003), 38.

23. Aimee Howley, Solange Andrianaivo and Jessica Perry, "The Pain Outweighs the Gain: Why Teachers Don't Want to Become Principals," *TC Record,* vol. 107, no. 4, 2005, http:www.tcrecord.org/PrintContent.asp?ContentID=11819, 3, 2.

24. Barbara Kantrowitz and Jay Mathews, "The Principal Principle," Newsweek, May 28, 2007, http://www.msnbc.msn.com/id/18754330/site/newsweek/page/0/, 4.

25. William G. Ouchi, *Making Schools Work: A Revolutionary Plan to Get Your Children the Education They Need* (New York: Simon & Schuster, 2003), 11, 13.

26. For retrospectives on New York's experience: Richard D. Kahlenberg, *Tough Liberal:Albert Shanker and the Battles Over Schools, Unions, Race, and Democracy* (New York: Columbia University Press, 2007); James Traub, "A Lesson in Unintended Consequences," *The New York Times Magazine* (October 6, 2002): 70–75. On Chicago's experience, see Anthony S. Bryk, "Policy Lessons from Chicago's Experience with Decentralization," in Diane Ravitch, ed., *Brookings Papers on Education Policy 1999* (Washington, DC: Brookings Institution Press, 1999).

27. Deborah Meier, *The Power of Their Ideas* (Boston: Beacon Press, 1995), 146.

28. William G. Ouchi, "Making Schools Work," Commentary, *Education Week* (September 3, 2003): 56.

29. David N. Plank and BetsAnn Smith, "Autonomous Schools: Theory, Evidence and Policy," in Helen F. Ladd and Edward B. Fiske, eds., *Handbook of Research in Education Finance and Policy* (New York: Routledge, 2008), 407.

30. Larry Cuban, "A Solution That Lost Its Problem: Centralized Policymaking and Classroom Gains," in Noel Epstein, ed., *Who's in Charge Here: The Tangled Web of School Governance and Policy* (Washington, DC: Brookings Institution Press, 2004).

31. See generally, Karen M. Killeen and Kai A. Schafft, "The Organization and Fiscal Implications of Transient Student Populations," in Ladd and Fiske, *Handbook of Research in Education Finance and Policy,* and E. D. Hirsch, Jr., *The Knowledge Deficit: Closing the Shocking Education Gap for American Children* (New York: Houghton Mifflin, 2006), 109–112.

32. General Accounting Office, *Elementary School Children: Many Change Schools Frequently, Harming Their Education* (Washington, DC: U. S. General Accounting Office, GAO/HEHS-94-45, 1994).

33. Hirsch, *The Knowledge Deficit,* 110.

34. Hirsch, *The Knowledge Deficit,* 110.

35. Adamowski, *The Autonomy Gap,* 5, 24.

36. Adamowski, *The Autonomy Gap,* 5.

37. Adamowski, *The Autonomy Gap,* 1.

38. Ken Futernick, *A Possible Dream: Retaining California Teachers So All Students Learn* (Sacramento, CA: The Center for Teacher Quality, California State University, 2007), 7.

39. Futernick, *A Possible Dream,* 57.

40. Baltimore City Public School System, unpublished data, October 2007.

41. Futernick, *A Possible Dream,* 59.

42. Chester E. Finn, Jr. and Michael J. Petrelli, "Foreword," in Adamowski, *The Autonomy Gap,* 10.

43. Catherine Gewertz, "Easing Rules Over Schools Gains Favor: State, district leaders debate when to grant autonomy," *Education Week* (March 16, 2007): 14–15.

44. Lynnell Hancock, "School's Out: For New York City Chancellor Joel Klein, Corporate Reforms Trump Democracy," *The Nation* (July 9, 2007): 16–22.

45. Sobol is quoted in Hancock, "School's Out," 17.

46. For a recent overview of the development of EMOs and the issues surrounding them, see Gary Miron, "Educational Management Organizations," in Ladd and Fiske, *Handbook of Research in Education Finance and Policy.*

47. Alex Molnar and others, *Profiles of For-Profit Education Management Organizations, Ninth Annual Report 2006–2007* (Tempe, AZ: Commercialism in Education Research Unit, Arizona State University, 2007).

48. Julie Bennett, "Brand-Name Charters, " *Education Next,* vol. 8, no. 3, (Summer 2008).

49. Michael Dobbs, "Corporate Model Proves an Imperfect Fit for School System," *The Washington Post,* December 5, 2004, A3.

50. Patricia Sellers, "Schooling corporate giants on recruiting," *Fortune Magazine* (November 27, 2006), http://money.cnn.com/magazine.furtune/fortune_archive/2006/11/27/8394324/index/htm.

51. Sam Dillon, "2 School Entrepreneurs Lead the Way on Change," *The New York Times,* June 19, 2008.

52. www.tntp.org/aboutus/overview.html.

53. Bryan C. Hassel, "Attracting Entrepreneurs to K–12," in Frederick M. Hess, ed., *The Future of Educational Entrepreneurship* (Cambridge, MA: Harvard Education Press, 2008), 58.

54. Lynn Olson, "Harvard Course Yields Education Entrepreneurs," *Education Week* (June 13, 2007).

55. Hassel, "Attracting Entrepreneurs to K–12," 61.

56. David Nakamura, "Fenty To Oust Janey Today," *The Washington Post,* June 12, 2007, A1.

57. Brian Gill and others, *State Takeover, School Restructuring, Private Management, and Student Achievement in Philadelphia* (Santa Monica, CA: RAND, 2007); Molnar, *Profiles of For-Profit Education Management Organizations,* 16; Paul E. Peterson, "The Philadelphia Story," *The Wall Street Journal,* February 23, 2007, A11; Martha Abele Mac Iver and Douglas J. Mac Iver, "Which bets paid off?", *Review of Policy Research,* vol. 23, no. 5 (2006): 1077–1093.

58. Alex Molnar, "For-Profit K–12 Education," in Hess, *Educational Entrepreneurship*, 115.

59. Frederick M. Hess, "Politics, Policy, and the Promise of Entrepreneurship," in Hess, *Educational Entrepreneurship,* 256.

60. John E. Chubb, "The Bias against Scale and Profit," in Hess, *Educational Entrepreneurship.*

61. Steven F. Wilson, "Opportunities, but a Resistant Culture," in Hess, *Educational Entrepreneurship.*

62. Larry Cuban, *The Blackboard and the Bottom Line: Why Schools Can't Be Businesses* (Cambridge, MA: Harvard University Press, 2004), 3–4.

63. Cuban, *The Blackboard and the Bottom Line,* 4.

64. Childress, Elmore and Grossman, "How to Manage Urban School Districts," 56.

65. Miron, "Educational Management Organizations," 483.

66. Mac Iver and Mac Iver, "Which bets paid off?"

67. The Abell Foundation, *Baltimore's 'New' Middle Schools: Do KIPP and Crossroads Schools Offer Solutions to the City's Poorly-Performing Middle Schools?* (Baltimore, MD: The Abell Foundation, 2006).

68. Abell, *Baltimore's 'New' Middle Schools,* 22.

69. For instance, if a school's positive impacts are attributed to extra funding, that can help to make the case for more money for all schools or the re-allocation of existing budgets. KIPP, basking so brightly in the national limelight, has a special obligation to be forthcoming.

Part VI

Interim Report Card

The concluding two chapters summarize the hope for school reform. In the first, light is shone on the urban school systems that show the most promise of achieving successful "turnarounds." These systems have sown the seeds of transformational change, including new kinds of leadership and management capacity. But most have been planted only recently, and there is no proof that they will grow success on a large scale. Their chances will be greater if undergirded by national resolve and a New Education Federalism.

The final chapter forecasts the political prospects that these reforms will come to pass. The outlook is indisputably buoyed by the election of Barack Obama as president. It is no sure thing that he will stand firm on his educational platform and become a staunch educator-in-chief. Many barriers—including the education establishment and the division within the Democratic party over education policies—stand in the way. But his post-ideological political brand, if stamped on public education policy and blended with a new focus on classroom instruction, could lift school reform to new heights.

Chapter 13

Turnarounds or Merry-Go-Rounds

According to an old axiom, there's nothing so practical as a good theory. Or better still, a good theory of action. Unfortunately, central to this book is the reality that there are many competing theories of action for school reform, but none has succeeded or established its clear superiority to the others. In particular, no large urban school system has come close to enabling the majority of its students to meet high academic standards.

Nonetheless, a few urban school districts are in a class by themselves in the promising systemic "turnaround" theories of action they are pursuing, and the lessons to be learned from them.[1] The most prevalent theories have appeared in various contexts in earlier chapters. They include:

- Governance Reform. This includes replacing elected school boards with boards appointed by mayors, or, as in New York and the District of Columbia, a full mayoral takeover in which the school board is abolished. Governance reform is also closely associated with the hiring of non-educators as superintendents.
- School Autonomy. Also known as school-based management or decentralization, the school principal makes most or all decisions about the school budget, instruction, and personnel.
- Portfolio Schools. School districts reach outside the system to enter into agreements with private for-profit or non-profit organizations that operate, with considerable autonomy, sizable numbers of charter and "contract" schools.[2]
- More Money. Schools get adequate funding that could buy more and better instruction.

Proponents of each of these theories tend to claim that their prescription is sufficient by itself to be "the solution."[3] When confronted with evidence disproving their claims, each counters that its initiatives have been thwarted by opposition or haven't been tried in the pure form and on the scale that's needed. I don't buy these excuses. There's no reason to believe that any one of these theories of action can, by itself, enable any school system to reach a brave and bright new world of student achievement. On the other hand, they *might* succeed more if some or all of them were combined.

That hope is inspired by the ambitious turnaround strategies in several large city districts. Excellent background is found in a 2007 report *The Turnaround Challenge* by the Boston-based Mass Insight Education and Research Institute. "Turnaround," the authors conclude, demands "an atmosphere of crisis" that leads to "dramatic, transformative change."[4] Change embraces familiar elements like strong leadership, relentless focus on hiring and staff training, and additional school time. But what sets the report apart is its cutting-edge call for public school systems to work *"outside of traditional public education structures"* and *"against [the norms of the] system* (emphasis supplied)."[5]

Can these anti-establishment strategies survive the opposition of the entrenched insiders? *The Turnaround Challenge* calls upon states to prod or force low-performing school districts to undertake them. But states haven't done so. The authors assert that none of the states studied for the report "had been able to marshal the broad leadership commitment, sustained public investment, and comprehensiveness of strategy required to bring about effective turnaround at the scale of the need."[6]

But the good news in the report is that a few urban districts have made promising strides on their own. "[M]uch of the bolder work on organizing school turnaround to date has happened at the district level, where a handful of entrepreneurial superintendents, driven by extreme performance challenges and political pressures, have jumped in front to create some dramatically different new strategies."[7]

The Turnaround Challenge report profiles four districts regarded at the time as out in front of the pack: Chicago, Miami, New York, and Philadelphia. Guidance also comes from a collection of articles in a penetrating book published in 2008, *The Transformation of Great American School Districts—How Big Cities Are Reshaping Public Education.*[8] The articles propound principles for institutional change and survey how the process is working in Philadelphia, Chicago, New York, the District of Columbia, and Los Angeles.[9] These pacesetting districts of the past decade have in common high percentages of low-income students of color, and each turnaround venture was fueled by desperation among parents, politicians, and the city as a whole. (Educators expressed less sense of urgency.) But otherwise, the districts vary considerably in their size, demographics, politics, other local circumstances, and mix of strategies.

As I looked over the school reform landscape in early 2009, several school districts appeared to have the most upside potential. Two are familiar reform landmarks: New York and Chicago. These cities have been in their current turnaround modes for a substantial number of years, they have been most closely studied, and the trend lines are fairly positive (Chicago, while dwarfed in boldness by New York, is also of special interest because of President Obama's selection of its superintendent, Arne Duncan, as secretary of education).

On the other hand, two other cities that make my short list of most promising districts are relative newcomers on the national radar: D.C. and Baltimore. Being a former member of the Baltimore school board and down the road from D. C., it might seem that I am simply rooting for the home-town teams. But their rejuvenations, though in relatively early stages, seem especially geared to generate a second wave of turnarounds that builds on the experience in New York, Chicago and elsewhere.

There are, however, no sure bets on the horizon. Will the most hopeful turnarounds turn out to be, like the many hyped reform efforts that preceded them, merry-go-round rides that leave the school systems where they started? It's too soon to tell, but there is much to learn in the meantime.

THE PACESETTERS

New York City

The New York City school system is the place to start. No full book has been written about the Big Apple's turnaround strategy. But one should be. In my view, it has surpassed all school districts in the United States (not just urban ones) in the audacity and comprehensiveness of its reforms—beginning with leadership at the top.[10]

Immediately after his election as mayor in 2001, Michael Bloomberg did something unprecedented in the annals of the modern relationship between a city hall and a public school system: he sought and took full charge. He persuaded the New York state legislature to abolish the school board (which he called "a rinky-dink candy store"), declaring, "I want to be held accountable for the results, and I will be."[11] He wanted history, he said, to judge his tenure as mayor first and foremost on whether the school system made great progress.

He appointed as chancellor (superintendent) a former U. S. Justice Department antitrust lawyer with no previous experience in education administration, Joel I. Klein. "It's not an education job," Bloomberg said, foreshadowing the management overhaul to come.[12] Radical, non-incremental change became the order of the day for the Bloomberg/Klein regime. Klein was the CEO, but Bloomberg was fully involved and out front, like the active chair of a one-person governing board.

They proceeded first to reorganize the bureaucracy. In the first stage, tighter central control was imposed. Thirty-two community boards were replaced by ten regional districts, and major instructional decisions—like district-wide reading and math curricula, reading and math coaches in every school, and a strict policy to limit the "social promotion" of students who did not meet passing standards—were centralized. At the same time, Bloomberg/Klein hired a phalanx of outside managerial consultants and employed a corporate model of top-down governance and management.

Then about three to four years into their stewardship, Bloomberg/Klein reversed the course of centralization. Beginning in 2006, principals were given near autonomy over their budgets, instructional programs, and hiring of teachers (accompanied by stricter accountability). The authors of the *Turnaround Challenge* report rank the four districts they profiled on a centralization/decentralization scale that ranges from "Centralized/Tight" to "Decentralized/Loose." New York is ranked the loosest.[13]

Bloomberg/Klein have not explained why they changed course. Some observers note the inconsistency between their boasts of substantial academic progress in the early years and their decentralization about-face. And some have alleged that the plan all along was to dismantle the bureaucracy and put private managers in charge of residual central functions.

Portfolio Schools were also a priority. Some had gotten started with impetus from foundations before Bloomberg/Klein took over, and their growth accelerated thereafter. Through 2006, over 200 "new small high schools of choice" were initiated.[14]

Other features of the New York turnaround landscape, however, are more distinctive. One is the large amount of additional state aid that resulted from the court ruling in the long-running, mega-publicized New York adequacy lawsuit.[15] A lot of it made its way to teachers as Bloomberg/Klein undertook to alter the district's relationships with the politically gargantuan teachers' union, the United Federation of Teachers (UFT). The 80,000 teachers in the New York City are a staggering number (there are about as many teachers in New York as students in Baltimore), and the UFT probably exceeds in power any teachers' union in the nation.

From day one, Bloomberg/Klein and UFT president Randi Weingarten engaged in knock-down, drag-out negotiations and public posturing. The scorecard: teachers won large pay increases and higher pension benefits while the school system gained more leverage over teacher assignment and evaluation procedures and was able to put in place a merit pay system, albeit a weak one. "Which side has won overall?" asks Peter Meyer, author of a well-balanced account of the Bloomberg/Klein record. His answer: "Neither yet, and the battle is far from over."[16]

All things considered, how well have Bloomberg/Klein succeeded? It depends on who you ask. In 2007 the New York City school system won the prestigious Broad Foundation Prize for Urban Education awarded annually to the urban district seen as making the most progress in raising student achievement.[17] The authors of *The Turnaround Challenge* and Meyer give generally high marks. And public opinion supports Bloomberg's hands-on public-schools leadership.[18]

On the other hand, Meyer mentions the litany of complaints of many detractors. For instance, that test scores are inflated, parents and communities are shut out of the governance process, and there has been "constant institutional disarray."[19] The most high-powered critic is Diane Ravitch, New York City's nationally-renowned resident education expert. To Ravitch, the New York reforms have been "both costly and ineffectual," and "the test scores mainly flat or declining."[20] But her conclusions have been hotly contested.[21]

In the state tests for 2008, which came after the positive and negative comments mentioned above, New York City students made significant gains. For example, 57.6 percent scored at or above grade level in reading, up from 50.7 percent the year before, and 74.3 percent scored at grade level or above in math, up from 57 percent two years before.[22] Still, naysayers point out that other cities across the state also posted big gains, and, most of all, the huge disparity between the scores on the state tests and on the nationwide National Assessment of Education Progress (NAEP) tests.[23] On the last round of NAEP tests in 2007, only one-third to one-fifth of all New York students scored at or above the proficient level in reading and math, and the scores were even lower for Black and Hispanic students.[24]

Whether one sees this cup of progress as half full or half empty, both admirers of Bloomberg/Klein—and I am generally one of them—and detractors need to probe more. Why haven't minority students done even better over the past seven years? What are lessons that other districts might learn? I offer these possible answers.

One, schools *by themselves* in New York (or elsewhere) are incapable of accomplishing much more unless there are larger social and economic improvements in the lives of poor children, families, and communities. In my view, as discussed in chapter 6, this is a partial explanation. At the same time, it should not be allowed as an excuse for the depth of the failings of urban schools. There is probably an invisible ceiling at some height because of socio-economic circumstances, but students in New York and elsewhere in America haven't come close to reaching that point.

Two, the sheer size of New York City and its powerful entrenched interests, particularly unions and other liberal groups, make its school system extraordinarily difficult to turn around, even with Bloomberg steering the ship.

Three, it will take more time for the reforms to fully blossom. In their damn-the-torpedoes approach, perhaps Bloomberg/Klein went too far too fast, though one can validly respond that a slower pace would simply have given interest groups more time to shore up their fortresses of resistance.

Four, too little attention has been paid to centralized curricula design and capacity for management of the delivery of instruction. Or stated another way, School Autonomy has been taken too far. (In chapter 12, I indicated my own strong preference for retaining central control over major instructional decisions.) Arguably, Bloomberg/Klein shifted from centralization to decentralization because (a) school autonomy is politically popular with educators and communities and (b) it spared them the uncertainty and conflict over which instructional policies and programs to centrally prescribe and how to devise a supportive instructional infrastructure. Before they decentralized, they got caught up in the "reading wars" and were attacked by traditionalists over central mandates.

Five, Bloomberg/Klein, even with the large revenue increases from the lawsuit, have not had enough money to pay for all the necessary reform elements, like smaller class sizes, expensive instructional interventions, and after-school and summer programs. The Big Apple is so big that the additional one-plus billion dollars represents less than an 8 percent increase in the school system's total budget; the state governor and legislature cut drastically the $5.6 billion remedy ordered by the trial judge in the settlement of the lawsuit.

No one can say with any assurance at this point which of these possible explanations, singly or in combination, are most plausible. Or if any are. Or what will happen in the future. A lot more will be known if Bloomberg succeeds in being re-elected in 2009 for a third term and Klein stays on. In any event, Bloomberg/Klein have broken much fresh ground, they have done as much as any on-the-ground reformers to challenge the education establishment, and the nation should admire and learn from their courageous governance.

Chicago

The contemporary winds of school reform have been blowing longer in the Windy City than anywhere else, and their impact has been well-documented.[25] In 1988, shortly after then U.S. secretary of education William Bennett famously said Chicago had the worst public school system in the nation, the state legislature, under pressure from mayor Harold Washington, parents, advocates, and the business community, mandated a radical decentralization. Each school was governed by an elected council of parents, community representatives, teachers, and the principal. But the pace of progress did not satisfy mayor Richard M. Daley who was elected in 1989. In 1995 he persuaded the state legislature to give him the right to appoint the board of education and the CEO.

Daley hired his aggressive budget director Paul Vallas as CEO and urged him to shake things up. Vallas did. Charles Payne, a professor at the University of Chicago and a longtime activist in Chicago public school affairs, writes that "Vallas brought to the office a level of energy it had not seen in decades and the subtlety of a Sherman tank."[26] His mile-a-minute initiatives included fiscal reform, high-stakes testing, a pioneering program to end "social promotions," mandatory summer school for struggling students, placing many schools on probation (and reconstituting some of them), and a high school redesign plan. But increases in test scores leveled off, Vallas got into a power struggle with the local school councils,[27] and in 2001 Daley replaced him with another non-educator, Arne Duncan.

Duncan's professional career began as a basketball player. He had no experience as a teacher and only three years as an education administrator before becoming CEO. Still, leading up to his promotion by president Obama, he earned excellent grades as a reform-minded leader whose signature steps were in the direction of closing or reconstituting failing schools. The goal of the flagship portfolio initiative begun in 2004, called Renaissance 2010, was to open 100 new schools by 2010 that include charters and contract schools.[28] A new Office of School Turnarounds was created. As of the end of the 2007 school year, sixty new charter or contract schools had been opened and another twenty-one were slated to open in fall 2008.[29]

In addition, he announced in 2005 that high-performing schools would be granted substantial autonomy. The aim, said Duncan's chief administrative officer, was to turn the central office "into a support center, rather than a command and control center. Ideally we'd like to have all 600 schools doing this."[30] Thereafter Duncan expanded the number of schools enjoying autonomy, but in 2007 *Catalyst Chicago,* an independent journal on the Chicago schools, reported that the effort was lagging.[31] *Catalyst* expressed apprehension about the "curious blend" of Duncan initiatives in school choice, autonomy and accountability, and compared them unfavorably to the reforms underway in New York.[32] "In our backyard," *Catalyst* wrote, "it's difficult to know what's going on, and so far, the available data don't shed much light."[33]

Scores on state tests show large, though (as in New York) disputed, gains. In 2007 between 53 and 78 percent of Chicago students achieved at or above proficient on the state tests, but only 16 to 17 percent of the students achieved at or above proficient on the 2007 NAEP tests.[34] Also, while graduation and dropout rates have improved, the gap between Black and White students increased between 2002 and 2006; for Blacks in 2006, the graduation rate was only 51 percent.[35]

Payne concludes that despite all its reform efforts, Chicago "is still very much a failing system." As in other cities, he notes, "we can point to some improvements, yet we have come up well short of fundamental change. It is a long way still from the kind of revolution Chicago reformers thought they were authoring in 1988."[36] That seems to me a fair appraisal, and it is bolstered by the judgment of an academic expert on the history of the Chicago schools. Dorothy Shipps, who wrote the Chicago chapters in *The Transformation of Great American School Districts* and an earlier volume on urban districts, refers to Chicago's more or less "familiar solutions . . . we should be skeptical about the likelihood of their improving the life chances of the immigrant, black and low-income children who attend Chicago's schools."[37]

Why has Chicago not scaled greater heights even though it has had mayoral ownership and two unusually talented non-traditional CEOs? The break in continuity between Vallas and Duncan may be one reason. Also some of the explanations for New York's limited progress—such as socio-economic barriers, too much decentralization, too little capacity to manage the delivery of instruction, and not enough money—would seem to apply to Chicago as well. And don't forget local politics. Duncan, as secretary of education under president Obama, has advocated bolder reforms than he apparently felt able to promote in Chicago.

District of Columbia

The national spotlight in urban school reform is shining on the D. C. public schools, and miracle of miracles, it's mainly because the system is being lauded for aggressive leadership and high hopes. Until 2007 D. C. was usually cited for its political wrangling, turnover of superintendents, all-around mismanagement and a rate of student failure at the bottom of the pit even among low-performing urban districts.[38]

But now the capital city has come up with a mayor and chancellor whose daring school reform deeds may surpass those of the Gotham duo of Bloomberg and Klein. The D. C. one-two punch is mayor Adrian M. Fenty and chancellor Michelle Rhee. Fenty was a former D. C. Council member, only thirty-five years old and an avowed reformer when he was sworn into office on January 2, 2007. Still, the political and education power structures and the public were unprepared when the next day he announced his bombshell plan, not disclosed in his election campaign, to take over the public schools. Like Bloomberg, he not only wanted to abolish the school board and take the reins himself; he said flat-out that he was willing to stake the future of his mayoralty on school reform.[39]

In doing so, he was plunging into political waters even more shark-infested than New York City's. Governance of the D. C. schools had been in constant disarray for decades, with the D. C. Board of Education and its elected school board subject to authority of the Congress, the D. C. Council and the D. C. Financial Control Board, and buffeted by powerful union, corporate elite, and grassroots interests. Fenty's predecessor as mayor had offered a similar takeover plan but it was shot down, with Fenty ironically voting against it as a Council member.[40]

Fenty, too, ran into opposition, but to the surprise of many, the D. C. Council, driven by the mayor's determination and the sense that things were so bad there was nothing to lose, approved his plan by a large majority. Under the plan, the elected board of education was abolished, and while a separate elected "state" board of education was created, it had relatively minor functions. Fenty was clearly in control and wasted no time in exercising it.

The takeover took effect on midnight. The next morning he summarily fired the superintendent and announced the appointment of Rhee as replacement. The rude treatment of the dismissed superintendent, the stealth manner of the actions and Rhee's qualifications were immediately attacked. Rhee was at the time head of the New Teacher Project that she had founded. The Project recruited and trained teachers to serve in urban systems including New York and D.C., and had a sterling reputation. On the other hand, she was then thirty-seven years old with only three years' teaching experience and no experience as a public school administrator. Moreover she was a Korean-American in a school system that was 85 percent African-American, and its first non-African-American superintendent in about 40 years. And she was an out-of-towner.

But from the outset neither Fenty nor Rhee gave any ground. Fenty declared, "This system needs radical change; it really needs a shake-up. We did not want to pick someone to tinker around the edges."[41] A year later Rhee was recognized in D. C. and nationally as a fearless change agent who, as a reporter for the *Washington Post* summarized, had led "a tumultuous year of unprecedented change" and become "perhaps the most polarizing figure in District government."[42]

At the center of the hurricane she unleashed was a determination to change the culture of low expectations. That meant cleaning house fast of the people and schools that didn't appear up to the task of making "D.C. the highest performing urban school system in the country."[43] According to one account, in the first year, she closed twenty-three under-enrolled schools, finalized overhauls at twenty-six under-performing schools and fired 150 people.[44] Most of those fired were central administrators after she overcame union opposition and gained D. C. Council approval to fire them without cause.[45] But that was a warm-up for what became her most audacious initiative: a new contract with the teachers' union that would revolutionize teacher pay and tenure.

In a proposal, like "no other in the country" according to the National Council on Teacher Quality,[46] teachers could get huge pay increases— enabling many to earn over $100,000 a year in five years—if they were willing to give up tenure. But after prolonged negotiations and squirming by its leadership, the union balked. Whereupon Rhee, making good on her threats, announced her intention to bypass labor negotiations and to impose, by other means, tough provisions to evaluate teachers and to fire quickly those deemed ineffective.[47]

All the while, she took numerous other controversial steps. She replaced principals at a rapid rate, fired large numbers of teachers and teacher's aides who didn't meet a deadline to obtain certification, pushed to expand Pre-K–8 schools, made plans to turn over the management of failing schools to privatized operators, took away considerable authority from principals over school budgets, launched a weekend academic program, and offered students cash incentives for good performance.

In the process, she was blunt and defiant. When asked why she would risk alienating teachers and others by publicly "airing so much dirty laundry" about the system's failings, she replied, "You know what? . . . I really don't care, though. I also talk about how we have lots of people who work hard, but it doesn't mean that I am not going to talk about the dangers of having people working here who are not for the kids. If you're going to get your panties in a bunch about that, that's on you."[48]

No surprise, she made a lot of enemies. Chief among them was the local teachers' union with the national head of its parent body, the American Federation of Teachers, joining in the chorus of criticism and local negotiations. There were also frequent squabbles with the D. C. Council and parents' groups. Still, Fenty stayed by her side, and she worked tirelessly, attending in her first year 370 community meetings and responding to 95,000 emails.[49] Student test scores rose, and the achievement gap between African American and white students narrowed.[50]

What's clear is that whatever the mixed reaction at home, she became "From Charlie Rose to Katie Couric to Newsweek . . . the national media's go-to-figure for discussions of what ails big-city schools."[51] A long profile on her in *The Atlantic* portrayed her as "the most controversial figure in American public education and the standard-bearer for a new type of school leader nationwide."[52] She was on the cover of *Time Magazine* and on the mind of the new president of the United States. In the third presidential debate in 2008, Obama said that the D. C. school system has "a wonderful new superintendent there who's working very hard with the young mayor there."[53]

Is this hype and hope warranted? One year is infancy in the development of turnaround districts. Will Fenty and Rhee have enough time to grow their revolution? Will they be able to keep Congressional and local politics, the unions, the awkward power-sharing arrangement with the "state" board of education, and restless community activists at bay? And how will Rhee's theory of action evolve?

There are many similarities in her style and substance to those of Bloomberg and Klein in New York and Andres A. Alonso, as shortly canvassed, in Baltimore. But Rhee's theory of action, reflecting her prior experience at the National Teachers Project, appears to be even more emphatic on fast action to improve the quality of teachers—so much so that she has been quickest to risk a dramatic shoot-out with the teachers' union. Only time will tell, but she and Alonso, to whom we turn next, seem to be the frontrunners among the current class of risk-taking school reformers.

Baltimore

I have saved the best, in my judgment, for last. I believe Baltimore under Alonso offers the most hopeful turnaround in progress. But readers should be on the lookout for any bias and parochialism on my part. As a member of the Baltimore City school board, I was one of the 9–0 votes to hire Alonso as CEO beginning on July 1, 2007. And I had a front row seat as a member of the board during his remarkable first year.

Over that first year, he battled the teachers' union over his insistence that teachers spend more of their planning time in collaboration with principals and other teachers. In developing his first budget, he absorbed a budget short-fall of over $50 million, in large part by eliminating over 300 central office positions. He revolutionized how funds were allocated to individual schools, wiping out inequitable practices that shortchanged schools with the greatest needs. He radically increased the powers of school principals, devolving decisions over school instruction, budgets, and personnel previously made by central administrators. He created five "transformation" high schools through contracts with private operators, planned a series of other innovative schools that would house grades 6–12, and initiated several alternative programs and schools for over-age "problem" youth, including a school on the first floor of the central office headquarters.

He put pressure on principals to reduce suspensions which dropped dramatically. He insisted that high schools with selective admissions give second or third chances to students who weren't meeting standards before transferring the students. He overhauled and expanded programs to involve parents and communities, in part replacing staff through contracts with community-based organizations. He instituted cash incentives for high school students in an effort to boost their performance on exams needed to earn a graduation diploma. He told staff and community, quoting racing driver Mario Andretti, that if things were under control, they weren't moving fast enough. He made 240 school visits. His emails to staff, board, and others started around 5 a.m. and ended around midnight.

In the process he rattled the teachers' union, infuriated the administrators' union, upset several members of the City Council, prompted the mayor to suggest that he was moving too fast, and invited skeptics to label him (since he was the sixth CEO in ten years) just another short-term flash in the pan.

Yet, the school board was thrilled, as were most parents and community groups. There were a few bumps as the board got used to his style. But bottom line, he was delivering the shake-up of the status quo that the board envisioned when it rolled the dice and unanimously offered him a contract for the maximum four-year period allowed under state law.

We knew he was a non-traditional and risky choice. He was a first-time superintendent who was an out-of-town Hispanic-American in a school system that was 90 percent African-American, only 2.5 percent Hispanic-American, and where the community expected an African-American to replace the previous white CEO. Also, the board was opting for a full-throttle change agent at the top even though, unlike almost all other school systems where mayors and non-traditional superintendents led turnaround efforts, we were not in a crisis situation.

In the ten years preceding Alonso's appointment, student test scores had risen steadily. In a journal article, co-author Sam Stringfield, a Baltimore school board member during much of that time and an education researcher at the Johns Hopkins University, compared favorably Baltimore's record of incremental progress to other cities with a similar low-income and minority student population.[54] Alonso was replacing a permanent CEO and an acting CEO, each of them a well-liked, home-grown, and competent traditional educator.

But the board wanted more. We aspired to move the city school system to a new plateau of student achievement locally and nationally, and following a national search, we found Alonso.[55] His personal and professional history told a lot.

He emigrated from Cuba to the United States as a 12-year-old, graduated from Columbia University and Harvard Law School, went to work in a Wall Street law firm, and then abandoned the legal profession to teach emotionally disturbed children in the Newark, New Jersey public schools. After eleven years in the classroom, he decided to become an administrator, earned his doctorate at the Harvard Graduate School of Education, and went to work in the New York City school system. In four years there, he catapulted to the position of Deputy Chancellor of Teaching and Learning, making him, in effect, second in command under Chancellor Klein.

In New York, he earned rave reviews and almost overnight became a hot candidate for the superintendency of any school system (and being a Hispanic-American would have been especially appealing to cities like Los Angeles, Houston, and Miami). But he chose relatively small-town Baltimore for a number of reasons. We were a bird-in-the-hand job offer. He wanted to stay along the eastern seaboard for family reasons. And he grasped that Baltimore's relatively small size, our relatively stable political environment including a harmonious appointed school, and our foundation of progress in prior years made it an especially viable place for the launch of a second wave turnaround theory of action.

But now, notwithstanding all he accomplished in the first year and since,[56] comes the hard part. Across the country over the past decade, other reform-minded CEOs have daringly sought to turn around beleaguered school systems. Most got off to whirlwind starts only to stumble later. Rise-and-fall examples were Alan Bersin in San Diego, Roy Romer in Los Angeles, Paul Vallas in Chicago and Philadelphia, and Rudy Crew in Miami. Will Alonso succeed where they didn't? It depends. Will he stay long enough? He has promised to stay at least through his four-year contract and acknowledges that transformation will take five to ten years.

One variable is whether he will continue to be supported by the school board. I am confident he will.[57] Another is the mayor's support. The current mayor made some veiled threats to interfere but backed off due to Alonso's community support and political savvy. But most important, assuming all these pieces are in place, will his theory of action work?

Alonso never presented his theory in a comprehensive, multi-year plan of specific actions and timetables. As he sees it, what may be lost upfront in the lack of precision planning is outweighed by the need to move quickly to forestall resistance to reforms. Still, the mainstays in his game plan are fairly obvious, and most follow the New York City playbook which he helped to write.

The hallmarks include a no-excuses, high-expectations culture, uprooting the local education establishment by firing many top central administrators and eliminating the jobs of many others, and by bringing in outsiders to operate Portfolio Schools and to serve as management consultants. But more than anything else, he is wagering on the power of School Autonomy.

In his doctoral dissertation, Alonso approvingly drew attention to the idea that **"the single most important lever for superintendents is the choice, development and socialization of principals** (bold letters are in the original)."[58] He is not referring to the ideological faith in decentralization discussed in chapter 12. Rather it's a hard-nosed calculation of the best way to cut through the old culture and to create new expectations and means of enforcing them. Principals get almost full authority (whether they want it or not), and Alonso looks to them to deliver. He has made clear that he will fire those principals who don't measure up.

That's the thrust of his theory and it sounds plausible. But there's a big caveat: To repeat the lesson taught in chapter 12, there is no past evidence that full School Autonomy/decentralization/school-based management is a sufficient strategy.

To give it a fighting chance, a fresh and large pool of able principals must be recruited and retained. The Alonso force-fed principals must not only do what principals have always been supposed to do; they must do a lot more. They must assume responsibilities previously borne by central staff. Chief among them are the selection of instructional programs and methods. They must also draw up from near-scratch the school budget, and assume control of operations previously centrally managed, such as custodial services and procurement of equipment and supplies.

Yet, as earlier analyzed, it is questionable where there are enough principals who are up to all these tasks and willing to undertake them. Still, Alonso is confident he can overcome these obstacles. In year one, he chose new principals for nearly one-third of city schools. And in the search process, he is relying heavily on the pipeline of New Leaders for New Schools, a national organization that has an anecdotally strong track record of finding mainly young educators, training them, and putting them on a fast track to become principals. He has also created fifteen "principal coaches," experienced principals who will mentor peers. The principal coaches will still run their own schools but with the help of an intern recruited by New Leaders. In addition, an enhanced Leadership Academy will offer further training to the principals.

Alonso also believes the supply of candidates for the job of principal will grow in quantity and quality when principals are given more control and better training. On the other hand, the opposite could happen if the principals under Alonso are overwhelmed by all that's expected of them and are unable to produce the big leaps in student achievement that are expected. Which scenario will occur is a crucial question. The answer probably lies in the extent to which Alonso can calibrate the balance between expecting the principal to act autonomously and providing the principal with central directives and sufficient support for improved management of classroom instruction.

Principals have been given guidance documents that contain high expectations for everything from core instructional models to interventions for students with special needs to school safety to procurement of technology and other school components. But the guidance documents are vague, leaving principals considerably in the dark about exactly how they are to provide all these essentials within current budgets and what rate of progress is expected. Some principals are already complaining privately that they are overloaded with responsibilities and pressure.

Alonso recognizes these strains and will no doubt address them in the years ahead. I think he has felt the tactical need to go overboard early on expectations in order to substitute a we-can-do-it-no-matter-what mindset for the culture of complacency that reigned in Baltimore (as it does in other school systems). Thus, he dismisses principals' complaints that they don't have enough money, even though he knows that more money is badly needed. But this approach, in my opinion, must evolve. In the future, principals will have to receive more support in the selection and implementation of instructional programs and interventions for students who are struggling, and sound benchmarks for progress will have to be set.

I said when casting my vote to hire him that I was convinced that if any urban school system could reach a new plateau of progress, Baltimore could under his smart and intrepid leadership. I still think so. And so far so good. In his two years so far, test scores jumped to record heights and the graduation rate soared to its highest level in decades.[59] And school enrollments have increased for the first time since 1969.[60]

Sure, as Alonso is the first to say, there is still a long way to go. Still, it's a sign of his confidence that he agreed for Baltimore to participate in 2009 for the first time in the urban NAEP tests and be subject to the truest and stiffest measures of progress. The results aren't in, but I'm betting that he will survive and students will thrive.

LESSONS LEARNED

In addition to New York, Chicago, Baltimore, and D.C., other cities have been regarded in recent years as turnaround models. Most familiar, as earlier noted, are Philadelphia, Boston, Miami, and Los Angeles, but none has been an exemplary trendsetter.[61] In addition, San Diego deserves honorable mention and Houston deserves dishonorable mention on the reform honor roll. Houston was the showcase of the "Texas Miracle" in education, as touted by then governor George W. Bush. But the miracle turned out to be a mirage.[62] San Diego is a different and meritorious story.

Between 1998 and 2005, the non-traditional superintendent Alan Bersin, a former U. S. Attorney for the Southern District of California that includes San Diego, and his imported chief academic officer Anthony Alvarado, who had achieved a national reputation in New York City District 2, led the longest and, prior to Bloomberg/Klein, the most ambitious reform effort in the nation. A book *Urban School Reform: Lessons from San Diego,* edited by Frederick M. Hess, is a revealing autopsy.[63] Like other contemporary reformers, Bersin and Alvarado thought it necessary to apply quick shock treatment to the system. However, their theory of action was different from others.

It was about, to borrow from real estate development, instruction, instruction, instruction, and highly centralized.[64] Based on Alvarado's prior experience, it involved a common curriculum and a laser-like focus on "upgrading the skills and knowledge of teachers, principals and district leaders through intensive system-wide professional development."[65] Regional superintendents were replaced by regional "Instructional Leaders," and resources were poured into school-based coaches for teachers.

But Bersin/Alvarado clashed constantly with the school board and teachers' union over the top-down, rapid change. Resistance snowballed. Alvarado bailed out in 2003 and Bersin was forced out in 2005.[66] Their legacy, in Hess's appraisal, is "a mixed record, with some evident successes and a complement of disappointments and frustrations."[67]

A city that is trying to break the mold entirely is New Orleans. Even before Hurricane Katrina, the public school system was a swamp of student failure and administrative incompetence, with eight superintendents in the eight preceding years. Since Katrina, it has been envisioned as a showplace of school privatization, "unlike any other" school system in the United States.[68] To conservatives especially, it is a dream that might come true. Most of the district schools are run independently with more than half being charters that enroll around 60 percent of all students. Education entrepreneurs like Teach for America and KIPP and foundations are flocking to the Bayou. And, as one observer proclaimed gleefully, the "New Orleans public schools are now largely union-free."[69] The seemingly ubiquitous Vallas was hired as CEO in 2007, and the education world is watching to see what happens.

What, then, are the accumulated lessons from the districts that are, or were not so long ago, most promising? All registered significant gains in student achievement on state tests. On the other hand, the gains were usually confined to elementary grades, large achievement gaps between minority and other children persisted, and the students scored much lower on NAEP tests than on state tests. All told, each with a track record over several years (that is, excepting Baltimore and D. C. where it is too soon to tell) fell short of its ambitious turnaround goals. So stronger medicine is needed. Under my theory of action, the turnaround strategies to date must be altered and/or augmented by the recommendations in this book.

The local starting point is Governance Reform through mayoral leadership and, presumptively, non-traditional superintendents. Baltimore is the only one of the limelight cities where the revolutionary impulse to hire someone like Alonso began with the school board. But that board is the exception which proves the rule, and as a general rule, school boards should be abolished.

Another trademark of the turnaround pacesetters is the leaders' ability to dramatize the urgency of radical change, and their willingness to put the accelerator to the floor in driving their reform strategies. Most slashed and overhauled central bureaucracies, and New York, Chicago and Baltimore have banked heavily on School Autonomy. Several have invested also in Portfolio Schools operated by outsiders. All have emphasized improving the supply of teacher and principal applicants.

Still, in my analysis, New York and Chicago have failed to achieve their potential (and Baltimore may too) in part because of their failure to focus more closely and smartly on the design and implementation of classroom instruction. This suggests a word of caution to reformers about the tightrope they must walk. They should not overdo the shake-up and housecleaning of the central bureaucracy.

True, deadwood needs to be pruned, a message needs to be sent that business as usual is unacceptable, and management talent must be imported. But in assessing the capacity of the bureaucracy, an essential distinction must be drawn between people and job positions. No doubt there are many central administrators, a.k.a. bureaucrats, who don't do their jobs well. They may be incapable. But there are also many who burn out because the jobs are poorly designed, staff are overworked, and there is poor management supervision.

As important as it is to bring in outside management capacity, quick consultant fixes are too often short-lived unless internal capacity is developed simultaneously.

However, even if all these local governance and management steps are taken, they will, I believe, fall short without other elements (beyond entrusting mayors and eliminating school boards) of the New Education Federalism. That means credible accountability under national standards and tests, robust R&D, and enough money. Anything less than this full local and national turnaround package is unlikely to lift poor schoolchildren high enough.

Can our nation deliver this politically high-voltage package? Yes, we can, as highlighted in the final chapter.

NOTES

1. The term "turnaround" is borrowed from the business world and, in the context of school reform, can mean anything from turning around individual failing schools to entire school systems. It is in the latter sense that I use it, with excellent guidance from a landmark study, Andrew Calkins and others, *The Turnaround Challenge* (Boston: Mass Insight Education & Research Institute (2007). See also Emily A. Hassel and Bryan C. Hassel, "The Big U-Turn," *Education Next*, vol. 9, no. 1 (Winter 2009): 21–27.

2. If well-known education professor Paul T. Hill had his wish, school systems would be composed entirely of Portfolio Schools, none run directly by school systems. Hill, *Put Learning First: A Portfolio Approach to Public Schools* (Washington, DC: Progressive Institute Policy Report, 2006).

3. There are many other "theories of action" than those outlined. And there are many ways to configure each individually or in combination with one or more others.

Accountability, the biggest educational idea of the past twenty years, is not on the list because its basic components—academic standards, testing and consequences—have become school policy fixtures under NCLB and state laws. Whatever the fate of NCLB, there's no turning back from the accountability movement, and there shouldn't be.

Several other exclusions from the highlighted theories of action also warrant explanation. The most glaring omission is teacher quality. I don't disagree with the paramount importance of excellent teachers and principals (though there is dispute over the best ways to attract, retain, support and evaluate them). But the quest for teacher quality, like accountability, is assumed as an indispensable priority in each turnaround theory of action.

Another big idea that I have left out is school integration based on family income, as touched upon in chapter 6. Research shows that low-income students gain academically and middle-income students do not lose ground when socio-economic integration occurs. But the rub is political opposition since low family income is usually correlated with race, and the nation's resistance to racial integration is all too shameful and seemingly intractable. The leading voice for socio-economic integration, Richard D. Kahlenberg, an astute liberal education analyst, perseveres because he believes that it is more powerful than other theories of action, left or right. See, for example: Richard D. Kahlenberg, *A New Way on School Integration* (New York: The Century Foundation Issue Brief, 2006); Jennifer Jellison Holme and Amy Stuart Wells, "School Choice beyond District Borders," in Richard D. Kahlenberg, ed., *Improving on No Child Left Behind* (New York: The Century Foundation Press, 2008). I don't disagree with its potential. I just am convinced that it's not politically possible on a nationwide scale.

4. Calkins and others, *The Turnaround Challenge*, 8.

5. Calkins and others, *The Turnaround Challenge*, 11.

6. Calkins and others, *The Turnaround Challenge*, 56.

7. Calkins and others, *The Turnaround Challenge*, 32.

8. William Lowe Boyd, Charles Taylor Kerchner and Mark Blyth, *The Transformation of Great American School Districts—How Big Cities Are Reshaping Public Education* (Cambridge, MA: Harvard Education Press, 2008).

9. The precursor to both *The Turnaround Challenge* and the *Transformation of Great American School Districts* is a 2003 volume that includes case studies of Boston, Chicago, Philadelphia and Seattle. Larry Cuban and Michael Usdan, *Powerful Reforms with Shallow Roots: Improving America's Urban Schools* (New York: Teachers College Press, 2003). Among other recent volumes on urban school reform: Charles M. Payne, *So Little Change, The Persistence of Failure in Urban Schools* (Cambridge, MA: Harvard Education Press, 2008); John Simmons and others, *Breaking Through: Transforming Urban School Districts* (New York: Teachers College Press, 2006); Pedro Noguera, *City Schools and the American Dream: Reclaiming the Promise of Public Education* (New York: Teachers College Press, 2003).

10. For a balanced overview, Peter Meyer; "New York City's Education Battles," *Education Next*, vol. 8, no. 2 (Spring 2008): 11-20. For sharply critical views, Norm Fruchter, "'Plus Ca Change . . .' Mayoral Control in New York City," in Boyd, *The Transformation of Great American School Districts*, and Diane Ravitch and others, *NYC Schools under Bloomberg and Klein* (New York: Lulu, 2009).

11. Meyer, "New York City's Education Battles," 13.

12. Meyer, "New York City's Education Battles," 15.

13. Calkins and others, *The Turnaround Challenge Supplement*, 33.

14. Fruchter, "Plus Ca Change," 97.

15. The eventual payoff amounted to over $1 billion per year, and the school system budget soared from $13 billion in 2003 to nearly $20 billion in 2008. Meyer, "New York City's Education Battles," 16.

16. Meyer, "New York City's Education Battles," 14.

17. Kathleen Kennedy Manzo, "N.Y.C. Wins Award for Strides in Student Achievement," *Education Week* (September 26, 2007): 12.

18. Meyer, "New York City's Education Battles," 20.

19. Meyer, "New York City's Education Battles," 13.

20. Diane Ravitch, "Mayor Bloomberg's Report Card," *Education Next*, vol 8, no. 3 (Summer 2008): 6–7.

21. Diane Ravitch, "Reading scores in New York City: Achievement stalled," *The Education Gadfly*, vol. 7, no. 22 (June 7, 2007): 3–6. In response, David Cantor, the school system's press secretary, accused Ravitch of "blithely unprincipled" and "absurd" statements; Ravitch counter-responded without backing down. Cantor and Ravitch, "Gotham City Showdown: Ravitch and Cantor on NYC Reading Scores," *The Education Gadfly*, vol. 7, no. 26 (July 12, 2007): 3–7.

22. Jennifer Medina, "Reading and Math Scores Rise Sharply Across N.Y.," *The New York Times*, June 24, 2008.

23. Medina, "Reading and Math Scores Rise Sharply Across N.Y;" Jennifer Jennings and Sherman Dorn, "The Proficiency Trap: New York City's Achievement Gap Revisited," *TCRecord*, September 8, 2008, http://www.tcrecord.org/Content .asp?ContentID=15366.

24. National Center for Education Statistics, U. S. Department of Education, *Reading 2007: Trial Urban District Assessment Results At Grades 4 and 8*, http:// nces.gov/nationsreportcard/pubs/dst2007/2008455; National Center for Education Statistics, U. S. Department of Education, *Mathematics 2007: Trial Urban District Assessment Results At Grades 4 and 8*, http://nces.gov/nationsreportcard/pubs/ dst2007/2008452. See also Meyer, "New York City's Education Battles," 16, 17.

25. For general background: Dorothy Shipps, "Neo-Progressivism as School Reform in Chicago," in Boyd, *The Transformation of Great American School Districts*; Simmons, *Breaking Through*, chapter 1; Shipps, "The Businessman's Educator: Mayoral Takeover and Nontraditional Leadership in Chicago," in Cuban and Usdan, *Powerful Reforms with Shallow Roots*; Calkins and others, *The Turnaround Challenge Supplement*, 34–41; Julie Woestehoff and Monty Neill, *Chicago School Reform: Lessons for the Nation* (Chicago: Parents United for Responsible Education, 2007); Designs for Change, *The Big Picture: School Initiated Reforms, Centrally Initiated Reforms, and Elementary School Achievement in Chicago (1999–2005)* (Chicago: Designs for Change, 2005); Anthony Bryk, "Policy Lessons from Chicago's Experiment with Decentralization," in Diane Ravitch, ed., *Brookings Papers on Education Policy, 1999* (Washington, DC: Brookings Institution Press, 1999).

26. Payne, *So Much Change, So Little Reform*, 11.

27. Under Vallas, the school system "was simultaneously decentralized and recentralized." Payne, *So Much Change, So Little Reform*, 12.

28. Calkins and others, *The Turnaround Challenge Supplement*, 35–37.

29. Shipps, "Neo-Progressivism as School Reform in Chicago," 68.

30. The official is quoted in Simmons, *Breaking Through*, 16.

31. For an extended account of Duncan's autonomy plans, see "School autonomy all over the map," *Catalyst Chicago* (a special supplement), vol. XVIII, no. 5 (February 2007).

32. *Catalyst Chicago*, "School autonomy all over the map," 1.

33. *Catalyst Chicago*, "School autonomy all over the map," 1.

34. *Reading 2007: Trial Urban District Assessment Results At Grades 4 and 8; Mathematics 2007: Trial Urban District Assessment Results At Grades 4 and 8.*

35. *Catalyst Chicago*, "School autonomy all over the map," 18.

36. Payne, *So Much Change, So Little Reform*, 14.

37. Shipps, "Neo-Progressivism as School Reform in Chicago," 83.

38. For background: Jane Hannaway and Michael D. Usdan, "Mayoral Takeover in the District of Columbia: The Need for a Shake-up," in Boyd, *The Transformation of Great American School Districts;* Clay Risen, "The Lightning Rod," *The Atlantic* (November 2008): 78–87; April Witt, "Worn Down by Waves of Change," *The Washington Post*, June 11, 2007, A1.

39. V. Dion Haynes, "Better or Worse, It's Rhee's School System Now," *The Washington Post*, August 25, 2008, A1; Hannaway and Usdan, "Mayoral Takeover."

40. David Nakamura, "Fenty's School Plan Marks a Turnabout," *The Washington Post*, December 8, 2006, B4.

41. David Nakamura, "Fenty To Oust Janey Today," *The Washington Post*, June 12, 2007, A1.

42. Haynes, "Better or Worse."

43. Brian Westley, "New chief seeks to fix D. C. schools where others failed." *USA Today*, August 28, 2008.

44. Haynes, "Better or Worse."

45. V. Dion Haynes and Yolanda Woodlee, "D. C. Schools Chief Fires 98 Workers," *The Washington Post*, March 8, 2008, A1.

46. "Dream Contract: D. C. Goes For Broke," *Teacher Quality Bulletin*, July 30, 2008, http://www.nctq.org/p/tqb/viewBulletin.jsp?nlIdentifier=245.

47. Bill Turque, "Rhee Bypasses Talks, Imposes Dismissal Plan," *The Washington Post*, October 3, 2008, B1; Turque, "Long Battle Expected on Plan to Fire Teachers," *The Washington Post*, October 25, 2008, B1.

48. Leslie A. Maxwell, "D.C. Chancellor Makes Her Case," *Education Week* (August 25, 2008): 22–25.

49. Haynes, "Better or Worse."

50. Bill Turque, "D.C. Schools Show Progress on Costs," *The Washington Post*, July 14, 2009.

51. Turque, "Rhee's 'Plan B'."

52. Risen, "The Lightning Rod," 78.

53. The Third Presidential Debate transcript, http://elections.nytimes.com/200/president/debates/transcripts/third-presidential-debate.html, 21.

54. Samuel C. Stringfield and Mary E. Yakimowski-Srebnick, "Promise, Progress, Problems, and Paradoxes: A Longitudinal Case Study of the Baltimore City Public Schools," *American Educational Research Journal*, vol. 42, no. 1 (Spring 2005): 43–75.

55. My respect for my diverse colleagues on the board is unbounded. The way we came and stayed together under the leadership of our chair Brian Morris to hire and support Alonso was remarkable and one of the most rewarding experiences of my professional life.

56. In his second year, nearing an end as this book goes to press, he stumbled once in an aborted attempt to hire the departing school board chair as his chief of staff. But

otherwise, he continued full-speed ahead with his reforms, community support solidi-
fied, and, as shortly noted, student test scores and graduation rates continued to climb.

57. I withdrew from consideration for reappointment to the board because I wanted
to free up more time for other educational advocacy work and writing. But I would
not have withdrawn if I were not confident that Alonso's board support was firm.

58. Andres A. Alonso, "Leadership in the Superintendency: Influence and Instruction
in a Context of Standards-Based Reform," An Analytic Paper Presented to the Faculty of
the Graduate School of Education of Harvard University, 2006, unpublished, 88.

59. Liz Bowie and Arin Gencer, "City pupils' test scores rise," *The Baltimore Sun*,
July 22, 2009. The incline in graduation rates and decline in dropout rates is in a press
release from the Baltimore City Public Schools, September 21, 2009.

60. Sara Neufeld, "City Enrollment headed up," *The Baltimore Sun*, November 6,
2008, A1.

61. Boston, with the retirement of the its celebrated traditional superintendent Thomas
W. Payzant, and Los Angeles, with the ouster of its non-traditional superintendent Roy
Romer, ceased to be in the reform spotlight. In Philadelphia, a respected, traditional
superintendent succeeded Paul Vallas who lit sparks there after leaving Chicago; but the
City of Brotherly Love is rarely that when it comes to its public schools, and its future
course of action—particularly whether it will continue as the nation's largest demonstration of Portfolio Schools privatization (in the face of controversial but lukewarm
results)— remains to be seen. Miami, under Rudy Crew, a traditional superintendent who
drew mainly plaudits as head of the New York City school system before the Bloom-
berg/Klein era, pursued a fairly top-down, centralized approach that stands in contrast to
the trend elsewhere towards decentralization; but Crew departed under fire in September
2008, and Miami's outlook too is uncertain. Another school system often praised by
observers is Atlanta; it has not been studied like others mentioned, but it should be.

62. "We now know that Houston falsified data." Simmons, *Breaking Through*, 210.

63. Frederick M. Hess, ed., *Urban School Reform: Lessons from San Diego*
(Cambridge, MA: Harvard Education Press, 2005). See also Larry Cuban and Michael
Usdan, "Fast and Top-Down: Systemic Reform and Student Achievement in San
Diego City Schools," in Cuban and Usdan, *Powerful Reforms with Shallow Roots*.

64. Amy M. Hightower with Milbrey W. McLaughlin, "Building and Sustaining
an Infrastructure for Learning," and Jennifer O'Day, "Standards-Based Reform and
Low-performing Schools: A Case of Reciprocal Accountability," in Hess, *Urban
School Reform: Lessons from San Diego*.

65. Hightower and McLaughlin, "Building and Sustaining an Infrastructure for
Learning," 71.

66. Bersin was never supported by more than a 3–2 majority of the elected school
board.

67. Frederick M. Hess, "Conclusion," in Hess, *Urban School Reform: Lessons
from San Diego*, 340.

68. James Peyser, "The schools that Katrina built: How New Orleans could end up
saving public education in America," Opinion/Ideas, *The Boston Globe*, October 14,
2007.

69. Peyser, "The schools that Katrina built."

Chapter 14

The Audacity of Hope for All Schoolchildren

This book is about K–12 education policy: what it is, what it isn't, and what it should be. But politics drives policy, and, therefore, contrarian policy reform must be viewed through the prism of what is politically feasible. Through that prism, a plan along the lines of the recommendations in this book is more politically feasible than conventional educators and politicians think.

The prospects brightened on November 4, 2008 with the election of Barack Obama as president and large Democratic majorities in the House of Representatives and Senate. I rang doorbells and made phone calls for Obama in the general and primary elections. I believe he has the unique potential to transform the culture of American politics and to reshape domestic and foreign policy. Still, it is far from certain that he can redeem the dream of equal educational opportunity for all American schoolchildren.

One obvious barrier is other national priorities. The economy, Iraq and Afghanistan, health care, energy, and the environment, to name just a few. But it is more than competing priorities that hinder national school reform. For much of the past two decades, public education has been at the top of the nation's domestic policy concerns; yet, little change has occurred. So it's not will that holds us back.

Instead, it's uncertainty, policy complexity, a reactionary education establishment, and ideological extremism that stand in the way. So do demographics. The massive academic failure of low-income students is likely to get worse before it gets better. According to a recent report, "low-income students constitute as much as 45 percent of U.S. public enrollment," and if current population trends continue, "the United States could have a majority of low-income students in public schools within the next 10 years."[1]

Recall too, as set out in these pages, the education policy and practice distance to be traveled to get us near to the day when all our children, particularly the disadvantaged, will be able to read, write, compute, think, connect to and compete in mainstream society. Focusing just on classroom instruction, the engine of school reform must have many more re-tooled and well-meshed parts—among them, better teacher recruitment and retention, more research-based curricula, academic and behavioral interventions for struggling students, extended school hours, and smaller class sizes.

What's more, management leadership and systems for the delivery of classroom instruction must be re-engineered. This will require recognition at long last that the fatal flaw in American public education is a woefully weak instructional infrastructure. Educators themselves—rarely self-critical and almost always out of touch with management norms in other fields—don't know what they are missing. They don't know how better design, supervision, and evaluation of teaching and learning could make their jobs more rewarding.

Nor can we forget that, under the best of management circumstances, educators can't do the whole job on their own. Families and neighborhoods must be purged of the scourges of poverty, drugs, crime, and inadequate health care and housing that suppress student achievement. The nation must remove the barriers of alienation and dashed dreams that separate so many poor school-children from the rest of America. So we have a long way to go.

Nonetheless, it is equally apparent that we can make more progress than we have. At present, well over half of all children in urban school districts are not meeting academic standards and at least one-third are dropping out. Suppose, to set modest goals for the next five years, we were able to bring another 20 percent of the students up to high achievement levels and to decrease the dropout rate to 20 per cent. That would dramatically change the course of life for millions and millions of children.

We should, of course, aim higher. Virtually every child *can* be an academic achiever. On the other hand, we must not reach too far beyond our grasp. We must set achievable goals. Unrealistic targets, like the expectation in NCLB that 100 percent of students achieve proficiency by 2014, become demoralizing and immobilizing. Already too many reformers seem stuck in the same ideological rut, and too many educators, disillusioned by empty promises and false starts, are running on bureaucratic autopilot. A jump-start must be ignited by fresh leadership at the top, and that leadership, this book contends, is more likely to come from political officials than from the education establishment.

Education politics does not mean turning over school reform lock, stock, and barrel to politicians and the partisan political arena. However the executive and legislative branches have to break the policy stalemate over authority, accountability, and resources. A person who wants to set the nation on this course is President Obama.

POLITICS AND POSSIBILITIES

One would never suspect from the presidential campaigns in 2008 that Barack Obama was primed to become a forceful educator-in-chief. National education policy was almost completely absent in the primary and general election debates, although many people tried to push it into the spotlight. Education-oriented philanthropists Bill Gates and Eli Broad took the unprecedented step of creating a $60 million "ED in '08" fund to pressure the candidates to talk about public school reform.[2] But it didn't happen.

Despite the many rabid political differences between them, Obama and his opponent in the general election John McCain said—and differed—little on school policy.[3] Both tried to straddle divided public opinion over NCLB, and, when pressed, offered vague support. Their education platforms were built from run-of-the-mill planks: for McCain, school choice; for Obama, mainly more money for such programs as early childhood, after-school, dropout prevention, and teacher recruitment and retention.

Obama, especially, tried to stay as far away as possible from the ideological "education wars." As discussed in chapter 5, it is not just liberals and conservatives who battle each other constantly. Even worse from Obama's perspective, liberal Democrats are at war with themselves on everything from NCLB to classroom instruction. As a result, his impulse toward "change" was constrained by his desire not to alienate the powerful national teachers' unions and other establishment liberal forces, and his campaign education advisors were a mixture of education progressives and centrists. His positions on NCLB, vouchers, and merit pay and tenure for teachers became a political high-wire act in which he swayed to and fro.

But now in the White House, which way will he try to go, and how fast? Will he mount the bully pulpit, articulate the stakes, and lay out the principles and particulars of the federal government's responsibility for world-class national standards and tests, rigorous and relevant educational R&D, and adequate funding for school districts nationwide? And how far will he get with his signature blend of audacious goals and pragmatic pursuit of them?

The Political Lay of the Land

As discussed in chapter 9, the political odds for passage of a vastly enhanced federal role are more favorable than commonly supposed. National opinion surveys show that despite the furor over NCLB, most Americans want it mended, not ended. Opinion polls also reveal popular support not just for more federal funding but for national standards, tests and curricula. Our citizenry is pragmatic, and the emotional attachment to local control is trumped by the common sense logic and we've-tried-all-else-and-have-nothing-to-lose argument for greater federal power.

Political compacts—a "third way" through the battle-lines in the education wars—are attainable, as the original bipartisan support for NCLB shows. The framework of the New Education Federalism combines conservative high standards and tough tests with liberal resources. It safeguards against over-encroachment on state and local prerogatives by limiting the federal role to guaranteeing a floor (not a ceiling) for *what* students are entitled to; states and local districts remain entrusted with *how* national standards are to be met and how federal money is to be spent.

Republicans have already compromised their ideological purity on the subject of a larger federal role, thanks (or no-thanks in the minds now of most of the GOP) to George W. Bush's juggernaut infringements on state and local control under NCLB. Even prior to the 2008 elections, legislative compacts were proposed in which liberals would get more money earmarked for poor kids and school districts, and conservatives would get more accountability and choice and some relaxation of the hold of unions over teacher discipline, tenure, and merit pay.[4]

In this mobilization of post-ideological school reform, you would think liberal Democrats would be the first to enlist for the campaign. Think again.

The Left-Out Political Left

The American political system is stalemated generally. Witness the polarization and indecision over almost all foreign and domestic policy issues. Yet, surprisingly, school policy has been a partial exception. That's because for the past twenty-five years or so, conservatives have been in the driver's seat, their sights trained with passion and precision on accountability and choice. Liberals have been in the back seat aching to get their feet on the brakes and searching for an alternative "big idea" of their own (beyond more money).

Liberals are not wholly to blame for their predicament. Conservative education policies like choice and privatization were hitched to the pro-market, anti-government political bandwagon that got rolling in high gear under President Ronald Reagan.[5]

Still, liberals had only themselves to blame for the broken promises of their federal education initiatives. The political left could take credit for the enactment under Democratic President Lyndon B. Johnson of the first major federal funding for public education, the Elementary and Secondary Education Act of 1965 (EASA). EASA provided aid intended to demonstrate that K–12 schools could pull poor children out of poverty. And in the decade that followed, liberals were behind other federal measures. Some were payoffs to interest groups, but others were monumental accomplishments like Head Start and the federal law to provide services to student with disabilities (now known as the Individual with Disabilities Education Act).[6]

But the funding was modest. As later said, LBJ declared a war on poverty but financed a skirmish. More damaging, the federal funds sent to states and local school systems were spent haphazardly with education-establishment interests calling the shots. Big spending netted small gains in student achievement. Yet, liberals failed to pay attention. There was no accountability, and Democrats never made a point of it. Thus, the run-up to and the runaway success of conservatives in establishing accountability and choice as the dominant education reform movements. Two decades later, liberals are still stuck without a competing "big idea" of their own.

Quick quiz: On K–12 school reform, what do liberals stand for as distinguished from what they are against? . . . Well, if you can't think of anything besides more money, you're not alone. It's far easier to recite what many liberals are against: NCLB, testing, vouchers, and privatization come readily to mind. As incongruous as it seems, liberals have even allowed conservatives to steal their thunder on an expansive federal role to provide equal educational opportunity for minorities and the poor.

Over the past seventy years, Democrats blazed the trail on the New Deal, desegregation, the Great Society, and environmental protection. Yet, Republican George W. Bush pushed through NCLB, the flawed but most radical attempt to make the federal government the guarantor of the rights of all schoolchildren. Too many liberals, including Obama and the other Democratic presidential candidates in 2008, have been politically reluctant to embrace the necessity of a paramount federal role like the New Education Federalism.

That is where we find liberals today: adrift on K–12 policy, without a coherent platform, and politically paralyzed. One source of the paralysis has been the knee-jerk reaction to George W. Bush: if he was for it, liberals were supposed to be against it. Given Bush's overall job performance, that sounds justifiable. But as asserted throughout this book, NCLB and the underlying principles of accountability and choice deserve liberal support anyway.

A second explanation is the teachers' unions. As I have argued, the unions have been unfairly typecast as the villains in the story of school failure. Nonetheless, as also acknowledged, they are sometimes a negative force that restricts the hiring, assignment, and discipline of teachers, and resists accountability. With their tremendous political power within the Democratic party, they keep Democratic candidates on a close leash.

Exacerbating these tendencies is the underlying educational fratricide within the political left. Speaking for the frustrated liberals who are political progressives but education conservatives, centrist Andrew J. Rotherham has decried the "incoherence and ultimately the impotence of modern liberalism when it comes to addressing today's educational problems . . . When the issue is not school spending, liberals, in no small part because of politics, too often end up siding with the adults and not the kids."[7]

The best opportunity for liberals to reclaim the high ground is a New Education Federalism. And the time is ripe. Seismic political change has been occurring since the November 2006 elections when Democrats regained control of the House of Representatives. On top of that, of course, is the Democratic near-sweep in 2008. Yet, on the stalled reauthorization of NCLB, liberals remain divided. A writer for the liberal Center for American Progress points to the irony that "Resistance to federal power is now a progressive rallying cry in education."[8] In the 2007 national opinion survey cited earlier, more Republicans than Democrats supported amending NCLB to include national standards and tests.[9]

Still, some liberals want to preserve NCLB. They include President Obama so that view is virtually certain to prevail. But that's not good enough. Liberals should reach higher. Unlike conservatives, we don't believe that NCLB-like accountability, while a good thing, is sufficient by itself to reform K–12 education. But a New Education Federalism—national standards, tests, R&D, and funding guarantees, together with breaking up the education establishment and putting mayors in charge at the local level—is. It's the kind of educational policy "big idea" that liberals have been lacking.[10] Fortunately, President Obama seems to get the idea.

THE STIMULUS FOR RECOVERY OF PUBLIC EDUCATION

The rallying cry in the Obama administration in early 2009 was, never let a crisis go to waste. Consequently, the fiscal stimulus American Recovery and Reinvestment Act (ARRA) struck a balance between short-term economic recovery and longer-term investment in the nation's energy, health, and education systems. For school reform, the $100 billion ARRA allocation to public education represents a stunning, unforeseen, and possibly once-in-a-lifetime opportunity. While candidate Obama was evasive about whether he had any audacious change in mind for national K–12 policy, his ambitious presidential intentions are now beyond doubt. Whatever its impact on the nation's economy, ARRA could mark a historical turning point in school reform nationwide.

Part of its power is its largesse: it basically doubles prior annual federal aid. The funding includes about $56 billion in a State Fiscal Stabilization Fund designed mainly to prevent the layoff of teachers as a result of state and local budget retrenchments. It also includes about $13 billion more in Title I grants for low-income students and $12 billion under IDEA for students with disabilities, which is about 50 percent more under ARRA than the prior annual appropriations for each.

And then, most remarkably, there is the ARRA wild card: the $5 billion Race to the Top Fund. The secretary of education has almost complete discretion over how it is to be awarded, and it represents the big bait that Obama and Duncan hope will lure states and local school systems to reform their ways. Duncan says, "States that are simply investing [the Stabilization, Title I, and IDEA funds] in the status quo will put themselves at a tremendous competitive disadvantage for getting those additional [Race to the Top] funds." "I can't emphasize strongly enough," Duncan warns, "how important it is for states and districts to think very creatively and very differently about how they use" all the stimulus funds.[11]

ARRA lists certain applicant "assurances" that are obvious reform favorites of Obama and Duncan: addressing inequities in how teachers are distributed between high- and low-poverty schools; improving the use of data for instruction and teacher evaluations; raising the bar on instructional standards and tests; and strengthening or closing and reconstituting failing schools. And the watchword for Race to the Top runners is "innovation."

Innovation has a continuum of meanings. It can refer to experimental projects. Or, as Duncan has said, to programs with proven track records: "We have this magical opportunity to invest significantly in . . . best practices and scale up what works."[12] That sounds good to me. But is it likely to happen? The fiscal stimulus money for public schools will circulate in the economy, but will most states and local systems pass Obama's crash course in school reform?

In the near term, I fear they won't. Most of the money must be applied for in 2009 and spent fast. There is hardly any time for state and local departments of education, even if inclined to challenge the status quo, to get their act together and to plan and manage programs much differently than they do now. Even the Race to the Top funds, which are in part to reward school systems that use the other stimulus funds in innovative ways, are to be distributed no later than spring 2010. Yet, that's too soon to tell what, if anything, the earlier stimulus funds will have accomplished.

The short life span of the ARRA funds—only two to three years—also creates disincentives for school systems to spend the money where it might do the most good: especially on vital instructional add-ons, like reading specialists, longer school days, summer school, and smaller class sizes. Policymakers will fear that they could be stuck at the end of that time with large revenue shortfalls and have to jettison popular programs and lay off staff.

The lessons in this book about the management shortcomings of the education establishment are another cause for concern. How efficiently can the stimulus funds be spent on relatively short notice? Innovation may be the stimulus siren song, but remember the reform anthem sounded in earlier chapters: execution is more important to school reform than invention.

Finally, the likelihood that the stimulus funds will not live up to hyped expectations in the short run creates a longer-term and more serious danger: the absence of instant reform may sour the public and politicians on a permanent, expanded federal role.

Still, I foresee that not all the potential of the stimulus package will be lost. The most agile and aggressive school reformers will use the ARRA, including Race to the Top, funds to advance their turnaround agendas, particularly on urban fronts where the biggest battles must be won. These risk-takers will take the chance that the big increases in Title I and IDEA funds—because of their large, vocal constituencies—may not be sunsetted after all, and they will use some of the money to build in ongoing instructional improvements.

Another positive outcome from ARRA is that the political path to garnering Congressional votes for reauthorization of a ramped-up NCLB has been paved with fiscal stimulus gold. Reauthorization is likely to occur before short-term results are in and the gold runs out.

That reauthorization of NCLB will probably come with a new name, centrist amendments and more money. The mandate that 100 percent of students attain proficiency by 2014 will almost certainly be eliminated, states will be given more flexibility in determining "annual yearly progress," and the criteria for "highly qualified teachers" will place more emphasis on teacher effectiveness. The cascade of sanctions—ranging from tutoring and school transfers for students at low-performing schools to overhauling chronically failing schools via charter or other privately operated schools—is likely to remain substantially intact, with more emphasis on closing and replacing failing schools.

On funding, annual Title I and IDEA appropriations as well as earmarked grant programs for early childhood education, teacher recruitment and retention, and dropout prevention may add up to federal aid that is near ARRA stimulus levels. Equally important, the funding in the NCLB successor legislation is likely to incorporate carrots and sticks to prod states and local districts to adopt national standards and tests, assure funding guarantees for low-income school districts, and support charter schools and modified in teachers' union contracts.

That's a hopeful scenario, but let's not forget that even a more potent federal role won't be enough. The reform baton must be carried from the White House to City Hall and school system bureaucracies. While the president can't directly abolish local school boards and draft mayors as school reform leaders, Duncan has bluntly made clear that's what they would like to see happen. "At the end of my tenure, if only seven mayors are in control, I think I will have failed," he has said.[13]

Thus under a New Education Federalism, the White House and Congress should be at the top and mayors at the base of an accountable public-school chain of command. Mayors, for their part, must especially assure that school bureaucracies, energized by non-traditional managers, put most of their time and money on direct improvement of classroom instruction. (President Obama has set an example by appointing a non-educator with extensive management experience as deputy secretary of education.[14]) If these governance reforms come to pass, state departments of education, because of their weak will and management capacity, should be reduced to subsidiary, supportive roles.

This agenda is daunting but doable. Our nation can finally fulfill the legal and moral right of every schoolchild to equal educational opportunity. But it will only happen if contrarian ideas overthrow the education establishment and lead to transformation of management of classroom instruction.

That is the audacity of hope expressed in these pages. Hope springs eternal, but it is unconscionable to wait any longer. We owe it to our children and to our national self-interest and self-respect not to waste any more time and young lives.

NOTES

1. Debrah Viadero, "Low-Income Students are Public School Majority in South, Study Finds," *Education Week Online,* http://www.edweek.org/ew/articles/2008/06/18/42nces.h27.html.

2. David M. Herszenhorn, "Billionaires Start $60 Million Schools Effort," *The New York Times,* April 25, 2007.

3. The Third Presidential Debate, http://elections.nytimes.cm/2008/president/debates/transcripts/third-presidential-debate.html.

4. See, for example: Matt Miller, *The Two Percent Solution: Fixing America's Problems in Ways Liberals and Conservatives Can Love* (New York: Public Affairs, 2003), chapter 6; James P. Pinkerton, "A Grand Compromise," *The Atlantic Monthly,* January/February 2003: 115–116; Robert B. Reich, "The Liverwurst Solution," *The American Prospect* (November 6, 2000): 56.

5. Liberals, on the other hand, were paying a steep political price for their support for desegregation. Thomas Byrne Edsall with Mary D. Edsall, *Chain Reaction: The*

Impact of Race, Rights, and Taxes on American Politics (New York: W.W. Norton & Company, 1992).

6. Congressional Democrats must share credit with Republican president Richard M. Nixon for passage of the Education of all Handicapped Children Act in 1975, which was the forerunner to IDEA.

7. Andrew J. Rotherham, "Impotent Liberalism," *PPI 21st Century Schools Project Bulletin,* February 10, 2004, vol. 4, no. 3, http:www.ppionline.org/ppi_ci.cfm ?knlgAreaID=110&subsecid=900001&contentid=2523988, 2.

8. Robert Gordon, *Point-Counterpoint: Should We Repair "No Child Left Behind" or Trade It In?* (Washington, D.C: Center for American Progress and Economy Policy Institute, 2006), 6.

9. Michael J. Petrilli, "Conservatives love national testing," *The Gadfly,* vol. 7, no. 41 (October 25, 2007): 2.

10. For other views on the need for Democrats to get their act together: Kevin Carey, "How the Dems Lost on Education," *The American Prospect,* vol. 11, no. 9 (September 2008): 35–38; Robert Gordon, "Class Struggle: What Democrats Need to Say about Education, *The New Republic Online,* May 30, 2005, htt://www/tnr .com/docprint.mhtml?i=20050606&s=gordon060605.

11. Maria Glod, "With $5 Billion Fund, Duncan Seeks to Fuel Innovation in Schools," *The Washington Post,* March 29, 2009, A19.

12. Stephen Sawchuk and Eric W. Robelen, "First Education Stimulus Aid Flows to States," Education Week (April 1, 2009): 15. The Gates and Broad foundations have hastily assembled a blue-ribbon panel to recommend priorities for spending the stimulus funds. Coalition for Student Achievement, *Smart Options: Investing the Recovery Funds for Student Success,* April 2009, www .coalitionforstudentachievement.org.

13. News in Brief (The Associated Press), "U.S. Education Secretary to Push for Mayoral Control of Schools," *Education Week* (April 8, 2009): 5.

14. Alyson Klein, "Deputy Secretary Pick Brings Business Background," *Education Week* (May 13, 2009): 20.

About the Author

Kalman R. Hettleman has had a notable career on the frontlines of urban policy and politics. In public education in Baltimore, he has been a member of the school board, deputy mayor for education (and other social programs), and executive director of a large dropout prevention project.

He has also been a nationally acclaimed education analyst and writer. His education articles have appeared in *The Nation, Education Week,* the *Washington Post,* and the *Baltimore Sun.* His published policy reports include "The Time Has Come: A Federal Guarantee of Adequate Educational Opportunity," "The Invisible Dyslexics: How Public School Systems in Baltimore and Elsewhere Discriminate Against Poor Children in the Diagnosis and Treatment of Early Reading Difficulties," and "The Road to Nowhere: The Illusion and Broken Promises of Special Education."

He has further served as Maryland's cabinet secretary for social welfare programs and director of the Baltimore department of social services, taught at several universities, been a public interest attorney, and managed state and local political campaigns.